Joe Duffy is the presenter  of
popular radio shows in
working-class Dublin sub
one of the first people from his area to attend Trinity
College Dublin, where he became a student leader
advocating access to education and social justice. He
went on to a successful radio career with the *Gay Byrne
Show* on RTÉ Radio One, before becoming the
presenter of *Liveline* in 1999. Married to June Meehan,
he is the father of triplets and now lives in Clontarf in
Dublin.

JUST JOE

MY AUTOBIOGRAPHY

Joe Duffy

TRANSWORLD IRELAND

TRANSWORLD IRELAND
An imprint of The Random House Group Limited
20 Vauxhall Bridge Road, London SW1V 2SA
www.transworldbooks.co.uk

JUST JOE
A TRANSWORLD IRELAND BOOK: 9781848271005

First published in 2011 by Transworld Ireland,
a division of Transworld Publishers
Transworld Ireland paperback edition published 2012

Addresses for Random House Group Ltd companies outside the UK
can be found at: www.randomhouse.co.uk
The Random House Group Ltd Reg. No. 954009

Penguin Random House is committed to a sustainable future for
our business, our readers and our planet. This book is made from
Forest Stewardship Council® certified paper.

MIX
Paper from
responsible sources
FSC® C018179

Printed and bound in Great Britain by Clays Ltd, St Ives plc

Typeset in 11/14.5pt Sabon by Falcon Oast Graphic Art Ltd.

2 4 6 8 10 9 7 5 3 1

For Mabel, Jimmy and Aidan, then and now;
for June, Sean, Ellen and Ronan, for ever.

CONTENTS

ACKNOWLEDGEMENTS

Please, oh please do not do what I do when I see a page of acknowledgements at the start of a book – quickly glance through them in the belief that the author is simply nodding to those he forgot to mention in the text, or worse, those he has offended and wants to appease. These are not nods, but genuflections to those without whom this book would never have reached your hands.

On both knees firstly to my editor Brian Langan, who kept the book on the straight and narrow, reassured, cajoled and worked tirelessly, helping me make sense of a jumbled life and disjointed narrative. When self-doubt, lawyers and my own 4 a.m. wobbles kicked in, Eoin McHugh of Transworld reassured me with his calm demeanour.

A warm embrace to my relatives who have had to endure unusual questioning over the last three years – Aunts Renee, Monica and Patsy and Uncle Brendan for their great memories, in both senses of that word.

To my mother Mabel, my brothers James and Peter

and my sister Pauline for overcoming their initial bafflement and no doubt belief that I had once again lost the run of myself with this project; for their recollections and delving into our collective past and accepting that this is my story told through my eyes.

To June Meehan, Ann Farrell, Tara Doyle, Sebastian Hamilton and Gay Byrne, who read early drafts.

People like James Hickey, Barry Cullen, Liam Maguire, Noel Kelly, Tony Byrne, Harry Crosbie and Joe Moreau advised and supported me – and for some reason believed I was able to play 'senior hurling' with the best of them.

The *Liveline* crew – as with all I have worked with in RTÉ radio and television – never get enough credit for their daily work, loyalty and forbearance; this brief thanks cannot hope to make up for their dedication. My current team deserve special mention for their endurance: Siobhan Hough, Sorcha Glackin, Tim Desmond, Rachel Graham, Ger Philpott, Elaine Conlon and Sandra Byrne are the real stars around whom I orbit daily. And this thanks goes right up the line in RTÉ, to the powers-that-be who trusted me, gave me the break and place their faith in me every single day.

To the *Liveline* listeners, especially those who 'talk to Joe', sharing their lives, often with great intimacy; having delved in that direction in this book, I admire and have tried to emulate your honesty and bravery. Thank you for adding to the great national conversation. Frank Byrne's incisive research for his thesis on *Liveline* focused my own mind on the power of the programme.

To my immediate family, June, Sean, Ellen and

Ronan, who left me alone in my 'panic room'. This book is proof that I was not mitching from household duties, though I do now admit that I dusted a lot of my model fire engines during that time (they needed it). Whether or not the time was put to good use, I'll let you decide.

Through my eyes, this is how I saw it: the blinkers, jaundice, errors and omissions are all mine – though no doubt I will come to deny them!

Joe Duffy, August 2011

To go to Rome is little profit, endless pain,
The master that you seek in Rome
You find at home, or seek in vain.

'In time of crisis', ninth-century monk's prayer,
translation by Frank O'Connor

PROLOGUE

Footprints in the Custard

As the bus lunged around the corner on to Claddagh Green, the teetering pot of custard finally toppled over. The thick, bright-yellow coating spread slowly across the open platform. By the time we reached our stop, the floor was a sea of custard.

The conductor looked at his ruined bus. Facing the prospect of returning to the garage, he let out an unmerciful roar: 'Who left the pots of custard under the stairs?' Losing his shift halfway through the day meant a big drop in income.

We all knew which passenger had brought her aluminium pots to the stew house in Lower Ballyfermot to get the free food ladled into her pots. We all lowered our heads and glanced around furtively. By our silence we denied that we were poor. Even Mrs Pender, the owner of the pots and a neighbour of ours, kept her head bowed.

The stew house was a lifeline for so many people in

Ballyfermot, but you had to be on your uppers to avail of the free grub and be prepared for the public humiliation. Most of us would deny ever being in such a penniless state to need the help of the Little Sisters of the Poor who ran the facility. Bizarrely, even though the most well-off families in Ballyfermot – and that is not saying much – could only afford a dessert or 'sweet' on a Sunday, the stew-house users got pints of custard every day.

Our family of eight never had to go to the stew house. But we did suffer other public ignominies. The older Duffy boys – James, myself and Peter – regularly had to take a long trek through Ballyfermot for free fuel (and abuse) from the turf depot at the far end of the 'scheme'. This trip was a nightmare. We would queue for hours, only to be manhandled by the guy shovelling the turf into our bags. We would then set off on the long uphill trek from the bottom of Ballyfermot to our home near Cherry Orchard Hospital, the sacks of turf balanced precariously on our baby brother Aidan's pram. Thankfully, he wasn't in it at the time.

For those unfortunate enough to need the stew house, there were two ways of collecting the food: stack the pots and pans in the baby's pram or carry them on to the number 78 bus and store them under the stairs. And that is exactly what Mrs Pender, a small, strong woman with ten children, dressed in her overcoat and scarf, had done that day.

As the bus came to a standstill, the coagulating custard began to drip over the edge of the red platform on to the road. Who would be first to walk through the mess? Of course, it was Mrs Pender herself who stood up and, head held high, led the sludgy, yellowing march off the bus. Wiping our dripping soles, we watched her and realized that, while she had left her pots and food on the bus, she was walking away with her dignity.

Dignity was probably our most valuable possession in Ballyfermot.

The Boy from Ballyer

CHAPTER 1

Family

IF, AS THEY SAY, OUR LIVES FLASH BEFORE US JUST AS WE are about to leave this earth, it will be images of buildings that will dominate my life's movie: the Georgian house on Dublin's Church Street, where two rooms served as home for members of my father's family for well on sixty years; another tenement about a mile east in Mountjoy Place where I was born in 1956; add to that 6 Claddagh Green in Ballyfermot, Dublin 10, where I was reared; Trinity College, where my life was changed irrevocably; nearby Mountjoy Prison, where I was both prisoner and worker; and Donnybrook in Dublin 4, where I have spent most of my working life in radio, and you have a pocket atlas of my life story.

I had always believed that I was the quintessential Dubliner, mainly because we had no country cousins to visit during the summer school holidays. While our neighbours headed off to relatives in Monaghan or

Meath, the Duffys of Claddagh Green became the Duffys of Dollymount for a day each summer. We simply knew nobody outside of Dublin city centre. Our lives were encircled by the Grand and Royal canals, whose two placid, watery arms embraced the centre of the capital.

However, I later found out that, although my mother's mother, Grace, lived all her married life in many different addresses, all within shouting distance of the Liffey, she was actually born in India. My father's family did not have an Indian connection; they all hailed from those tenement rooms in Church Street in the heart of Dublin. But I was later to discover a link to Knockcroghery in Roscommon and nearby Athlone on my mother's side, and a very tenuous connection to Ballymahon in Longford with my paternal grandfather, also called Joe Duffy.

Still, my mother and father were reared in very similar circumstances in the Dublin of the newly founded state. My father was born in 1926, in the same tenement room in number 89 Church Street where his own mother, Agnes Carroll, also saw the murky light of day twenty-three years earlier. With a few hiccups in between, Agnes's family eventually left there in 1960.

I still find it hard to explain to my teenage children today that in the course of two generations we went from that existence to the comfort we have today. I have lived without doubt through the single most cataclysmic time in our history. In the space of five decades we have gone from rat-infested Dickensian conditions to become a modern, appliance-led, educated, well-fed nation. More so than most, my family has made that jump – and we ain't going back!

Church Street was at the heart of tenement Dublin. At one time, fifty thousand families lived in these inner-city tenements – old Georgian houses formerly belonging to English landlords, who, having fallen on hard times, simply rented out the many rooms in the tattered four-storey houses, now owned by the new Irish business class.

The corridors and stairwells were a riot of children, with the constant noise of teeming families – up to one hundred people in each house. Doors remained ajar; apart from giving an extra sense of much-needed space, people were always coming and going. The communal parlour was the street: all human life and more was there. Screaming, running, pushing, shoving, coughing, spluttering, wheezing, sneezing – scores of noisy young kids tumbled up and down the wooden stairways, invariably in bare feet.

There were four families sharing number 89: the Clarkes, Stephensons, Carrolls and Leeches. My granny's family, the Carrolls, as well as her uncle Christopher Leech and her two cousins, all lived in two rooms at the top of the house. The 1911 census records twelve people sharing this small space, with the youngest being my future grandmother, eight-year-old Agnes. They had no running water, no electricity or heating apart from the open fire that was also used for cooking. The single, shared toilet was to be found in the back yard, alongside an outside sink. There was little incentive to maintain the buildings. The only representative of the owners who visited, every week, was the rent collector. For some members of my immediate family these types of living conditions still existed in 1966, when my other grandmother, Grace, was living in the last remaining example of such housing in the notorious Keogh Square in Inchicore.

At that time, Dublin had the worst living conditions of any city in Ireland or Britain. In 1913, during the height of the Larkin lockout, when Dublin was brought to a standstill by a massive, bitter strike, the landlord called to a neighbouring tenement in Church Street. As he made his rent collections in the dusk, he heard an unmerciful roar and literally ran for his life as the tenement collapsed into the street opposite Father Mathew Hall. Two families were wiped out, with only one young child surviving. The tragedy was to lead to a massive upheaval in Dublin, but to little long-term effect. The subsequent inquiry uncovered political corruption and inaction. Sixteen councillors on Dublin Corporation owned tenements and endorsed 'light regulation'.

It took until the early 1960s, after two other tenements collapsed and an elderly woman was killed when a lorry ploughed into the already derelict building where my father's family was still living for that festering sore on the face of a so-called modern city finally to be eliminated. This was just a few years after the sixth child of Breda Fagan, one of the survivors of the 1913

Church Street disaster, wrote about poverty and triumph in the Dublin of the 1930s and 1940s; Christy Brown's *My Left Foot* is still a classic.

Most of the families lived in a single room; in some cases, two or more families shared the one space, separated by an indoor clothes line. Often a dozen people or more slept, cooked, ate and existed in a space no bigger than what we would consider today to be a normal living room.

The death rate among this class was 32 children for every 1,000 born. Contemporary descriptions of these conditions talk of rampant illness: bronchitis, rheumatism, tuberculosis, and many other infectious diseases. The home was the most dangerous place to be.

Little wonder that many men effectively lived their lives on the streets. Alcohol featured prominently in inner-city lives. My God, the warmth of the snug or the comfort of the wooden bar stool had to be a better option than squabbling for an upturned tea chest in a dark, dank, fetid, overcrowded room surrounded by sickly, snotty-nosed children! My father was among the many who chose the easy option: the public house rather than the private squalor. My grandmother Agnes would later recall that her own mother, Catherine, was a serious alcoholic who took to going to the funerals of strangers in the hope of a few free drinks.

There were only two ways out of tenement life: the British army or the British 'mainland'. Agnes's two brothers, Christopher and Tom Carroll, walked to the British army recruiting office in Brunswick Street – now

Pearse Street – in late 1914 and joined the Dublin Fusiliers. Christy and Tom were shipped off along with thousands of other Dubliners to the green fields of battle-locked France in early 1915. 'Uncle' Tom survived the war, returning to Dublin with a bullet still lodged in his shoulder. But Christy was not so lucky. Within weeks of arriving, he was gassed at Mousetrap Farm in Belgium. He survived but was sent to the Somme, where he was killed on 16 April 1916.

Eight days after Christy's death, Church Street was one of the centres of the Easter Rising. Irish people, including my granny, thought the volunteers who attacked the nearby Linenhall Barracks were, in her own words, 'mad'. Unbeknownst to his family, as the Rising threw his home city into turmoil, 23-year-old Christopher Carroll was being buried in a military grave in Bienvillers in northern France. He had died fighting for the army that the rebels in his home city were now attacking. Agnes Duffy was proud of her brother Christy and her family took out a pictorial front-page 'in memoriam' in the Freeman's Journal on his first anniversary.

According to my Aunt Renee, Agnes prided herself on the efforts she made as a 17-year-old in 1920 to help a young Kevin Barry after she witnessed him taking part in a botched ambush on soldiers who were collecting bread from Monks bakery in Church Street. Three soldiers were killed, and Kevin Barry was captured hiding under a truck – inadvertently betrayed by an un-suspecting neighbour, who warned the British soldiers:

'Don't drive over that chap under the lorry.' This poor woman was forever chided as an 'English-lover' by her unforgiving neighbours. Kevin Barry was later hanged by the British in Mountjoy jail. Agnes later took the Collins side during the civil war, and hated de Valera, whom she described as 'devious and sly'.

My paternal grandfather, John Joseph Duffy (Joe), a house painter originally from Ballymahon in Longford, lived further up towards Phibsboro. He first met Agnes at Doyle's Corner, which at the time was a gathering point. They were married in the early 1920s, and lived first with Agnes's family in the increasingly over-crowded tenement in Church Street. My father, Jimmy, was the eldest of their eight children. As with many families of the time, not all of Joe and Agnes's children survived: they had twins, one of whom, Anthony, died at just a few months old; another child, four-year-old Gerard, was hit on the head by a rock while playing on the street, and he was declared dead on arrival at the nearby Jervis Street Hospital.

Jimmy was effectively fostered out to his Aunt Kitty, who also lived in number 89. This was not unusual in those days; with the rest of her large family in two rooms, unmarried Kitty did the decent thing and helped her sisters Agnes and May with their kids. So Jimmy and his cousin Kathleen were reared by their aunt from an early age. Jimmy's siblings were jealous of the arrangement, as Kitty 'kept a good table' and had fewer stresses and outgoings than her sisters. Kitty, a formidable, stern woman with a soft centre, apparently lived off a British army pension and some earnings from moneylending.

Kitty's room also had the added attraction of a Mullard Radio, a big, brown contraption whose acid batteries had to be carried to a local garage and refilled on a regular basis. It was the only wireless in the whole house, and it began my father's lifelong love of the medium, something I inherited from him.

So my father was spoiled – well fed, well clothed, it seemed he wanted for little compared with his brothers and sisters, Joseph, Brendan, Vincent, Kevin, Rose and Renee. He went to North King Street primary school, around the corner from Church Street, but, like so many, he left to find work and earn money for the family. (His younger brother Brendan recalls using his deceased older brother Gerard's birth certificate so he could legally leave primary school even earlier.)

Tragedy was to strike the family again when my grandfather Joe Duffy died in his forties of a heart attack in 1948, leaving Agnes and the younger children destitute. The family faced eviction from their two rooms above a shop in Ormond Quay, where they had moved some years earlier. They found temporary accommodation in St Joseph's Place in Dorset Street, thanks to friends, but this was abandoned when the landlady turned out to be an alcoholic.

In the early 1950s, they found themselves living in Ballyfermot, when Agnes, in desperation, agreed to look after the four children of a widower. A short sojourn in

Drimnagh followed, but in the late 1950s their path again led back to Church Street, where they returned to the same tenement room in number 89! But Agnes loved living in Church Street; it was cheaper, for a start, and in truth was a wonderful location: a busy, bustling junction in the heart of the city beside the colourful fruit, fish and flower markets. To this day, it has firmly implanted Dublin city centre, especially the northside, in my DNA.

But when number 89 was hit and badly damaged by a truck in the early 1960s, the family was given emergency housing by Dublin Corporation in St Eithne Road in Cabra. At last, a place of their own. Going from two rooms in a shared tenement with no running water, inside toilet or electricity to a new three-bedroomed house in Cabra with its own kitchen, bathroom, toilet and a very large garden was, in the words of my aunt, 'like moving into a hotel'.

My father was lucky; apart from a brief stay with the family in Ormond Quay, he remained living with his Aunt Kitty in Church Street until her death in 1951. He had become a confident, gregarious man-about-town while the rest of the family moved from home to home around Dublin.

Meanwhile, a few hundred yards across the Liffey, in York Street, my mother was living in one of the many homes she was to inhabit – if only briefly at times – as a child. My mother's family led a nomadic life, moving from house to hovel and onwards. My aunts once counted that they had lived in nineteen different homes in and around central Dublin during their childhood.

Grace Murphy, my maternal grandmother, was born in India in 1904. Her father, Joseph Ganly, from Knockcroghery in County Roscommon, joined the Connaught Rangers in 1894 at the age of seventeen. Three days before Christmas 1896, he married Elizabeth (Lizzie) Dowling of Strand Street in Athlone – and was promptly dispatched to India, leaving his new bride at home. He marked his twenty-first birthday on the high seas, arriving in Bombay on 4 February 1897. He took the train inland from bustling Victoria Station to the massive British army fort in Ahmednagar, where he would spend most of the following twelve years. As a soldier of a colonial power, he lived a charmed life in occupied India. For most of his stay, there was no war on, no counter-insurgency, so Joseph Ganly had little to do except better himself – and, like other soldiers, drink.

Despite only being married seven months, his wife Elizabeth gave birth to a baby boy back home in Athlone on 31 July 1897. Jack Francis Ganly was five before he met his father. By that time, Joseph Ganly had been promoted to sergeant and so was entitled to bring his family out to India. His wife and child travelled by sea from Ireland, a journey that took a month. Within a year, Jack was to have a new brother, Edward. My grandmother Grace was born in 1904, almost exactly a year later, followed quickly by two other siblings, Christy and Mabel.

Their life in Ahmednagar was idyllic. The army barracks was a completely self-contained town, fortified by a massive, impenetrable wall and set apart from the impoverished, teeming nearby Indian town. It was more like a holiday camp than a military establishment. Life was easy, the climate temperate, and I have no doubt that my grandmother's first three years of life were simply her happiest. She would have played safely in the green fields of the fort with her brother Edward (or Arnold, as he was called by the family).

Elizabeth was busy rearing her young family, but with a school, hospital, food and accommodation supplied, she was enjoying life. Then, in 1907, tragedy struck: Arnold died suddenly, which effectively ended their idyllic existence in India and my grandfather's army career. Within four years, my grandmother's brother and mother were dead, she had returned with the remaining family to Ireland and to much reduced circumstances, her father had remarried and she had acquired a wicked stepmother.

How five-year-old Edward 'Arnold' Ganly died in India is still uncertain. All we know is that this young Irish boy never saw Ireland; he was born and died in Ahmednagar. There is a poignant photo of him perched – in full British army uniform – on his father's knee, watched by his doting mother.

In 2002, when she was ninety-eight and close to death (though it was not obvious at the time), I spoke to my Nana – Grace – about her past. I asked her if she had any regrets. She said she had always wondered about

Arnold – what happened to him and where he was buried. At that stage, we did not know for certain that Arnold had even existed, but Grace spoke of him so often, so movingly, we felt he could not be a figment of her imagination.

I eventually got to Ahmednagar in 2007, for an episode of the TV series *Who Do You Think You Are?* We found the beautiful whiteboard church where Arnold and Grace were baptized. We found her birth certificate and his death certificate, which testified that he had died of 'dysentery'. Nana had always argued that this mysterious brother had died from a snake bite – which would have been possible. Along with other deceased Connaught Rangers and their children, Arnold was buried in the nearby cemetery in an unmarked grave.

Arnold died on 13 August 1907. The family was back in Boyle within a year, and my great-grandmother Lizzie Dowling died in her late twenties, almost two years to the day after her second-eldest son. Grace always insisted that she died from an illness picked up in India. Fifteen months later, Sergeant Ganly, now living beside the Connaught Rangers Barracks in Boyle, married Gertrude Brown (nineteen), with whom he was to have three more children.

Mysteriously, in the 1911 census in Boyle, only Jack, his eldest child, was recorded as living with his father and his new wife. Where were his other three children, all aged under seven? The answer can be found in the same census: Grace (seven) and Mabel Ganly (five) are recorded as living in the Summerhill Orphanage in Athlone; I presume Christy (six) was there too.

Joseph Ganly left the army in 1920 and took up a job as a caretaker in the Kings Inns in Dublin. While the Gandon-designed building cuts a magnificent figure on Constitution Hill, my granny's family lived in squalor in the workers' cottages hidden behind the eighteenth-century complex. Nana recalled her life in the Kings Inns with horror. The living quarters for the serving staff were Dickensian – and it seems her stepmother did not treat her well. She told me that her cruel 'mother' fed her on chicken feed!

I have a strong memory of walking up Dublin's Henry Street when I was a teenager with my mother and Nana, and meeting a woman who had also lived in the servants' quarters of the Kings Inns, less than a mile away. Nana insisted on this stranger retelling the hard life they had working for the barristers' organiza-tion – including the chicken-feed story – to which this bemused but kindly woman vehemently assented. Indeed, she added that Grace was only telling us 'the half of it'.

Ironically, when I became president of the Union of Students in Ireland in 1984, one of the issues we were asked to take up was the living conditions of some staff in these self-same cottages. I found the Benchers of the Kings Inns formidable opponents, who lived up to their motto '*nolumus mutari*' – we shall not change!

In 1925, at the age of forty-nine, Joseph Ganly died of tuberculosis. By this stage, my granny had met and married Peter Murphy from Portland Place in the heart of Dublin, an employee of the Post Office. My grandfather Peter's family was unusual: his father married again after his first wife had died young, leaving a large number of children – but the widow he married also brought a bunch to the household, bringing the number of children to twenty-two. Not knowing many of his newfound siblings, apparently, my grandfather was warned by his own father to be careful whom he danced with in the local halls – as she might be related to them!

Grace and Peter married in 1922 in Arran Quay Church in the centre of Dublin, a few hundred yards from where my father's family was then living, the same church where a young Éamon de Valera had married Sinead Flanagan twelve years previously. Nana's first child died shortly after birth, but another four arrived within five years, including my mother, Mabel (named after her aunt), who was born in 1929 when Grace was twenty-five. With a number of miscarriages in between, four more children later arrived. With six daughters and two sons, it was a big brood and a tough existence.

My mother is uncertain where her family was living when she was born. In fact, from the North Circular Road and Dorset Street, via Kimmage, Crumlin, Inchicore, Cabra, Eccles Street, Summerhill, Ballyfermot, Russell Street, York Street and places in between, Peter Murphy and Grace Ganly lived the thirty-eight years of their married life on the move. Their eight children – Annie, May, Mabel, Agnes, Monica, Patsy, John and Willie – were shuttled around the grey city, packing, unpacking, finding their space in cramped accommodation, getting into a new school, settling into a new class, only to be uprooted again, at least once a year. Moving and not improving.

There is no doubt that it was evictions for non-payment of rent that propelled my mother's family from address to address, and it still deeply pains my aunts even to talk about this. In many ways, they are baffled by it; their father was a hard worker, if low paid. Neither of their parents drank to excess; indeed, my own mother seldom if ever takes a drink to this day.

Looking at the map of Dublin at the time, it seems the Murphy family was like a pinball in a gaming machine, bouncing around the city from room to room, within a three-mile radius of the Liffey, never settling for long in any community. I can't begin to imagine the fear and insecurity in my mother and her seven siblings with the constant evictions. Is it any wonder that, when I tried to encourage Mabel to move out of her house on Claddagh Green, literally fifty feet across the road to a magnificent new old folks' complex with support services, she fiercely and angrily resisted. She refused to give up her home of over fifty years, paid for week by week. At eighty-two, despite living in one address for the last fifty-three years, she had had twenty different abodes in her life.

No wonder my mother is still confused about where she was born. Mabel attended five different primary schools – including St Joseph's in Dorset Street, then across the city to St Agnes's in Crumlin, and on to York Street – even though her education finished when she was twelve. My mother recalls making her First Holy Communion in St Joseph's in the mid-1930s, but still wonders if she ever made her Confirmation, as she has no recollection of it. Neither did she do any exams: while school attendance had been made compulsory three years before she was born, the primary cert was voluntary until 1943. Up to the late 1950s, very few went on to second-level education, with fewer than ten thousand students sitting the Leaving Certificate each year at that time.

Grace took her daughters out of school at an early age, not telling her husband, so they could work and bring in money. This seemed to be the only objective – survival. My aunts talk with some anger about their mother making them chop sticks and sell them door to door for firewood when they should have been at school. It seemed a haphazard existence, but in many ways – apart from the constant evictions – was it very different from countless other families across the country at the time? Remember, children's allowance in any form was not introduced in Ireland until 1944, and even then it was a pittance paid to the father for the third and every subsequent child.

So, at an early age, like the rest of her family, my mother entered the world of work. She worked in a local factory, followed by a spell in Lamb's jam factory in Bluebell, and then moved on to the Post and Telegraph depot in John's Road, where she worked at repairing the Bakelite telephones, along with three of her sisters, Annie, Agnes and Patsy.

It was a busy household, and you would wonder how they ever got time to go to work or school. With six girls spread across eighteen years, there was a great liveliness and sisterly competition and conviviality between them, which made for interesting times, to say the least. With no electricity and no radio, and such cramped living conditions, the main source of entertainment for the six Murphy girls would have been going out to the 'pictures' or dances. It was at one of these dances that Mabel would meet Jimmy.

'Nana' Grace Murphy was a tough, resilient woman. Short, thin and wrinkled, and always wearing a turban-like hat to cover her thinning grey hair, when I knew her, she was very much the archetypal granny. Her life was deeply influenced by the fact that the material comforts of her time in India had disintegrated in the space of a few short years from the day she left India in 1908.

I remember walking to my home on Claddagh Green one afternoon to be accosted by Nana storming down the road. She started shouting at me, her finger wagging, instructing me to tell my mother, her daughter, that she would never talk to her again. I was dumb-struck as she yelled at me that she would 'not allow anyone to talk to me like that'. I was scared out of my wits. When I reached my hall door, I was shaking with fear and could not tell my mother of this encounter. What the row was about, I will never know.

Nana Murphy was at this stage living – not for the

first or last time – in Ballyfermot. Her husband Peter had died suddenly in January 1960, a day after my fourth birthday. My recollection of him is of a large, imposing, gentle man standing at the door of his house on Sarsfield Road in Ballyfermot. He was idolized by his children. His daughters subsequently insisted that their father was a good provider but that Nana simply frittered money away on frivolous things. Her daughters tell tales of her constantly redecorating or buying unnecessary household goods.

Within ten months of Peter's death, the newly widowed Grace was evicted again for non-payment of rent. At this stage, only two of her adult children, John and Patsy, were living with her. Patsy describes the feverish telegrams to Annie, the eldest daughter, living in Coleraine, to try to get money to pay the rent arrears to Dublin in time. It was not to be. Late at night, the sheriff arrived and Grace's furniture was loaded on to a horse and cart. John disappeared into the night and 20-year-old Patsy was left to her own devices. She landed on our doorstep in Claddagh Green, where she lived with us for two years. The family was finally sundered.

Patsy took this wrench badly. She was without doubt the daughter most open in talking about the difficulties with her mother. It was clear when I spoke to my aunts after she died that my grandmother was not a happy woman.

My granny ended up living in Keogh Square in Inchicore in Dublin, where the conditions were similar to those in Church Street, which my father's family had only left a few years previously. But Keogh Square really was the lowest of the low. In the Dáil in 1965, the then Fianna Fáil minister for local government Neil Blaney admitted that the houses in Keogh Square were 'substandard as regards their suitability for human habitation'. We seldom visited, but when we did, braving the dark stairs smelling of urine, we only stayed long enough for the novelty of a heel of batch loaf crisply toasted on an open fire.

Most of Grace's children took the earliest opportunity to get out from under her feet. A coming of age surely in all our lives is the realization that those whom we naturally adore – parents, grandparents, teachers – may not after all be superhuman, but in truth are like the rest of us, complete with flaws, weaknesses and foibles.

When her son John, who was regarded as vulnerable because of a childhood illness, fled to the UK, Grace promptly boarded the cattle boat to Holyhead, and did not rest until she got to London, tracked him down and brought him home. John spent a lot of his life in institutions, particularly St Ita's in Portrane, and Nana was devoted to him. She worried what would become of him if she predeceased him, as, inevitably, she felt she would. She never missed a weekly visit to him, right up to her death. I visited John myself in the controversial institution. He thought I was my father and seemed to be happy, once he had access to cigarettes. Nana was very close to her daughter May, too, and lived with her and her children for many years.

Grace died at the age of ninety-eight on 6 November

2002. Her son John died of natural causes thirty days later.

My father began his working life in his teens, with one of the biggest employers in the capital, Brooks Thomas, a builders' providers, whose yards and shops dominated the capital from Marlborough Street to Ballybough and much of Dublin's docklands. His father and many of the extended family worked there also. He later regaled me with stories of how the workers were dispatched from their Marlborough Street base to help out with the harvest after the Second World War or 'The Emergency', sitting in the back of open Brooks trucks as they bounced their way to the countryside to help with – or hinder – the harvest. He had no previous experience of rural life, and he loved it.

On another occasion, my father would recall how, during a strike at Brooks, he invented a new weapon to beat the 'scabs', as he called them. As the strike-breaking drivers waited to be dispatched from Marlborough Street, he would embed a nail in a matchbox and hide the upstanding weapon under the front tyre – which would promptly burst as it moved off.

By 1951, my father was back living with his mother in Ormond Quay, following Kitty's death. Jimmy was developing a drink problem, according to his sister. There was even talk of going to the St Vincent de Paul Society about the issue – though what they would have been able to do about what was surely a common problem in Dublin, heaven only knows.

Jimmy had by this stage 'moved on' from his job in Brooks Thomas – unusually, as his family was embedded there. A job as a barman in the Catholic Commercial Club in Upper O'Connell Street followed. But giving the bar to a man who was inordinately fond of the drink was letting the thirsty cat loose among the pigeons – so it wasn't long before the cat was out of the bag, and he departed. (He would often talk about this gentleman's club when we walked past the premises, which closed in 1954, but his main claim to fame is that he had taught the ten-year-old John Bowman how to play snooker, as his father was a member. Thankfully, John gave up the snooker cue and took up the microphone.)

My father then got a job in Wigoders wallpaper shop in Talbot Street, around the corner from Brooks. He worked as a sales assistant, complete with his brown shop-coat. I suspect he was rather good at this as, like my brothers James and Peter, he was brilliant at dealing with the public.

Jimmy seemed to be a real Jack-the-lad. He was always well dressed, in a Crombie and waistcoat. Indeed, in his sisters' words, 'That Crombie kept us alive.' His sisters Rose and Renee would head off every Monday morning to the pawn shop, unbeknownst to Jimmy, with his best Crombie, which gave Aggie her few bob until pay day, when the immaculate coat would be retrieved in time for Jimmy's weekend activities.

My parents were living close to each other in the city centre, and they met in the Ierne Ballroom in Parnell

Square, which in 1950 had a reputation as a dance hall for 'culchies'. Jimmy was slim, dapper, witty, a snappy dresser who took a drink and smoked and was apparently popular with women. My mother Mabel was not his first girlfriend. She was a bright, attractive, elegant, slim, blonde woman, and a fine dancer. Indeed, she herself was not without her suitors.

Jimmy was twenty-four, Mabel just over twenty-one, and they hit it off. They made a handsome couple, stepping out together. However, Mabel lost interest after a few weeks and called it off. It wasn't so much the hand of fate but a glove that brought them back together: Jimmy found one of Mabel's from their final date, reappeared with the missing item and their courtship was reignited.

Within two years, they were married, on 6 August 1952 in St Michael's Church in Inchicore. The reception afterwards was held in the back garden of my granny Grace Murphy's house in Sarsfield Road in Ballyfermot. Like most weddings then, it wasn't a lavish affair. My other granny – Agnes Duffy – recalled that she was back home by tea time!

After they were married, my parents lived for five years in a one-bedroom flat at the top of a tenement in Mountjoy Place in central Dublin, a few hundred yards from O'Connell Street and in the shadow of Croke Park. My aunts describe this attic room as disastrous. It contained only a bed, a chair, a table and a cooker; visitors had to sit on the bed. There was a second room available, but it was unusable because of dampness and cold. My aunts also recall that my mother was terrified of the dark – and, being at the top of the house, the stairs were always in darkness. On the other hand, having been born in the same tenement room in which his own mother came into the world, I am sure that the green space of nearby Mountjoy Square must have seemed like a savannah to my father.

I often wondered why my parents' first child, James, was born in the Rotunda Hospital in Parnell Square in 1953, while each of the five of us thereafter was born at home, either in Mountjoy Place, as in my case, or in Ballyfermot for my four younger siblings. Whenever I asked my father about this anomaly, he would quip, 'You were born at home because you wanted to be near your mother at the time.'

The truth only emerged years later. Apparently, when my 24-year-old mother went in to have her first child, James, it seems she was blissfully unaware of what lay ahead of her. My aunt reveals that, during a protracted and very painful labour, the midwife reacted to my mother's screams with force. My aunt insists that my screaming mother was slapped by the impatient hospital midwife. My mother, with her usual reticence and embarrassment, recalls the nurse being 'rough' and bruising her face while trying to get her to inhale pain-relieving oxygen. My father and granny were shocked by the bruising and complained to the Rotunda. I have no doubt that Grace would have been a formidable advocate, but nothing came of it – and what could have come of it in that day and age, a young working-class woman allegedly assaulted in a hospital?

But Mabel did take the issue into her own hands: she simply never went back to a maternity hospital to give birth. She was not advocating home deliveries, organic living or new-age birth techniques by shunning maternity wards; she was simply afraid.

CHAPTER 2

Rock-a-Bye, Baby

I WAS BORN INTO A GREY TIME IN THE HISTORY OF Ireland, in the dying days of January 1956, in that small room in Mountjoy Place.

The census taken in June 1956, where I was enumerated for the first time, recorded the lowest population in Ireland since records began. Ireland was in the middle of an economic downturn. Taoiseach John A. Costello's inter-party government was implementing savage austerity measures. Times were bleak and looking bleaker.

My only memory of Mountjoy Place is of a very tall building and a long climb to the top room. To my very young mind, it had a cosy feeling; after all, the whole family was in the one room. I was small, so the room looked big!

My father was working around the corner in Wigoders, and my mother also went out to work, as she had done since she was fourteen, so we were usually

43

minded by my Aunt Monica. I also have a vague recollection of being looked after by our downstairs neighbour, Mrs Cuddy, a kindly, gentle woman. For years afterwards, I recall the annual wait for Mrs Cuddy's birthday card, which would arrive exactly on time on 27 January. I would claw open the envelope in the hope of seeing the beautiful soft-green tones and imprint of a postal order, usually valued at half a crown, inside the card. Hers was the only card I got.

Mabel was now working for the Bradmola hosiery factory, and every morning she headed to their unit in Dublin airport to check the raw material being imported for the plant. She walked a lot, pushing her pram. She still talks about walking the four-mile journey from Mountjoy Place to the house her mother had recently moved to in Lower Ballyfermot, with James and me at either end of the Pedigree pram. In wet weather she would have to leave the pram in her parents' house because it was too big to bring on the bus. It would be left to her father to pull the lumbering, bouncing pram behind him, tied with rope to his bike, back to Mountjoy Place.

That Pedigree pram was the only vehicle in our early lives, as my family never owned a car. It had wonderful rocking suspension, four big, hard white rubber tyres and spoked wheels, and a strong cross-barred handle. Its depth and generous hood rendered it extraordinarily robust and provided fantastic protection from the elements. It was warm and deeply comfortable, with room for at least two, or (at a squeeze) three, young children. It was a constant feature of our daily lives and became in my mind an extension of my mother.

At this stage, we were on the corporation housing list – and with two children and two adults in one room with shared toilets, surely we were a priority? Not so; it seems the best we could do was get our name into a 'draw'. My father often recalled waiting outside the corporation housing offices beside City Hall in Dame Street as the local TD, Frank Sherwin, informed him that his name had been picked out of a hat and the Duffys were being offered a three-bedroomed terraced house in faraway Ballyfermot. We had won the lottery!

So, a week before Christmas 1957, we moved from our one-roomed bedsit to a terraced corporation house on Claddagh Green. My mother and father packed our few belongings, along with James and me, into a small van driven by one of my father's friends and made the five-mile journey to Upper Ballyfermot. Mabel even took the 'oil cloth' or lino off the floor of the bedsit and got our Uncle Bernard to cut it to fit the living room of the new house. We moved in on a Saturday – a decision my mother regrets to this day, because it is supposedly unlucky to move on the most obvious day of the week to pack your belongings! She was heavily pregnant at the time of the move, and her third son, Peter, was the first of us to be born in Claddagh Green.

Meanwhile, my father's time in Wigoders was running out; an expected, and deserved, promotion never came because, as often happened in such businesses at the time, Protestant workers were frequently promoted over the heads of their Catholic colleagues. Jimmy subsequently lost his job and that awful word 'idle' crept into our house. (Empty houses, with windows and doors nailed shut, were dressed in the same language as unemployed people in Ballyfermot – they were also 'idle'.)

Having lost his job and with no work opportunities in the Ireland of the late 1950s, my father had only one option – the cattle boat to England. Two of his brothers, Joseph and Brendan, had already emigrated; in the words of his younger brother, Brendan, 'I was forced like thousands of my contemporaries to leave my beloved Dublin city in February 1953 aged eighteen and a half.' Jimmy's mother Agnes wrote to Brendan, who was now a clerk on the construction site of the West Thurrock Power Station in London. Through Brendan, Jimmy quickly got a well-paid job as a labourer there. It was 1959, and my father was thirty-three when he emigrated. My mother was left in Dublin with three children under five.

Jimmy was gone for two years. He lived with Brendan, his wife, Kay, and their family in Canvey Island on the Thames Estuary, about forty miles from London. It was not an easy arrangement: Kay and Jimmy did not get on. It emerged that when Brendan had received the pleading letter from his mother, he had simply said yes, without consulting his wife. Jimmy would have a few pints on his way home every evening, and I presume a few more at the weekends. I can imagine the stress for

Kay, rearing three young children, having your husband's older brother living with you seven days a week. Given that my father was useless at domestic chores, he would have been no help around the house – only a burden.

My father was still drinking heavily. At one stage, his mother wrote to my Uncle Brendan looking for help with an outstanding electricity bill. Brendan gave Jimmy the money, as he was taking the boat home for the Christmas break. Imagine his surprise a few weeks later when Agnes contacted Brendan again asking about the unpaid ESB bill. Brendan then realized that Jimmy had, in his words, 'drunk the money'. My stomach dropped when he first told me this story, but it reinforced my memories that drink dominated my father's life. No matter how hard he tried, how hard he worked, drink diminished him.

We saw a lot of my mother's family when my father was away; they seemed to rally round. Nana Murphy was a regular visitor in the evenings to help with the three of us and to ease the loneliness for Mabel. And my mother regularly took us out to visit her sister Monica and her husband Bernard, who lived in a maisonette in Bluebell; Nana Murphy at this stage was in Keogh Square in Inchicore, and Agnes was in Lower Ballyfermot. We were a happy little group, Mabel and her three young boys, as we criss-crossed the city in the Pedigree pram.

My main memory of the time is the weekly phone call from my father, and my mother easing open the weekly 'registered envelope', its linen-like texture revealing fresh, crisp notes with the distinctive image of Queen Elizabeth, a welcome arrival in our household every week. I remember, every Saturday evening, my mother pushing the pram, myself and Peter in it and James holding on to the side bar, as we bounced up to the local butcher's, which had a public phone. My father would ring from London at six thirty. The brief conversation between my parents did little else but confirm that we were all still alive. We were then each passed the heavy black Bakelite handset and listened to our father's disembodied voice down a crackly line from another public phone in another country, his voice drowning in the noise of other early Saturday evening drinkers.

Whatever intimacy a phone call can offer, it was lost as people queued, and listened, in the busy, cold butcher's for their corned beef, chickens and brisket, while my father at the other end kept feeding the coinbox until he ran out of change. So the lifeline phone calls ran out, the conversation came to an abrupt halt, and we would set off again – this time into Boylan's sweet shop next door as Mabel tried to compensate us for our missing father with a bag of Dolly Mixtures and a lollipop, treating herself to a walnut whip. We could sense the sadness in our mother after those truncated phone calls – the only weekly contact between a husband and wife.

My father travelled home three times each year, for holidays at Easter, summer and Christmas, between 1959 and 1961. That was the full extent of my contact with him in those two years. But don't for one minute think I felt deprived. I knew no different; I had my imagination and was getting on with my childhood, thanks very much.

In January 1960, Mabel gave birth to a fourth son, named Brendan after my uncle. In 1961, my father was promised a packing job in the new Glen Abbey factory in Tallaght – to us at the time a small country town a long distance from Ballyfermot. It was closer than London, but just about. He landed back to a completely different family from the one he had left behind. When he departed, his children would all have fitted comfortably into our spacious pram; on his return, it was standing room only, not that the Pedigree pram could have withstood the weight of three strapping boys aged eight, five and three, and a one-year-old screaming baby. We were baffled at the arrival of this stranger seeking the attentions and graces of our mother.

CHAPTER 3

All In, All In

THE PILOT RADIO SAT RAISED IN THE CORNER ON ITS own specially built shelf, complete with cloth and meticulously tacked-on bead trimming; it had pride of place in our small sitting room in Ballyfermot. My first memory of colour as a child was this red-frilled decorative edging, which was only untacked for frequent washing by my mother.

The radio was our main connection with the outside world. It was the size of a small modern-day television. We were not allowed to touch the four big black Bakelite knobs that operated the radio once it had warmed up. Exotic place names like Hilversum, Luxembourg, London, Geneva, and even unknown Athlone, were finely printed on to the small glass screen – but the only station that ever seemed to be available was RTÉ. I still have that radio.

I recall gazing at this shiny brown wooden rectangular box (yes, we watched the radio!), and hearing the voice of John O'Donovan presenting *Dear Sir or Madam*, a public access programme – through letters only – broadcast every Saturday evening as, one by one, we were dispatched for our weekly baths. The letters, on any and every topic, were simply read out and commented upon briefly by the presenter. I often dreamed of getting a letter broadcast. For the early 1960s, it was a superb form of public access to the rest of the nation. (I have one thing in common with the great John O'Donovan: he won a Jacobs Award in 1974 – and I won one of the last awards given out before the sponsor, Jacobs Biscuits, ended them in 1993.)

Those warm, fragrant, safe Saturday evenings in our house on Claddagh Green are among my earliest child-hood memories – that hour between seven and eight sitting on the couch, smelling of Lifebuoy soap, the skin on our fingers wrinkled from the bath. Those sixty minutes were our main family time each week.

My father was always there. He would work a half-day in Glen Abbey on Saturday, visit Downey's pub before coming home, have a sleep, then he would get up again at tea time and potter around as we went through our bathing rituals. Then he would prepare for another visit to his second home, Downey's. This routine was to change dramatically as we got older and other siblings arrived, and my father seemed to be in consistently bad form every Saturday evening, presumably caused by his longing for a pint.

My mother always seemed to be busy in the house; she would rarely sit down and would seldom go out with my father to the pub. As the family grew and we all reached school-going age, she was up early every weekday, getting lunches ready, cooking the porridge and dispatching the six of us off to school – all before launching into her 'working day'. Naturally, she always seemed tired. She had no means of relaxation that I could see.

For most of my teenage years – for thirteen years, from 1970 to 1983, from five until nine every evening – she went out to work as an office cleaner in the massive Semperit tyre factory across the fields at the back of Ballyfermot. She worked hard, donning her blue smock every afternoon, assembling her chamois, sprays and sandwiches.

'Joseph' – she never addressed me any other way – 'will you have my slippers at the fire when I come in tonight.' Assiduously, I would have the slippers with the band of fur across the top sitting at the fire as the nine o'clock news began on RTÉ. I would put on the kettle in anticipation of her arrival home in the dark.

Semperit, one of the biggest factories ever built in the country, had opened in 1969. It employed nearly one thousand people, mostly from nearby Ballyfermot. The factory was so long that the first time I remember noticing it from our hall door, I actually thought I was looking at the sea. The long, thin, uninterrupted line of azure stretching endlessly across the horizon with the Dublin mountains in the background was a sight to behold.

Shortly after my mother left Semperit, when I was

working as a probation officer, I brought a group of young people on a tour of the plant. I will never forget it; it was my idea of hell. Miles of dark, windowless buildings, filled with the overwhelming smell of rubber, chemicals and furnaces; how anyone worked there I do not know. The extensive factory – which even had its own fire engine to cover the 72-acre site – eventually shut down in 1996, throwing 650 people on to the dole.

The only time I can ever remember my mother sitting in these later years was as she sipped her tea from her willow-patterned cup, still in her blue smock, watching telly. James would be out, while the younger kids were in bed. These were our intimate moments; just the two of us watching late-evening TV, Mabel in her favourite armchair by the fire, silently revelling in shared pro-grammes like *Kojak*, Les Dawson or the dramatization of Thomas Hardy's *Jude the Obscure*. (This drama – and the book – had a major influence on me. I was 16 and enthralled by this tale of a poor nobody, played by Robert Powell, yearning to make his mark as a scholar but encountering difficulties along the way, as if he never deserved anything better than what he was born into. Jude is surrounded by the constant refrain: 'You shan't learn, labour or love.')

Those evenings of closeness were only matched by rare summer mornings when, just the two of us in the house, my mother would dispatch me to Boylan's to buy a cream slice and a sherry trifle fresh from the Kylemore bakery. She would take down her treasured bottle of Irel, and pour two large spoonfuls into hot milk for a delicious, sweet, chicory-flavoured coffee – heaven. Never closer, Mabel and Joseph.

On workdays, my father was usually in bed by the time my mother arrived home from work. He always went up early, after reading his *Evening Herald*, to listen to his little bedside radio. He wasn't a communicative presence in the house. He didn't make lunches, cook, wash or sew; neither, in fairness, was he an enforcer. My mother never threatened us with his punishment – her wooden baking spoon on the back of the legs did that job effectively if needed. My father never hit us, despite the ravings of five boys, each of us born two years after the other.

He rose very early in the morning, as the route to the Glen Abbey factory in Tallaght involved two long bus journeys. Without fail, we would hear the strains of 'O'Donnell Abu' from downstairs as he turned on the radio, awaiting the first broadcast of the morning at 6.30. (To this day, I still get up at 6.20 a.m.)

Ours was not a particularly talkative household. My main interaction was with my brothers, James, Peter, Brendan and, later, Aidan, in our shared bedroom, and to a lesser extent with my sister, Pauline, who of course had the other bedroom to herself. The bedrooms were so small and close together that the ritualistic *Waltons'* 'Goodnight, John-Boy' would have been heard by all even if it was only a whisper. I shared a double bed with my younger brother Peter. I would snuggle up in my sleeping bag with my earpiece, listening to Radio

Luxembourg, eagerly awaiting their hourly 'powerplay' – the song they tipped to be a hit.

My childhood was as exciting, eventful and action-packed as any other. When we moved there in December 1957 Ballyfermot was a massive, buzzing estate, fast becoming the biggest suburb in Western Europe. Initially, the land was bought by the state for a tuber-culosis hospital during the epidemic of the late 1940s and early 1950s.

Opposite us on Claddagh Green, the signs of the newly built estate remained evident, as a large building still housed the builders' and painters' materials. It was quickly commandeered by the local St Vincent de Paul, who turned it into a youth club, which was to become one of the happiest, most influential forces in my young life.

For a suburb with a population the size of Waterford city, Ballyfermot had very few shops – but, luckily, we lived beside eight of them. There are sixteen houses in Claddagh Green and eight shops, a ratio that would bring tears to the eyes of any ardent shopper. But these shops were unusual in that the owners and their families lived above them.

Foremost among these was TJ Boylan's sweet shop where, at the age of twelve, I would begin serving behind the counter. I was lucky in that my best friend at the time, Peter Boylan, was TJ's son and lived above the store. A tiny rent office was squeezed between the sweet shop and Alex the butcher's, which also had the public phone, with its complicated instructions to press buttons A or B. Then there was Lavelle's, the vegetable shop, whose main claim to fame was that Mr Lavelle had a slew of very attractive daughters.

Across the green was Ruane's grocery store, beside Mahon's hardware shop, which had bizarre opening hours and the constant smell of Esso paraffin, his big seller for all the heaters that augmented our open fires. Beside Mahon's was Clegg's shoe shop, which subsequently became an Eastern Health Board family centre. Next door was another Boylan's, which sold sweets of a different kind: it was our local friendly chemist.

Mario's fish and chip shop was two doors away from our house, but it didn't open until five every day, noon on Fridays. The sharp smell of salt and vinegar on deep-fat-fried potatoes was a constant distraction and a great treat. Mario was an odd character, originally from Italy, with a fiery and unpredictable temperament. Short, stout and balding, he was always well turned out in his clean grey chef's jacket. We revelled in testing his temper. Once, we learned the Italian for 'fuck off' – and when we ran to the shop and shouted 'vaf-fan-cu-lo', he bounded over the high Formica counter and chased us back to our house.

On another occasion, a neighbour of ours, Mrs Doyle, having battled through sheeting rain to get to the chip shop, was surprised to see Mario wearing his trademark sunglasses. 'Jaysus, Mario,' she opined, 'I hope you get the weather you are expecting.' Again, he bounded the counter and, with a bowling skittle in hand, chased her across the green.

In all the years I lived in Ballyfermot, I still don't think Mario knew any of our names and, even though he lived less than twenty feet from us, we never visited each other's homes.

But Boylan's sweet shop was the biggest attraction, with its Dolly Mixtures, Cleeves toffee, liquorice strings, 'nancy balls' (aniseed), golfball chewing gums, sherbet dips and the penny lucky bags, which weren't even worth the penny. But Flash bars were my favourite: a strip of chocolate-covered toffee that could be tackled in two ways: either snapped off and chewed or, my preference, the chocolate trim edged off with hamster-like teeth movements, leaving the exposed toffee to be sucked slowly. Delicious.

We were well fed at home and we never wanted for food. My mother was good at cooking and is adamant we never had to resort to the 'stew house'. Even though my aunt worked in Batchelors canning factory and we often got damaged tins of beans and peas, Mabel insisted we would never depend on them. Butter was always on the table; not for us the cheaper Summer County margarine. Indeed, the presence of Summer County on a relative's table – or, worse still, Stork margarine – was seen as a distinct mark of poverty. But I do remember the sugar sandwiches, beans and sausages on a Tuesday; Sunday's left-over corned beef on a Monday; stew, mainly consisting of barley and carrots, a Thursday regular; fish for Friday; and a fry on Saturday.

For lunches, cold toast sandwiches were my mother's speciality.

We lusted after the bread pudding made by our next-door neighbour, Mrs Carroll. (I confess, I lusted after her as well!) My mother tried the recipe once and we all ended up laughing with her at the disastrous, rock-hard results. But Mabel's apple tarts were legendary; indeed, we had a 'sweet' once a week on Sunday, usually jelly and ice cream but, sometimes, as a treat, apple tart and custard. If my mother headed into town on a Saturday to meet her sisters, we might get a bag of Iced Gems or Toytown biscuits from Woolworths.

In tougher times, a packet of Jacobs' cheapest biscuits, Marietta, would suffice. We would press two of the plain biscuits gently together with slathers of butter between, and watch the worms of butter slowly emerge fully formed from the tiny pinholes. Dunking Marietta in hot tea without bits breaking off was a skill of inestimable exactitude. Scoring the raspberry jam from the central reservation of a Mikado mallow biscuit with a powerful tongue was another magnificent skill, honed over years of slow, deliberate practice.

The Carrolls, our neighbours in number 4 Claddagh Green, had a family that mirrored ours in age so, from day one, we were very close. Joe and Aileen had been married around the same time as my own parents, and had arrived, newly wed, to the recently built suburb of Ballyfermot. Aileen was young, attractive and friendly. Joe was totally different from my own father. He seldom if ever drank, never seemed to go out, held down a good job and practised endlessly on his fiddle.

Joe worked as a guillotine operator at a local printer's, eventually losing a finger to his trade. Yet this did not deter him from his music. He also loved books, and was evangelical about education. I remember Joe's entreaties to me to stay in education, not for their force but because I simply never heard it anywhere else.

Joe Carroll also had a car; first a Morris Minor with beautifully stitched grey leather seats; then a massive Ford Consul with bench seats front and back. And not only did they have a television, but they had an aerial bolted to their chimney pot, which meant they could receive a snowy BBC and ITV. TVs were a very moveable feast in the Duffy household. Firstly, at that time, most people simply could not afford to buy tellies; they rented them. The two main companies at the time were TeleRents and RTV Rentals. We used both but, within weeks, the black-and-white televisions, which only received the single RTÉ channel anyway, would be taken back for non-payment. Eventually, the only TV we were allowed had a slot in the back for a two-shilling (florin) coin. We might be watching *Bat Masterson*, the western drama, unfolding and be wondering if the TV would run out before the end of the episode, leaving a tiny, un-obliging white spot in the centre of the grey screen. Once, we bought the latest gimmick – a perspex sheet to be attached to the TV screen which would enlarge the picture. Disaster: it simply magnified the hazy image beyond recognition!

The 'coin meter' was nothing new to us; we were already using a slot machine to fuel the gas and electricity supply in the house. The gas meter under the stairs took single shillings, while we fed florins into the ESB meter located high above the front-hall door. Balancing on a chair in the dark after the electricity had expired, trying to fumble the coin into the tiny slot and turn the dial to bring the house back to life was a skill, like riding a bicycle, that once acquired was never forgotten.

Most kids got 'pay' every Friday evening. This was not guaranteed in the Duffy household, given the un-predictability about our father's arrival home with his wage packet. My mother usually scraped up something – threepence if you were under ten and a silver sixpence after you entered your second decade. When Jimmy came home with a few drinks on him, we might strike it lucky and get half a crown – five times the value of a sixpence.

Every now and again, a group of us, led by Peter Boylan, would save our 'pay' for two weeks so we could have a treat. In the garden behind the sweet shop, we would build a little cabin from empty Taylor Keith wooden mineral crates, with a painter's tarpaulin thrown overhead. Myself, the two Peters – Duffy and Boylan – and brothers Colm and Joe Carroll would gather in our secret hut and munch into our feast.

Another friend, Thomas Byrne, had turned his coal shed into a 'bat den', a concrete homage to the

American superhero. We would all squeeze into the windowless shed with the walls beautifully decorated with Thomas's own drawings – he had a true talent. But I wasn't into American DC Comics; I much preferred the feast in Boylan's.

Street games were our chief occupation. We played marbles, hunting high and low for the magnificent 'steelies' which had been smuggled out in the pockets of many of the employees of the local Inchicore railway works. We also played a game of skill using pennies called Maul, and Jackers, an incomprehensible game involving five pebbles and a small ball. Relievio was another regular street game, where two teams tried to imprison their opponents, or escape to the safety of a 'den'. 'All in, all in' was the victor's cry.

Then of course there was knick-knack, where you would have to knock violently on a neighbour's hall door and run away to a hidden viewing spot before they emerged. This was just too risky, and would lead, we believed, to serious delinquency and exile to Letterfrack or Artane industrial schools – names that struck fear into our hearts.

We never ventured to the 'far shops', except to go to the pictures in the cavernous Gala cinema, and then we could only go to matinees, to be safe. Cowboy films were, of course, a treat. The Gala was unusual, not just for its 2,000-seat capacity, but for its balcony. One Saturday afternoon, the five of us decided to pee over the balcony, drenching the kids below. Don't ask me why we did it; maybe it was just pure lunacy and mischief, or maybe we were sick of being harassed constantly by other gangs in Ballyfermot. Within minutes, Harry the Hippo, the rotund usher, was flailing around with his torch in search of the culprits. Of course, other than by conducting minute and scientific examinations, he could never prove whose urine it was.

We played soccer in the grounds of St Mary's youth club, directly opposite our house. But, in truth, I was dreadful – embarrassingly bad, pathetic. A group of us would gather, and usually the two best soccer players – Anto Doyle and my older brother James – were the captains who would pick the teams. One by one, the numbers diminished. I would be left with Martina Carroll and Ringo Carroll – their dog. Then Martina would be picked and I would grab Ringo by the string that doubled as his lead and head to the sideline. My spirits would temporarily be uplifted by a cry from Anto Doyle: 'Hey, Joe, come back.' I would bound back in expectation, only to be told, 'Leave Ringo here, he's been picked!'

On one occasion, having been rejected once again, I grabbed a sizeable rock and flung it towards Anto, hitting him violently on the ankle. He was so hurt and bruised he could not even retaliate. But it was a shameful, jealous act by me against a good friend. My embarrassment was enough punishment.

Being good at sports was a badge of honour in Claddagh Green. Even Gerard 'Gag' Dunne, who had been struck down by polio – one of a few on our estate who were hit by the epidemic of the late 1950s – was a great footballer. Gag would fly around the pitch dragging his crippled 'polio leg' behind him. When he got tired, he was put in goal, where his ball-stopping skills were worthy of a comic-book hero. At one stage, Gag even broke his arm while gymnastically trying to save a penalty. But even without an arm and a leg, Gag still got picked before me – or Ringo, for that matter.

It's long forgotten now, but the polio scare was dreadful at the time. We were all scared of getting 'the withered leg', which, we believed, was the result of not washing your hands. We were warned over and over about the scare, though we didn't need much warning, since we could see the victims around us. There are now 7,500 polio sufferers in Ireland, most of them in my age group.

From as early as I can remember, we tried to become members of the youth club in the converted corporation workers' canteen opposite our house that had been given to the St Vincent de Paul Society for the community. The square, gaunt building had no windows – they were always being broken – and the two doors at the front were constantly being reinforced with metal, after many attempted break-ins.

But if it resembled Hitler's bunker from the outside, it was Aladdin's cave inside, with table tennis, billiards and various board games, including draughts and chess. The club was divided between juniors and seniors, and we got two nights each – incredible! It was run by volunteers, or 'brothers'. That club introduced me to the only sport I was ever any good at: table tennis. I got on the club team, which meant trips to other clubs to compete . . . and be beaten. I learned a great life lesson from ping pong: after you execute a brilliant back-hander, you are naturally inclined to wonder and revel in the skill of your shot. Don't – because, in the mean-time, your opponent will probably have returned the shot and scored a point.

The big ambition for juniors was to be asked to go 'up' to senior level. I remember desperately – and un-successfully – begging to be allowed to go 'up' one time, because Bunny Carr, a TV star at the time, was giving a 'teen talk' for seniors only. I got into a verbal altercation with Brother Nolan about why we should be allowed into this vital talk – but it ended with the harassed leader telling me to get lost and calling me a 'wet sack of potatoes'. Jaysus, I was hurt for days! A few of us juniors hung around the club door, hoping to get in, but we were rejected – though I did manage to get Bunny's autograph.

Schools were overcrowded, so, unable to squeeze into the Ballyfermot facilities, we managed to get into the primary school in nearby Palmerstown. I have a vague memory of my first day and a caring teacher, Mrs Ward, taking my hand, though I did not need much coaxing. The only problem was that Palmerstown was three miles away. I spent five years travelling to school in a neighbouring parish and back each day, and had different friends in each. The shortest way to Palmerstown was through the fields. 'The Gaels' was a no-man's land between working-class Ballyfermot and lower-middle-class Palmerstown, separated by a ditch. The Palmerstown children were warned never to cross that ditch into Ballyer, on pain of severe retribution from either their parents or the Ballyfermot natives – whoever got to them first.

Along with my brothers James and Peter, I made the daily trek. The journey was enjoyably rural. Here we were near the centre of the capital, concrete everywhere, and still the Duffy trio arrived in St Lorcan's each morning with mucky boots, brambled and torn jumpers, the backs of our bare legs covered in nettle stings. Our rain gear consisted of wellies and smelly oilskin coats and hats. We must have looked like Captain Birds Eye's offspring, cast off from a passing trawler.

I enjoyed my early school years. St Lorcan's was not as packed as the schools in Ballyer and they had extra-curricular activities such as PE and elocution, though at sixpence a session the elocution classes were out of my reach. Not that you have ever noticed!

We had good teachers. I fondly remember a husband-and-wife team, the Wards, who were kindly and nurturing. Mrs Ward wrote to me a couple of years ago – she was in her nineties and still living in Palmerstown – warmly noting my radio accomplishments but insisting I must have been a very quiet boy, as she had no memory whatsoever of me.

Mrs Ward introduced us to wonderful stories like the

Three Little Pigs. When I bought the same book to read to my three children as toddlers, the memories just flooded back. The warmth I felt for that little tome, the hard, colourful cover, the glossy pages, the smell of the paper, transcended an affection for the story. Rather, it was a remembrance that the gift of reading was instilled in me by the maternal figure of Mrs Ward, for whom I developed a reverential affection.

As far as I can recall, my father never brought me to school. All the things we expect from parents today – going to school meetings, helping with homework or even taking a mild interest in their children's education – simply did not exist as far as he was concerned. My mother, who had been taken out of school early by her own mother, simply could not help us with our homework. As I said, she went to five different schools for the six years of her primary education; as she says herself, it is a wonder that she got *any* education. Mabel, like so many, has great difficulty reading and writing.

My first encounter with the curse of illiteracy came when I was quite young, travelling into the city centre on the number 78 bus. I noticed a woman opposite me reading a magazine – but she was holding it upside down. This baffled me, and I started to nudge my mother, who seemed oblivious – annoyed even – by my entreaties. Just as I was getting off the bus, it struck me: the woman could not read, but she was pretending she could.

I don't always assume that people can read and write. The illiteracy figures for Ireland are shocking, but big numbers mean nothing. It is the realization of the effect it can have on one person's life that has an impact. I invariably get emotional when I am asked to present certificates at adult learning centres; the injustice of it all is just too much. My anger and the regret at what might have been, embedded in my own experience of the wonder of the gift of reading, propels me in all directions.

CHAPTER 4

The Victor

ALTHOUGH HE NEVER EXISTED, ALF TUPPER WAS A HERO of mine. It was thanks to Anto Doyle (the budding sportsman I had tried to cripple in a fit of jealousy) that I came across this working-class, hard-as-nails runner whose abilities power him, despite hardship and sneering by his 'betters', to triumph on the running track. To say Alf was the underdog is an understatement worthy of another underdog. He worked by night and ran by day, invariably arriving at the track perilously late after overcoming a series of hurdles, such as rescuing people in distress, catching bank robbers, or simply being sabotaged by the puffed-up popinjay competitors from the private schools.

Alf worked as a welder on the uplifting wage of one pound and five shillings a week. His staple diet was fish and chips (he must have had a 'Mario's' near by as well) and he had to sleep on a mattress on the floor in his aunt's house. Oh, by the way, did I mention that Alf

Tupper was an orphan? Of course, Alf *did* better himself and got a high-powered job at an aircraft manufacturer's, where he continued to unearth saboteurs and take a lone stand against evil, while racing to victory on the athletics track.

I know; it all sounds too good to be true. You see, Anto introduced me to the wonderful world of comics. Alf Tupper was a character in my favourite one, *The Victor*.

These colourful, story-filled weekly magazines cost a full week's 'pay', so we regarded them as expensive, but once you got a few you could engage in the wonderful school of 'swaps'. There were only a few avid comic collectors in the area and it was difficult at times to find a friend with similar comic-book interest. Some only swapped *Superman* comics, which I could not abide, as they were too unbelievable. One or two teenagers with serious relationship issues liked *Look and Learn*, a worthy comic-cum-educational magazine loved (but not read) by mothers but generally frowned upon by us 'real' aficionados.

Our mothers did at times frown on the comics, but not necessarily for the reasons you'd suspect. Given her spotless household, my mother worried that the second-hand comics, which had been through many more sweaty teenage hands than the most popular and willing local girl, carried infections or, worse still, the dreaded 'hoppers'. These little red bugs, which left tiny blood specks after they had bitten, were the bane of our lives. Five boys in one small bedroom is some territory to keep clean. My mother was also convinced that the free turf we got was another launching pad of the dreaded hopping hopper.

Anyway, it was these comics that introduced me to regular reading. As well as *The Victor*, my other favourites were the *Hotspur*, the *Beano*, *Dandy*, *Beezer* and the *Topper*. If I ran out of swaps, I must confess I read *Bunty*; I soon became an avid follower of the 'Four Marys' and their weekly adventures in St Elmo's.

It was through these swapped, used, tattered and torn comics that I first discovered the joy of reading – that private, intense, intimate world I could enter. Just me, the page, the imagination – bliss.

The first book I ever got was the *Victor Book for Boys*, at Christmas 1966; I was ten. These annuals always looked brilliant; there was invariably a soldier on the colourful cover in some precarious life-threatening situation. The smell of the paper was more mesmerizing than any expensive perfume. My Christmas was time-tabled around the slow unveiling of each story, pacing myself so the annual would last beyond my bedtime reading on Christmas night, snuggling into my sleeping bag, my transistor radio earpiece in place and my little torch on full power.

Our Uncle Bernard was a big part of our lives – more than I think he ever realized. We would always know he had been in the house the moment we woke up. Either the front room, or the kitchen, or the hall, stairs and landing would be newly wallpapered. When he called, he came to work. A small, balding man with wafts of fair hair and a cherubic face, he portrayed his total abstinence from alcohol with pride through the Pioneer pin on his lapel.

Because he worked in the nearby Clondalkin Paper Mills, Bernard would usually arrive late at night, when his wallpapering, painting and general maintenance could be done without interruption from the six young children in our busy household. He was our man about the house. But this was tantamount to betrayal to my father. I suppose I can understand my father's barely disguised tolerance of the teetotaller Bernard. But Uncle Bernard and Aunt Monica were a strong and stable force in our young lives. And they had a car.

On Sundays, they would arrive over with their three children, Lucia, Brenda and Regina, and pile all the Duffy children, as well as my mother and, sometimes, my father, into their Austin A40 and head to Poulaphouca or the Curragh. Thirteen people in such a small car would today stand a good chance of getting into the *Guinness Book of Records*, but in 1966 it was our only way to travel.

I remember at least four of us sitting on blankets in the boot, with the parcel shelf removed, giving us a view out the small back window. The smaller ones would be on their mother's lap in the back row, while Aidan would be balanced on my father's knees in the front passenger seat. Add to this the egg and onion sandwiches, Bernard's Primus stove and the fumes from its methylated spirits, a couple of foldaway chairs, a tartan picnic blanket spread out on the grass, and we were in heaven!

While the kids played around Donnelly's Hollow in the Curragh or on the verdant grass around the woods beside Poulaphouca reservoir on the Blessington lakes, Bernard would get the stove fired up so we could all enjoy a hot cup of tea with beans and bread and the wonderful egg and onion sambos. The sense of space was paradise to us. Six of us were old enough to run off on our own, while the three younger children stayed with their parents.

With the weight of the thirteen of us in a car only slightly bigger than today's Mini Cooper, something would invariably go wrong on the journey home – a flat tyre or a broken fan belt. I remember, when the car overheated, Bernard galloping off on foot into the night to get help. (We always made the most of the daylight hours.) He eventually returned covered in muck with tales of falling into ditches on his nocturnal trek, but with the spare part in his hand. Once, he commandeered a pair of tights to use as a sturdy substitute fan belt.

But I mostly associate Uncle Bernard with Christmas. Regardless of circumstance, Christmas is always a nerve-tingling, uplifting time in childhood, and ours was no different. The lead-up was full of the sparkling joy and expectant fervour that grips all children. For months beforehand, the nightly conversations under the blankets in the boys' bedroom were all about what we hoped for and desired from Santa. They were warm, intimate, cosy chats, completely self-contained and all embedded in a child's world of no worries and glistening hope.

Mabel would start cleaning; the pungent fresh smell of Mansion floor polish wafting through the house was as sure a sign that Christmas was imminent as any fragrance of holly. My mother, on her hands and knees, would redden the doorstep with polish and lots of elbow grease. Then came the windows, as she, her blue smock straining, stretched to lather the glass, bringing it up to a brilliant shine with old copies of the *Evening Herald*, the only newspaper read in the house.

But the visitations of Uncle Bernard with a paintbrush in one hand and a turkey under his arm heralded the real beginning of Christmas. Oftentimes this would be for last-minute improvements, but for some reason he also 'organized' the turkey. Leading up to the big day, we would hear him debating the weight of the bird with Mabel. Bernard also made and put up many of our Christmas decorations, even sewing a star for the top of the tree and fixing the Christmas lights. He was our fairy godfather!

Christmas was the only time alcohol was allowed in our house – outside my father's stomach, that is! It was my mother who organized the small supply. On Christmas Eve, James and I would be hastily dispatched with Aidan's empty pram – the same one we used to get free turf – to the 'far' shops, where alcohol could be bought in Liptons off-licence. The load was pretty harmless – a few dozen bottles of stout, Smithwicks, sherry and a couple of bottles of Babycham. But of course we needed an adult to purchase the booze. That dilemma was easily solved, as we simply stopped outside Downey's pub, parked the pram and one of us would dart in and commandeer our father for the 500-yard dash to Liptons. His function complete, he would retire to Downey's for the last of the Christmas Eve libations while we headed home with the laden pram.

When he was safely home from the last few drinks in Downey's, my father would give his annual Christmas concert. He would stand in front of our new radiogram and begin his little recital with 'Those April Showers', moving through the seasons. The highlight would come when he launched into his version of 'The Little Boy that Santa Claus Forgot', singing with a quivering mixture of vulnerability and pathos. His three eldest boys would be lined up on the couch, mesmerized, as he slowly sang the Christmas hit made famous by Nat King Cole.

By the time the song got to the line about the little boy having no daddy, tears would be streaming down his face. My often-distant father was suddenly giving us a glimpse into his own childhood.

Despite his emotions, he made it through the song uninterrupted, such was its power and sentimentality. It's a song without a happy ending; by the final line the little boy still hasn't got a daddy, or a mammy for that matter. This sharing of vulnerability and pain had an enormous impact on us: firstly, that he had chosen to perform it for us meant that, as a family, we were blessed and together; and secondly, the fact that the words obviously left him feeling vulnerable was, to us, generous and sharing. But he did not insist that we listen, he just commanded attention. He had a good voice, and although he had drink taken, he remembered every single word. I suspect it had a lot of meaning for him. It was a ritual, this Christmas Eve glimpse into his soul. To this day, Nat King Cole's version of the song still fells me and brings tears to my eyes.

Christmas morning with six children in the house was noisy and exciting. Nana Murphy would cook a Christmas pudding for us every year, boiled for hours on her open fire, but it usually arrived at the last minute on the big day. She would dispatch her adult son John on the bus from Keogh Square with the pudding still sagging in its steaming cloth. We would sit at the window in Claddagh Green with our eyes peeled for the next bus. Our eyes would light up when John arrived, like the proverbial stork delivering the newborn baby. This treasure in white muslin was to us the centrepiece of our day.

Our father would then take us on the bus for a short visit to his mother's house in Cabra. Jimmy would be offered a bottle of stout, and we would slurp sharply fizzy Taylor Keith orange in beautiful art deco-stippled half-pint glasses. We would rush back across to Ballyfermot for the Christmas dinner. (For some reason, we always regarded my father's family as being much better off than our mother's. Nana Duffy used to bring one of us into town every year to buy clothes for us. Accompanied by our aunts Rose and Renee, we would head towards the shops around North Earl Street – Bolgers, Boyers, Clerys and Guineys. It was a real treat and, to us, a magnificent gesture.)

The rest of Christmas Day was peppered with the smell of sulphur from our new cap guns or playing out on the road comparing what Santa had brought us as we tried not to dirty our new Christmas clothes. But Christmas Day came to an end – and that magic simply was never recreated.

Much later, when I was attending a weekly group meeting for Adult Children of Alcoholics, we reminisced about the simplicity and warmth of Christmas Day – without alcohol. Somebody nonchalantly asked, 'Why can't it be like that every day?' He was right: those warm, loving feelings are all free and should be with every family every day. But every family is not so lucky.

On occasional summer Sundays, if Uncle Bernard, his Austin A40 and Primus stove were unavailable, my parents would take us on a day trip to the beach. It usually involved last-minute panic; we simply could not plan anything with my father's moods. There was no way of knowing if, after a Saturday night's drinking, he would be in any humour to go to Dollymount or Portmarnock the following morning. We would wake early, check the weather through the curtains and gingerly cajole my mother into going. Egg sandwiches would be prepared, flasks filled and buckets and spades retrieved from beneath the detritus under the stairs. Eventually, after many false starts and threats of abandonment, we would get on the 78 bus outside our house and hit town. We would cross O'Connell Bridge on foot, maybe even being snapped by the trilby-wearing photographer; if we remembered three weeks later, we could collect the black-and-white photo from his dingy basement studio in Talbot Street.

For the whole trip, there would be an undercurrent of niggling going on between my parents. By the time we got to the number 30 bus terminus in Abbey Street, we would be on tenterhooks. We would only have positioned ourselves in the front upstairs seats when the row would start, over God knows what.

Sometimes, before the bus departed, my father would storm off, leaving us stranded like passengers on a transatlantic liner whose father had jumped back to shore just as the ship sailed. He would be gone, and we would be off to Dollymount. I think he didn't like Dollymount because the pub was too far away from the beach. It was a long walk up the bull wall, across the wooden bridge and up the Clontarf Road to Dollymount House. (Drinkers like my father would be more distressed when, at low tide, a massive painted sign would emerge on the sea wall saying 'Pub this way'!)

He seldom stormed off the Portmarnock bus – there was a pub fifty yards from the beach there, and we were more than happy to beaver away on our own, digging, dipping, chasing, hiding, paddling and relishing our egg-and-onion sandwiches; Mabel was happy and Jimmy was safely ensconced in the nearby pub, relaxing.

A day trip to Bray was rare, but would be the highlight of our summer holidays. This was a much more exotic outing, as it involved the train. The beach was stony, but we could spread our rug on the large grass esplanade. There was candyfloss, periwinkles and amusements galore, from bumpers to slot machines, all in the shadow of magisterial Bray Head. The tea stalls seemed of a better class and the train journey was a treat in itself.

How we envied the Carrolls when they revealed that they were about to spend a whole week in Bray for their summer holidays; how we pined as we watched their massive light-blue Ford Consul complete with six children and a makeshift roof-rack gently bounce its way out of Claddagh Green for the long drive south.

In fairness, my father did make the effort to bring us to the annual parades every St Patrick's Day and Easter Sunday, a ritual I still force on my own three children. The only exception I remember is the Easter parade in 1966, the fiftieth anniversary of the Rising. Nelson's Pillar had been blown up earlier that year and Jimmy had heard rumours that there was going to be trouble. I yearned to go to the 1916 commemoration, mainly because I had developed an unhealthy interest in trucks, tanks, armoured cars and assorted military vehicles, and the '66 parade was to be the biggest display of its kind in years – but it was not to be.

Three years earlier, the visit of John F. Kennedy to Ireland in June 1963 marked a watershed for me in my childhood memories. It was a festive, glorious summer's day as my father gathered his three eldest boys on to the number 78 bus to see the President of the United States of America. I was seven years old. My mother stayed at home with three-year-old Brendan and nursing her two-day-old daughter, Pauline.

We did not have a television at the time, but such was the fame of JFK, we all knew his visit was going to be stratospheric. The bus got as far as Christchurch Cathedral before succumbing to the heaving weight of humanity filling the roads and footpaths. Instead of getting up near the GPO – our normal vantage point during St Patrick's Day and Easter parades – we made it as far as City Hall, with a long view down Dame Street towards Trinity College and a long wait for the arrival of this superstar.

I could see the small Volkswagen vans of RTÉ, a cameraman perched on top; the excitement was mounting. Then came the sweep of the cavalcade: Garda outriders in peaked black helmets, President Éamon de Valera's empty black Rolls-Royce Silver Wraith, then the black Ford Consul of the Gardaí, dwarfed by the enormous rafts of American secret service cars, as up to ten trenchcoat-clad agents hung on for dear life from the running boards on each vehicle.

The first thing that struck me about JFK was his tan

– he almost looked orange – and that he was wearing neither an overcoat nor a hat as he stood in the car and waved. Beside him sat Éamon de Valera, dressed in black, looking twice the age and two generations away from his beaming passenger. I was surprised that I got such a good look at him as his open-topped limousine swept around on to Parliament Street, across the Liffey and up the Quays towards a rapturous reception in Áras an Uachtaráin.

The day was topped off by our usual 'parade ritual': first, a visit to an ice-cream parlour in O'Connell Street, with treats so headache-inducingly cold that it was a double-edged sword, but so, so gorgeous. Then it was back across O'Connell Street to O'Mara's of Aston Quay. We waited outside under the watchful eye of the fruit seller while our father had a few pints. In fairness, he always sent out a Club Orange and packet of King crisps each to myself, James and Peter.

Six months later, JFK was shot dead. Like so many others, I remember where I was that day. I was seven years old, behind the counter of the sweet shop with Peter Boylan on a Friday evening in November 1963 watching one of the few tellies in the area, when news-reader Charles Mitchell delivered the bad news on the six o'clock news.

Ironically, I have attended each subsequent visit of an American president in one role or another, but never again as innocently.

CHAPTER 5

Longing and Longer

BY THE TIME I GOT TO THIRD AND FOURTH CLASS, numbers in Palmerstown school were increasing and some classes were moved to the parish hall in deepest Palmerstown – even further away from my beloved mother and Ballyfermot. This was in effect a large community hall divided in three by shaky free-standing panels. The time spent here was varied, to say the least.

One of my friends was obsessed with whether or not we wore underpants, the presence of which he regarded not simply as unhygienic but as a sign of homosexuality. He took every opportunity to lure fellow pupils to the back of the school, where he would surprise them by pulling down their trousers to jeer at their underpants. Mother of God, such lunacy!

There were other humiliations in the classroom itself. Firstly, our teacher, Mr Sweeney, noticed that none of the Duffys could recite the Angelus. He picked a pupil to say it aloud each day at noon. When it came to his turn, James got off to a stuttering start but expired in tears by the second line. Since we were all being taught in the same big room, Mr Sweeney then dragooned the next eldest member of the Duffy clan – me – to continue. I was also spluttering and in tears within seconds of the Angel of the Lord appearing unto Mary. At that stage, he seemed to be enjoying this slow crucifixion of the boys from Ballyfermot, and Peter, the next in line, didn't have a prayer (literally). So the word was not made flesh, nor indeed did the handmaid of the Lord pour forth and dwell among us; the Duffys were not worthy.

If you want a glimpse of the power of the Church in Ballyfermot in the 1960s, just look at the size of their premises – the massive, cavernous Church of the Assumption at the main roundabout in the scheme. Ballyfermot was run – in a very real sense of the word – by a big, gruff, red-faced, silver-haired Kerryman, Canon Michael Charles Troy. He was born in Listowel in 1895, and legend had it that he ministered to some of the prisoners in Kilmainham jail, where he was chaplain in the 1920s.

He was a larger than life country parish priest transplanted into a sprawling, uncontrollable, volatile urban area with the population of a small city. One of his first acts was to savagely quash attempts by a group of locals to open a co-op shop to bring down prices. (There was no supermarket in the area.) Troy smelt a whiff of communism in the 'co-op' notion and bullied people into turning against it.

However, the Church, through the local de la Salle brothers, did help set up Ballyfermot Credit Union in 1963, and our greatest claim to fame in Claddagh Green came when our next-door neighbour, Joe Carroll senior, was elected president of what surely was one of the best things ever to happen to the area. Canon Troy had also 'invited' the de la Salle brothers and the Dominican nuns into the rapidly expanding community to establish three major schools in the area.

But Canon Troy's life's wish was to have every family in Ballyfermot reciting the nightly rosary on our knees on the cold linoleum floors, and he began a high-powered campaign to that end. Leaflets, scapulars, beads and holy pictures were distributed. If his spin was to be believed, every evening at six, a reverential hush would gently descend on Ballyfermot as thousands of families knelt in unison to recall the passion of Christ – instead of worrying about whether the batch loaf would stretch until the morning. The priests of the parish were all deployed by Canon Troy to make lightning visits each evening to check on the preparations for the rosary. I recall my mother attempting the ritual a few evenings, but the leaflets were gobbledygook to her and it was soon abandoned.

To give him his dues, Canon Troy, along with the fledgling Ballyfermot Community Association, battled hard against the negative image of the area in the media. A massive row broke out in March 1971 when the flagship RTÉ TV current affairs programme broadcast a 'special' on the 'problems of Ballyfermot', featuring young people drinking cider on the 'glass road', beside the stew house. RTÉ argued that the programme focused on the lack of amenities in the massive estate – but locals said it had 'degraded and demeaned the decent people of Ballyfermot'.

By now, it was clear that the local community leaders were simply fed up with the negative image of the area. When one newspaper ran a story under the headline 'Ballyfermot man gets six months for wife beating', locals complained, and it later emerged that the offender actually lived in Cherry Orchard and had only moved to the area ten days previously!

There were darker sides to some of the clergy based in Ballyfermot. It would take many years to uncover the fact that two of the priests in the area in the 1970s and 1980s, Father Tony Walsh and Father Bill Carney, were serious serial paedophiles, as the Murphy Report would outline in November 2009. Tony Walsh officiated at my father's funeral in 1984 (along with Fr Michael Cleary). In 2010, he was convicted of sexual abuse and sentenced to 123 years.

Father Bill Carney had inveigled his way into our lives through the local tech, where he was chaplain. He then latched on to St Mary's Youth Club and performed the marriage of my older brother James in 1977. (I was best man.) Carney was a real 'Father Trendy', with a fluent use of the language of the street. My mother would innocently use the phrase 'he's an awful man' about his ribaldry; little did we know how close to the truth she actually was. He was in and out of our house for a long period. Carney was moved to the North Dublin parish of Ayrfield in the 1970s, after complaints of child abuse, which he was to continue with abandon until 1992. But Bill Carney was eventually defrocked and fled to Scotland, where he married and lived variously there, in England and the Canaries.

Why did these paedophile priests mostly focus their attentions on children in Ballyfermot and other working-class areas in Dublin? It can only have been because their victims were more vulnerable because of their backgrounds, and their abusers got away with it for so long because it was a lot easier to cover up when the good people of these areas were voiceless and powerless.

On the scale of 'sins', Father Michael Cleary's were different from those of Walsh or Carney. I had few dealings with him as a teenager, when he was a curate in Ballyfermot. I do remember one later occasion when, during the Dublin bus strike in 1974, I was trying to travel to work. I had headed to Chapelizod to avoid the massive scrum for the army lorries in Ballyfermot which were ferrying workers into the city centre. Cleary obviously had the same idea and left Ballyfermot via the quietest road. As he spun around the corner on to the Chapelizod Road in his white sports Volkswagen Sirocco hatchback, cigarette dangling from his lip, he spotted me standing alone at the bus stop with my thumb outstretched – and sped by!

I recall him officiating at funerals in Ballyfermot,

where he was terrific and down-to-earth – though on a couple of occasions he didn't turn up. I remember his spirited performances on *The Late Late Show* in the 1980s, where he coined the phrase 'yellow-pack workers' to describe the new policy of the banks of hiring young people to do the same work as the current employees but paying them much less – much like the cheap, generic, unbranded supermarket products. I sub-sequently met Michael Cleary in RTÉ on a number of occasions. He was an unusual and in many ways an enigmatic character, constantly smoking, veering wildly in his views from strict Catholicism on matters such as divorce and contraception to lunatic notions on drugs.

Shortly after Father Cleary died, in 1993, it was revealed that he had led a double life when his house-keeper Phyllis Hamilton claimed that he was the father of her two children. When the revelations about Michael Cleary's personal life came out, I interviewed Phyllis Hamilton on *The Gay Byrne Show* in 1995. She struck me as a fragile, gentle woman who had been manipulated and used, to the point where she had grown steely and determined. I subsequently inter-viewed Michael Cleary's sisters, and I know without a shadow of a doubt that those good, decent women did not know about, nor could they even come to believe, the secret life that their brother had lived.

I stayed in the school in Palmerstown until the end of fourth class. Making my First Communion there was memorable because the parish – unlike my native

Ballyfermot – threw a cake party in the local hall after the ceremony. The rest of the day was spent on the bus, as I was paraded around the various relatives, from Crumlin to Coolock and Cabra, to collect the few bob for my 'Communion money'.

However, I look back at my communion and confirmation photos baffled (not only at the fact that I was in short trousers for both) by the absence of one parent for the former and both for the latter. My father did not attend my communion. When it came to my confirmation, neither my mother nor father was there. I can only presume that, because it was a weekday, my father was working; my mother was unwell at the time. So on the morning of my confirmation in 1967 – which took place in the Church of the Nativity, a beautiful old church on the banks of the Liffey in Chapelizod – my brother James took the place of my parents.

I was to be confirmed by Archbishop John Charles McQuaid. The fear of McQuaid cannot adequately be communicated to my children's generation. By the time I made my confirmation, he had been the dominant cleric in Ireland for forty years. The main difference between our First Holy Communion and confirmation ceremonies was the fact that you could be asked a question by the archbishop during the latter. So we had learned our green catechism off by heart – it was as important a book in our schoolbags as any Irish, arithmetic or English book – just in case Archbishop McQuaid threw a question at us.

Dressed in our new suits, we crowded into the small

church, jostling for a mid-row position where McQuaid could not reach us to ask a question. About an hour later, the archbishop swept in and presided from the altar. We were eventually all marched up with our sponsors (mine being James). We quaked in our Little Duke shoes until His Grace tapped us on the cheek. No questions asked; though on the way out of the church he did ambush a few of my classmates – but his question was no harder than 'Who made the world?' We all knew in Ballyfermot that Sisk, the builders, made the world!

By the time I got to fifth class, a place had been found for me in my local school in Ballyfermot, run by the de la Salle order. I was in the same room for my two-year stay in the 'Deeler', overlooking the main road that ran through Ballyfermot, and I also had the best teacher I ever encountered, Mr Michael Long. I can honestly say that they were probably the best two years of my education.

'Longer', as we nicknamed him, was bright, effervescent and quite small. Yet, patrolling the rows of old school desks, he still managed to control a class of nearly fifty pupils. He was always immaculately dressed in a grey suit, complete with tailored waistcoat, braces and grandfather watch. Each hour, he would meticulously slick back his silver-grey hair with his neat comb, in beautifully measured strokes.

I was chuffed when one day he declared that I was 'the most curious boy in the class'. The double meaning did not hit me then; I took it as a compliment. But he instilled in us a sense of curiosity and learning that stays with me to this day. Because of Mr Long, I still relish the unread book, the yet-to-be-seen painting, the soon-to-be-met stranger, the unheard piece of music. I say to people in their darkest moments, just think of all the things you have yet to see, eat, drink, love, hear or experience. Life is worth enduring and experiencing for all the surprises ahead.

Every Friday, Mr Long set for us a quiz and a crossword. His crossword was ingenious. He would draw the black-and-white grid on the blackboard and we would studiously copy it into our lined exercise books. Then he would reveal the clues. The first to complete it would win a small prize – each one of us having contributed a 'thrupenny bit' to the prize fund. His quiz was a much more robust affair. Each one of us vied for his attention with 'Sir, Sir, Sir', as our hands shot up with bullet-like speed in our attempts to display our knowledge of the events of the week.

He was a strict teacher, but he had an avuncular way about him; I idolized him as if he were a father. He gained an extra air of mystery about him when we discovered that he lived near Portlaoise, making the daily 120-mile round trip in his cream-coloured Ford Prefect.

My new school had other advantages; because it was on the bus route from Claddagh Green, I could get home for my lunch, passing the aforementioned stew house. Also, because it was in the Dublin corporation area, we would get a free bottle of milk and a sandwich every afternoon, and a currant bun on Wednesdays. The small, ice-cold bottle of milk was gulped down in class as Mr Long frisbeed the corned beef or cheese sandwiches to every gagging boy in the class. He wasn't aiming for our open mouths, but we must have looked like begging sea lions from Mr Long's vantage point.

Even though a lot of religious brothers taught in the de la Salle school, I had little or no contact with them. Unlike in Palmerstown, the only religious pronouncements were confined to a daily communal prayer, which, for my first couple of months in that school, seemed to be a prayer for the canonization of a Blessed Brother Benildus. Here I was, aged eleven, daily praying that a young man from the south of France who had devoted his life to educating poor boys through the religious order founded by his compatriot Saint John Baptist de la Salle would become a saint.

Our prayers were answered in 1967 by Pope Paul VI, who, having heard the pleas from the boys in Ballyfermot, canonized Pierre Romançon, elevating him to Saint Benildus and raising us all up as we marched to the nearby, cavernous Church of the Assumption for a long, boring thanksgiving ceremony – our impatience and lack of interest only diluted by the prospect of free choc ices in the school afterwards to mark another remarkable achievement for the Order – and for us!

I liked the de la Salle secondary school, but I had one serious disadvantage there: I had no big brother. James had gone straight from Palmerstown to the new technical school on our estate. Because we only arrived in the school in our last years there, my brother Peter and I tended to pal around together – and indeed we still do to this day.

Peter and I were very close. We even went on the mitch together – once. After about two hours of hiding in a local park, we simply could not face the fear of our mother finding out, which she invariably would, so we headed home and made up some cock-and-bull story about the school being closed early. Mabel, with her Miss Marple detective skills, quickly rumbled us, and we were sent tearing up the stairs, with the wooden spoon flailing behind us.

There was only one fly in the ointment during my wonderful two years under Mr Long's short gaze, and that fly was not easily swatted.

You know when someone latches on to your vulnerability and, no matter where you hide, or how anonymous you make yourself, they are still drawn to you like a magnet? In my case, one local gurrier was out to get me and so I nervously tried to ingratiate myself with him. It's hard to describe the fear this bully inflicted on me. It got to the stage where I was nearly pleading with him to beat me up and get it over with! He was like a cat playing with a mouse.

'Hey, Duffy,' he would yell. 'Come over here.' I would lower my head and approach; bigger than me and with an intimidating skinhead haircut, he would engage in a series of meaningless, cul-de-sac questions: 'What are you doing here?' he would goad. 'You called me over,' I would reply, proving to him of course that I really was a wimp.

And so I waited and waited for him to attack. I knew I would get over the bruises, but the waiting was killing me.

Finally, without warning, he did it one day outside the Church of the Assumption as the statue of Our Lady looked on, unmoved. It wasn't as bad as I had dreaded, but I hated that thug. Afterwards, though, I felt great: the hiding was over! And that was the end of it; he never came near me again.

As I grew, so did our family. Pauline had arrived in 1963, and Aidan three years later. By the time I left Mr Long's class, Mabel was rearing six children aged between three and fourteen.

I was always very close to Aidan. I was about to celebrate my tenth birthday when I first heard his cries from the upstairs bedroom on 19 January 1966. The Angelus bell was tolling on our rented black-and-white television as he was born, and *Labhair Gaeilge Linn* with Eoin Ó Súilleabháin was about to start.

Aidan was very ill as a child, suffering from the whooping cough. I remember my ashen-faced mother returning from a visit to him in far-away Clonskeagh Hospital and whispering to her sisters that the two-year-old Aidan had been confirmed. We were puzzled as to how he would fare when the rest of his class would eventually make their confirmation; could he legally or morally go out collecting money on his confo, when he had made it ten years previously? Little did we know that his young life was in mortal danger. But he pulled through and grew healthy.

For a number of reasons, it fell to me to look after Aidan. 'Take Aidan with you' my mother would order as I headed off to knock for my pals, Joe Carroll and Peter Boylan – as if Aidan was in our gang. So I would wrap the baby up in his beautiful blue cardigan – a hand-knitted gift from his godmother, Mrs Carroll – his tight bonnet framing his round, pudgy face. I would sit him up in his pram and bundle it down the steps on to the street. I don't remember this being anything of a burden, but being the age I was, I was about the right side of embarrassment when it came to wheeling him around in his new pram. All the gang got used to Aidan being with us. Apart from shoving a bottle or a soother in his mouth every few minutes, he was no bother. In truth, it was like having a son.

CHAPTER 6

Jimmy and Mabel

I WAS SURPRISED WHEN MY FATHER'S FIST PUNCHED through the window. After all, it was no ordinary glass but was reinforced with wire mesh. It was a normal Saturday afternoon in our house.

Even though, as children, we all see our parents as big – in every sense of the word – I only now realize that my father was in fact a small man, nimble on his feet, not overly stout, his short black hair always slicked back with Brylcreem, balding but not bald, with a rugged round face, button nose and prominent teeth. He always dressed formally in a shirt, tie, suit jacket, braces and trousers; he never wore jeans. I only ever saw him in a buttoned T-shirt and sandals on bank holidays. He smoked untipped John Player cigarettes, so a stale tobacco smell always lingered around him.

Jimmy at his best was a witty, deeply intelligent man, with beautiful flowing handwriting. He was insatiably curious about the world around him, an avid reader of newspapers, interested in politics, sport and current affairs. Everyone who knew Jimmy – or 'Chez', the Lord Mayor of Glen Abbey, as he was called in work – described him as a character, larger than life, always with a tale to tell or a sharp riposte.

My Uncle Brendan tells a story about Jimmy and him having a drink one day in Madigan's in Moore Street in the heart of Dublin. A 'moocher' – a man looking for a free drink – inveigled his way into their company and asked for a loan. Fumbling in his pocket, my father produced a button, handed it to the moocher and urged him to 'sew a suit on to that'.

But the drink was killing Jimmy inside, eating him up, driving him to acts of mental cruelty. There was not a big drinking culture in our extended family. My Granny Duffy, Jimmy's mother, never drank; I doubt if she ever entered a pub. My Nana Murphy, equally, never sipped alcohol, and there is no evidence within her family that she tolerated it either. So why was my father different?

In my view, alcohol ruled, ruined and ended my father's life. Our week ebbed, flowed and eventually drowned in his drinking timetable. He was not a daily drinker: Mondays, Tuesdays and Wednesdays were totally alcohol-free. But then came the gathering storm.

Thursday was for a long period a similarly alcohol- and hassle-free zone, until some pioneering bureaucrat decided that wages should be paid on that day, rather than Friday, to facilitate cheque-cashing – even though most workers were paid in cash and most people did not have a bank account. For my father, as for many Irish men, this simply meant another night's drinking.

He didn't always hand up his pay packet every week. My mother would wait anxiously for him to stumble up the footpath on payday; he always went for more than a few pints on his drinking days. Then the screaming would begin, the 'tug of war' between my parents: she looking for money, he refusing to hand over. In desperation, we would often rifle his pockets or hope that spare coins might have fallen from his discarded jacket and he was too drunk to notice.

Every week, my mother threatened to meet him at the Glen Abbey factory gate. (By this time, he had moved from Tallaght to their premises opposite St Patrick's Cathedral, closer to our house.) Indeed, she did get the number 78 bus to Thomas Street and walk around to the factory gate. But he was not to be embarrassed into submission.

On a regular basis, as we got older, my mother would exclaim, 'I'm leaving.' It was, I know now, a throwaway remark to force my father to hand over the wages. But this threat instilled fear into our hearts. We saw that she had good reason to depart, so we believed her. Here I was, a worrier by nature, fretting about my mother leaving us with a father who hadn't a hope of coping with us.

But Friday nights were not the worst. That weekly tug of war would be eclipsed by the Saturday-afternoon horrors. My father would always work a half-day on Saturday – and despite his previous night's drinking he was never late. After his half-day, he would head for the pub, then home around three and promptly off to bed. When he would get up two hours later for the big row of the week, he would be, to put it mildly, 'in the horrors', as my mother so eloquently described these episodes.

'You are like an antichrist,' she would say to him. And he was.

What would unfold was, I now realize, simply a ruse by my father to get back out to the pub. After my mother had fed him with a hearty fry, he would invariably engineer a shouting match with her. God knows we all say stupid things, especially in drink, but Jimmy came up with some bizarre gems during those outbursts. I didn't know whether to laugh or cry.

This happened so often, it almost became the norm – but it was so grotesque, there was no way it could remain so.

On this particular Saturday, I decided that enough was enough. I must have been about twelve. As my father stood in the kitchen in his starched white shirt shouting abuse at my mother, I quickly pushed open the back door, lunged at him and propelled him backwards into the garden. He was a strong man, but with a low centre of gravity, so one push was enough. He was in so much shock at my actions that he even stopped shouting. There was silence.

Quickly, I locked the door. And waited. I could see his shape through the frosted glass, his white, open shirt and vest, his unslung braces and dark trousers. My mother pleaded with me to let him back in, but I refused. I honestly did not expect what happened next.

Suddenly, his fist came through the reinforced glass. I could see the shards shearing up his arm, blood spurting everywhere. I unlocked the door and let him back in. He was now subdued, breathing heavily, like a boxer realizing he was beaten, his arms hanging down by his sides, one of them bleeding profusely. The sour stench of drink and tobacco, mingled with the ever-present pungency of Old Spice, was overpowering.

I was totally unafraid. I had stood up to him at last. Making my move had put me a step above him, not below.

It was still broad daylight on a busy Saturday evening when the screams of my mother and the younger kids enveloped the house. He refused to allow us to call an ambulance; he simply put on his jacket and stormed out, heading for the pub, blood dripping from a clean white hanky which he had wrapped around the wound.

My mother instructed me to run after him as she fumbled to give me the bus fare to bring him down to Dr Steevens' Hospital. I caught up with him just outside the house, waiting for the 78 bus to take him to Downey's. I got on the bus with him and pleaded with him to stay on it as far as the hospital. At this stage, the hanky was soaked red – and he finally realized that he needed blood more than beer.

Sitting in the accident and emergency department, he was back to his 'normal' self. He told me all about the history of the hospital and about Dr Colles, the world-famous surgeon who had worked there in the nineteenth century. We talked about everything except why he was there – and sport. He loved sport: I hated it, and he knew it.

But I knew that even this sojourn in Dr Steevens' would finish back up in Downey's. And so it was: his wound staunched and bandaged, we got back on the bus to Ballyfermot and he got off at the pub. Fumbling coppers into my hand, he said little. No explanation was needed for my mother when I arrived home alone; she knew where he was. He was back to normal. And so were we.

He always sat in the front bar, only populated by men. There was a running gag in Ballyfermot at the time: Downey's was closed for renovations for a few weeks, and 200 local men were made homeless. I remember once meeting a man in Ballyfermot who told me he knew my father from Downey's. I had never met or seen this man before. It was as if my father was from another world – Planet Downey's. I once got a glimpse of where he used to sit, furtively sticking my head in the door as someone left. I was thoroughly disappointed that the smoky, all-male, stale-smelling bar looked so uninviting, dark and small. I had never been in the pub – still haven't – but that glimpse certainly did not whet my appetite.

My childhood was one of trying to maintain dignity by denying or hiding embarrassments like these. Our pals would slag us about Jimmy's drinking. They told us our babies' milk was dispensed in used Guinness bottles with a rubber teat on top!

We used to keep vigil at the door for his arrival home, which was heralded by the creaking hinges of the garden gate and then the three steps up into the pathway which were the most difficult obstacle. Too often, a passerby would knock at the door to tell us that there was 'a man lying in your garden'.

A few weeks before the fist incident, with a few drinks on board, my father had fallen and got trapped on the floor between the toilet bowl and the wall in our tiny toilet. We were woken by his shouts of 'Mabel, Mabel,' and ran down to find him helpless and trapped. We tried to pull and push him out, to no avail.

My mother decided that the only hope was to get the fire brigade to free him. I ran to the main road, hoping the nearest public phone box would be working. I remembered my mother's entreaty to make sure to tell the firemen not to put on the 'bells' as they approached our house. The darkness helped, but my mother's fear was that the neighbours might hear the commotion. A fire service ambulance arrived quickly and quietly, the two firemen came in, ushered us away, and with one pull they freed my father. He was none the worse for wear, dusted himself down and headed off to bed. The whole episode, as usual, took more out of us than him.

My parents seldom went out together; we never saw them kissing or holding hands. I remember once staying overnight – the only time it ever happened – in the house of a schoolmate, John Holland, in Chapelizod. The following morning as we left, I saw John kiss his mother goodbye. The moment is frozen in my memory. I could have fallen over with the shock, the longing and the hurt of what I was missing. I almost thought it embarrassing to see 12-year-old John being so non-chalantly kissed and hugged by his mother.

When my parents did go out, which was usually confined to the Sunday of a bank holiday weekend, the evening would normally end with my mother returning to the house alone and upset.

It's hard to explain the feelings such encounters engendered in me; a sense of fear and embarrassment, certainly, but also a feeling of impotence and a desire to get out. These episodes made me feel awkward and further distanced me from my father. After all, my mother was saying that my father had made her life difficult! Looking at Jimmy through the eyes of a 12-year-old, I could only see the truth in what she was saying.

What a burden to place on a young boy. But the energy that emerged from these episodes would, I was sure, eventually propel me to try to better myself and get away from Claddagh Green. And we all hug and kiss my mother every time we see her now.

My mother did trust me and laid responsibility on my shoulders, including sending me on the bus journey to make the weekly payment to Harry Golden, who we knew as the 'Jew moneylender'. It would become a regular Saturday lunchtime trip, but on the first occasion Peter and I spent nearly an hour looking for North Great George's Street, where our mother told us that he lived in one of the three-storey terraced Georgian houses. The trip was important, because if we missed the weekly repayments, not only would the extortionate interest rate rise but Harry Golden would arrive at our house in his grey Austin Wolseley to collect his money, embarrassing us in front of the neighbours.

This first journey to pay Harry was also severely hampered by Peter's diarrhoea. Our mother had given us strict instructions to mind each other – and on no account to lose the vital ten-shilling note (just over fifty cents in today's money). Stepping off the 78 bus on Aston Quay, we immediately had to look for a loo. We remembered O'Mara's pub on the quay from our trips into the parades. We knew where the toilets were, so ten-year-old Peter darted straight in and down the back of the pub before the barman could stop him.

O'Connell Street was some challenge; at that time, Europe's longest main street had only one pub and toilet, the Long Bar in the basement of the Metropole beside the GPO. But the holy hour was still in force, when pubs closed between two-thirty and three-thirty in the afternoon, so it was a long dash to the top of O'Connell Street – but could Peter make it without a disaster? There were public toilets near the spot where Nelson's Pillar had reigned until a year earlier, though our mother had warned us, on our lives, never to go near them.

We dashed up the street, weaving in and out of the crowd, me clutching the red ten-shilling note, Peter clutching his sphincter. Every now and again he would let out a cry – 'Joseph! Joseph!' – and I would try to spot an escape. I remember a quick dart into the lane off Cathedral Street, behind the Pro-Cathedral, for some relief.

Of course, every house on North Great George's Street is a three-storey Georgian edifice; but, luckily, Peter recognized Harry's Wolseley. Harry Golden, a tall, thin man who looked uncannily like the comedian Harry Worth, came to the big door wearing his trade-mark grubby, once-white, buckled trenchcoat. He peered at us over his horn-rimmed glasses, took the money, pencilled it into his book and gave us a receipt.

Peter and I headed back towards O'Connell Street, his diarrhoea having miraculously subsided. We decided to treat ourselves to a cake in the Kylemore bakery. We spotted these white, fluffy confections with the sign 'meringues', which we had never seen, heard about or eaten before. In we trooped and asked for two 'mer-in-goos', as the staff fell around laughing.

Just around the corner at the junction of North Earl Street and Marlborough Street was the other source of emergency income. Carthy's Pawnbrokers had the familiar three brass balls hanging over the front door, and I remember my mother wrapping my father's over-coat in brown paper, tying it with twine and pushing it up on the high wooden counter for the few bob to be handed over – just as his own sisters had done twenty years previously.

Through my young eyes, there seemed to be a lot of good-natured banter in the long queue – all women – with mostly clothes and shoes being pawned. The pawn shops were the working-class banks of their day. It appeared to me that the pawnbroker (they were always male) gave out more money than the item was worth, but he was working on trust. Then it was back in with the docket at the end of the week for retrieval – if we could afford it.

Every Saturday evening, the 'cheque man' from the Provident Cheque Company would call to 6 Claddagh Green to collect his weekly payment. These cheques were worth £1 each and cost one shilling plus a shilling a week for twenty weeks. They could only be spent in shops displaying the 'Provident' sticker, such as Sloan's or Frawley's. My mother would get a Provident cheque twice a year, in August and December. Ray Rothery, the 'cheque man', was smart and gregarious with a lovely manner. He was always welcomed into our living room when he called.

The most popular daily caller to our block was Mr Long, the bread man. He would trundle up in his distinctive Johnston Mooney and O'Brien electric van and fill his wicker basket with fresh bread for his delivery to the Carrolls. We often stood as he opened the rear doors of the brown and white van, just to get the sensation of the crusty baked bread's aroma wafting toward us.

The other weekly caller to the house was the

'insurance man'. The insurance money was sacrosanct – but, in truth, the policies were practically worthless. Recently, my mother, now in her eighties, asked me to check the value of these policies. None of them was worth more than a few hundred euro on her death. If she were to redeem all the policies she paid for over the decades, they wouldn't pay for her coffin, let alone her funeral. When I think of the fear and dread she went through to get the weekly payment together, my blood boils.

One thing you did not do if you came from Ballyfermot is plan. The other thing you did not do, if you came from the Duffy household, was to show the confidence or arrogance to predict that you were going to do well. For some reason, my mother seemed to feel guilty about good things happening. While I have never fully understood this, I have now at least come to terms with it.

Was it her own difficult, almost nomadic upbringing that makes her believe that her lot is not going to be an easy one? Though she has instilled in us a great sense that we are no better – or no worse – than anyone else, none of us who came out of 6 Claddagh Green has a superiority complex, and this has served us well. In fairness, the road she has travelled was not a smooth, clear one. It was a tough life, and she was tough but fair on us and we benefited from it.

We still have a laugh at her expense as we remind her how she would search for us at night if we didn't happen to be at home when she arrived back from working in Semperit. She would cut a commanding figure in her blue smock as she herded us back, torch in hand, to 6 Claddagh Green at ten o'clock. We were always the first home. Fear of that wooden spoon certainly put some pep in our step!

So where did this urge to better myself come from? Was it a tenacious, deep-seated propulsion to improve myself and to show the world – or my father – that I could be somebody? To improve myself, to learn more, to know more, to escape, understand more about the world we live in – it really is a burning desire. I remember walking by the dressing table in my mother's bedroom when I was about ten and catching a glimpse of myself in the mirror. Suddenly, I realized that I was a person, separate and individual, and could have influence, power over the choices I made and, above all, control over my own life. It was my existentialist moment of discovery: the realization that we are essentially alone to make our own choices, to make a difference, to decide what to make of ourselves, and that I could make a difference primarily to my own life and, with hard work and effort, to the lives of others.

So I determined to study, to improve, to break free, to be somebody.

CHAPTER 7

33,716

Apart from its wonderful people, I can't say there was much to like about Ballyfermot in the 1960s and 1970s. It went from a population of 619 in 1936 to 33,716 in 1966 – at the time, bigger than Waterford and Limerick cities. To me, living in Ballyfermot was the most natural thing in the world; only later did I see the lack of planning and foresight in the massive, cramped city three miles from the centre of the capital. Viewing it from above, you see thousands of terraced houses, relatively sparse green areas and the unending, boring uniformity of many of the narrow streets, all built around one main road. The estate is squeezed between the Liffey and the Dublin–Cork railway line, with modest public facilities – which, thankfully, improved dramatically during the Celtic Tiger era, hard won by the great community.

Ballyfermot had a terrible reputation at the time. Lugs Brannigan, the (literally) hard-hitting Garda, was often seen in the area. His black Bedford van, with silver-haired Lugs in the passenger seat, would pull up outside the Gala cinema or Nalty's, the rowdiest local pub. Lugs would slide the door open and step out, pulling on his black leather gloves, a bit like de Gaulle entering Paris in 1945. His imperious figure would instil fear, and calm, among the Teddy Boys acting the maggot!

Of course, living in Ballyer, we had very little idea of its outside reputation, just as you do not fully understand or appreciate poverty, or your accent, until you move in different circles. So, while the Ballyfermot of the time may have been sullied by notorious criminals such as John Gilligan and kidnappers John Cunningham and Thomas Freeman, in the main the people were good and decent.

Many of the characters at the time ran shops in the area. 'Dirty Aggie's' was owned by a tall, strong country woman, who was neither called Aggie nor dirty! Mrs Louise Moran – to give her her proper name – hung sticky fly papers in her shop, which seemed to attract a lot of the pests, but had the disadvantage of giving the impression of dead flies on display rather than hygiene. But at least she made an effort. She seemed always to be harassed and in bad humour; but maybe that was because she was always being unfairly tormented by us local kids.

One person who was always in good humour was our regular bus conductor, Noel Harrington – or Noelly, as we all knew him. His dark-blue uniform, with leather money bag and ticket machine criss-crossing his chest, was always brightened by a flower in the lapel. Noelly was constantly bubbly and bright, singing at the top of his voice as he collected the fares.

The local celebrities were the Furey family, who lived a couple of blocks away on Claddagh Road. They lived in a corner house and their hall door was always open – night and day. They also kept a horse outside! When these talented folk musicians would return home after a glamorous tour in some exotic place such as Scotland, they would head to Mario's chipper for a good feed of fish and chips. The word would fly around the road like wildfire. We would all head up to have a good stare at Eddie, George and Finbar in their afghan coats – after all, according to some papers, the lads had gigged with Paul McCartney and Billy Connolly. The Fureys were simply the most famous people ever to come out of Ballyfermot – until Mary Byrne exploded on to X-Factor, that is.

Often, Mario's was out of bounds for us because of gangs hanging around. The local gurriers would challenge us and rob the money our mothers had given us for the 'messages'. Even though they were no older than us, they terrorized us viciously. Indeed, the sight of Thomas Freeman outside Mario's was enough to make us prisoners in number 6. He finished as he started, becoming a notorious criminal on the Irish gangland scene, specializing in vicious tiger kidnappings.

One Saturday evening, our next-door neighbour Colm Carroll was set upon – once again – by a gang outside Mario's. Suddenly, the Carrolls' hall door was flung open and Jimmy Brennan, boyfriend of Colm's older sister, bounded across our garden, over the wall, pounced on and pummelled the attackers, Clint Eastwood-style. I remember the sense of jubilation and excitement I experienced as Jimmy, dressed in jeans and black cowboy boots, pinned the two gurriers to the ground. I still get a shiver up my spine in admiration.

I was a nervous wimp by nature and experience; I would sneak a look out our open hall door to see who was hanging around, as I would rather not go to the shops than risk a hiding from these gangs. However, the one time I did pluck up the courage to engage in a fight, I was shown up to be an underhand coward who would hit someone when they were down – and I was caught by an adult I idolized.

TJ Boylan, the local newsagent and father of my best friend, Peter, was very good to me. He had a knack for encouraging and helping out local lads like myself and our bright neighbour Anto Doyle. TJ offered me an after-school job behind the counter in the shop. I was thrilled, mainly because it meant he trusted me with money.

I would run up to Boylan's at four o'clock and work until seven. I mostly worked on the sweet counter. I didn't gobble up all the sweets around me, as the whole reason for working there would have collapsed. TJ's wife, Patricia, was rightly strict about this. I enjoyed the work; it was much-needed money, and I was treated well, though the long hours standing were tough on the legs.

As well as working in TJ's shop, I was also included on some of the Boylans' family trips. I often travelled in their blue Ford Escort to Oldtown in north County Dublin, TJ's homeplace, on Sunday afternoons. It was there I received my first and only education about horse racing, as the legendary Arkle was trained by Tom Dreaper near by.

But at times I was mortified in the company of the Boylans, who were better off than most of us on the block. The family of five – Peter, his sisters Patricia and Bernadette and their parents – lived above the shop for many years and, on special occasions such as birthdays, we would be invited upstairs.

On Hallowe'en night, we would be diverted from our normal routine of door-knocking by an invite from Mrs Boylan for some Hallowe'en games, such as Snap-apple, where we were blindfolded and had to bite a swinging Granny Smith apple – whoever managed the first teeth incursion being the winner. Then Mrs Boylan would float apples in a deep bowl of water while we queued to take turns dunking. One year, just as it got to my turn, I noticed that the boy before me had left evidence of his presence: a number of head lice were floating on the surface. I hated these 'nits' with a vengeance and they were the bane of our young lives. I was so embarrassed that Mrs Boylan might spot them that I immediately scooped them out with my hand to be discarded. Even thinking about it makes my stomach churn. But at least, as with Mrs Pender and her pots on the bus, I didn't suffer any indignity!

But back to my moment of shame: one evening, we got into a stand-off with a group of boys who lived on the next block. These were not the thugs who hung around the shops. The row was probably over something earth-shattering like a robbed set of marbles or a disputed football match. I picked up the side of a wooden orange box and struck one of the Reids across the head as he was being held on the ground. TJ witnessed me inflict the wound and promptly told me it was a cowardly and cheap act. I was more devastated than if it had been my own father. It taught me a lesson; I never raise my hand in anger.

Of all the violent episodes in Ballyfermot, and there were many, the most memorable for me came years later, during a harmless party in the Carrolls' when their parents were out. A knock came to the hall door and a few of the local gurriers tried to force their way into the house. They were challenged by Colm Carroll, who had the misfortune, in Ballyfermot, of being tall and gangly. The attackers promptly dragged him into the garden and, draping him over the small brick wall, one held him powerless in a headlock while the others proceeded to whip him mercilessly with belts. I stood screaming at them as Colm tried to protect his face from the flailing metal buckles. Alerted by the screams, my mother ran out of our house next door with the sweeping brush in hand, but still the evil thugs would not desist. It eventually ended, and the attackers fled. But we knew them.

Eventually, someone was brave enough to run to the nearest coinbox and dial 999 for an ambulance and Gardaí. Colm was taken off, deeply bloodied and shocked, to Dr Steevens' Hospital. I was determined to take a stand by identifying the thugs. So along with Liam Maguire – an unlikely but fearless superhero – I was bundled into the grey Zephyr Garda car, and it sped off in pursuit.

Cruising up nearby Oranmore Road, an eagle-eyed Garda spotted someone hiding under a car. A short chase followed and the first of the attackers was caught. He was promptly flung into the back of the cop car, beside a terrified Joe Duffy and a resilient Liam Maguire. He immediately began to threaten the two of us that if we 'went witness' against him, he would kill us. Liam told him bluntly that if they came near us, he would kill them; Liam meant it – though how he could carry out the threat was beyond me, and Liam!

We sped to the local police station and the culprit was dragged inside. Waiting in the back of the car, the two of us could hear screams from inside the station, though I can't speculate as to who was screaming or why. A few minutes later, the Gardaí raced back out, jumped into the squad car and sped off once more to Oranmore Road to pick up the other thugs.

For weeks afterwards, I lived in total fear. The Gardaí came and took a statement. The gurriers stopped and stared at our house each evening, letting us know in no uncertain manner that we were in for it if we testified. But Liam, as on so many other occasions, was courageous and determined.

We eventually went to Kilmainham court. One of the assailants turned up in his army uniform, accompanied by a supporting superior officer who gave a character reference. I can still recall stepping up into the witness box and being calmly asked by the prosecuting Garda to reveal what happened and to identify the culprits. They were found guilty and got a three-month suspended sentence.

For me, it was a pivotal moment. Firstly, I was determined to stand up and be counted; and, secondly, I could not wait to start a new life, away from such fear.

CHAPTER 8

Leaving

IT WAS 1968, A YEAR OF CHANGE, TURMOIL AND TUMULT. One era was coming to an end, a brave new world was opening up, and I was distraught. I was twelve and leaving my beloved master, Mr Long, behind.

It was by no means obvious that I would get to second level – never mind beyond – as it was not a common achievement for teenagers in the Ballyfermot of the late 1960s. The local de la Salle secondary school, St John's College, was the main option at the time. Attending their primary school was no guarantee of entry to second level, though: firstly, they did not have enough places; and, secondly, like most second-level schools at the time, it was fee-paying. A scholarship scheme was in operation, but competition was fierce. After all, it was the only way to get beyond primary school without money. (The local VEC school had just opened, but at that time it was regarded as second best to St John's, the 'Cecils' school.)

Then, as if by magic, in 1968, Minister for Education Donogh O'Malley abolished fees for public second-level schools. One day I was dreading the 'scholarship' exam; overnight, literally, St John's became an option. Modest though they were, we did not have to fork up the fees, which would have been unmanageable.

St John's was, in the main, a good, academic school, with good teachers. But my abiding memory of secondary school is the complete (and unspoken) acceptance that none of us would go beyond the Leaving Cert, at best. It was that total absence of aspiration that subsequently so annoyed, angered and astonished me about St John's. I know this has changed now – as indeed has the whole second-level landscape in Ballyfermot – but the expectations at the time were not great. The summit was the Leaving Cert, a peak achieved by few. I was determined to stay on in school and get my Leaving Certificate.

While the principal of the school, Brother George, lived in the adjacent monastery, all the staff in the school were lay teachers, apart from one other, junior, brother. In my seven years in the hands of the de la Salle brothers, I never once felt the touch of their leather straps or hands. However, it seemed to us that the lay teachers all jumped into their cars at three thirty and drove as quickly as possible out of Ballyfermot. As far as I could see, there were no teachers, gardaí, civil servants or bank officials living in Ballyer – or, if there were, they kept a very low profile for fear of being identified as such.

In the main, the staff were good. There was 'Mousey' Smith, a small, stooped, energetic waistcoated teacher who made business organization an easy pass in the Leaving Cert; Ivor Mathews taught me maths, history and geography – the latter being my two favourite subjects – though at times he was simply too placid for the wily Ballyfermot teenagers. Irish was taught by a tall, strong, deeply political teacher, Mr Henphy, whose favourite form of discipline was the 'cheek grab': the side of your face pinched between his thumb and forefinger, he could lead you up to the blackboard without any resistance. Mr Cullen, with creaking shoes and a 1950s demeanour, tried to enthuse us about Shakespeare, Yeats and, my favourites, Sean O'Casey and Frank O'Connor.

We had some memorable teachers, such as Mr Timoney, the tall, thin, mischievous geography teacher who taught me the importance of knowing what the examiners were looking for rather than the answer you wanted to give. It's a lesson that I still apply today in all aspects of my life. Mr Hughes, the black-haired, dark-complexioned Irish teacher, took us all running in his spare time. He pushed us to our physical limits, but reminded us that we could soar.

When the first female teacher arrived, we all tried to transfer into her class. Ms Murphy was young, blonde and attractive; we knew it, she knew it. But her femininity backfired one day when one of my classmates, Harry Saul, observed that 'Miss, you're sweating'; she daintily replied, 'Horses sweat, men perspire and women glow,' to which Harry responded, 'So, why are you sweating?'

Any sign of affection or encouragement from any of the teachers to individual pupils was reciprocated – in spades. But sometimes this was an illusion. One teacher in particular seemed to take a shine to me. He seemed to be good-natured and supportive. For his first few weeks, he would leave the school each afternoon with his briefcase and head for the bus stop. One day he arrived in a sporty Triumph Herald; low, sleek and fast, the car suited him.

I thought this teacher liked me, until one shocking day when he sprang a quick test on us, which we thought was of no great import. Imagine our horror, after he corrected the test, to see him open his briefcase to reveal a bamboo cane, tightly coiled like a snake; the case was otherwise empty. He then called most of the class up one by one and caned each of us on the hand with an energy and animation that was frightening beyond belief. He gripped the cane with its curved handle, raised it above his head, his feet leaving the floor on impact, his victims dancing on one leg as they tried to shake the pain off their hand as if it was burning liquid. I was sure I would not be called up – but he coldly bellowed my name and, with no signs of emotion or recognition, whipped my right hand into burning, red, flaccid weakness. I clamped it under my left armpit to try to smother the pain, but this was nothing compared with the hurt and betrayal I felt. I was devastated.

Yet still craving his affection and attention, I stood in

the yard that afternoon to bid him goodbye. He emerged with another teacher and strode off arrogantly, clutching his briefcase, through which, in my mind's eye, I could only see the snake-like cane that had destroyed any feeling of warmth I had for him.

It was in St John's that my first stirrings of social and political activity emerged. I was thirteen when the 'Troubles' broke out in the North in 1969 but, apart from a school trip to Newry a few years earlier, we knew little about this 'foreign country', except they had a different currency, nicer sweets and red postboxes. I had just turned sixteen when Bloody Sunday happened. Immediately, a group of the more mature lads, led by Barry Cullen, decided to join a protest at the British Embassy in Merrion Square. I helped to make placards, but my mother forbade me from going in case there was trouble. There was: the embassy was burned to the ground.

A few of us then had the idea of forming a students' council, electing class reps who could have a say, however small, in the school. Although the teachers reacted benignly to the idea, it fizzled out. But it did not quench my own desire to change things.

I led attempts to set up a library in the school, and even managed to get time off each day to help organize the Dewey system, but it soon disintegrated, as the messers realized that this was a great way to skip classes. They wrangled their way on to the library roster and, instead of sorting and leafing through musty books, these sessions turned into fights, peppered with trips to the cloakroom to steal from the pockets of other students. Brother George copped on to this carry-on pretty quickly and, while the library was not abandoned, the unsupervised daily cataloguing was terminated.

Brother George used to patrol the corridors keeping an eye on teachers who could not control a class. One particular teacher brought more mayhem to the school. Within days of his arrival, the disruption to his class was ratcheting up. A secreted transistor would be turned on for the RTÉ lunchtime news and passed under the desks as the hapless teacher tried in vain to identify the source of the sound. Ball bearings would be pelted around the class; to get a smack of one of them in the eye, as I did, is a pretty frightening sensation. Unable to control the class, the teacher, who did not use a cane, would make the offenders stand outside the classroom door for a ten-minute 'penalty'. Before long, the corridor would be teeming, with more outside the class than in.

Brother George would creep around the hall in his soutane, spot the madding crowd and immediately remonstrate with his colleague – who in turn came up with a way of keeping the delinquents out of the corridor: he sent them across the hall to an empty class-room for punishment. But this turned into a living hell. The messers in the class devised a plan to get the smaller students disciplined by falsely accusing them of various crimes, which of course would ensure that they would be sent across to the detention room. The bait was quickly followed by the ringleaders, who would proceed to terrorize their prey, away from the prying eyes of Brother George.

On one occasion, I was part of the bait, and I became terrified when they started to rough up one of my best friends, who was of small stature and an easy target. I ran for help to the bemused teacher, who quickly followed me into the room to rescue him. But the victim could not be found; the others claimed that he had 'gone to the *leithreas*'. The baffled teacher retreated, berating my false alarms, while the others retrieved their prey from outside the second-floor window, out of which they were dangling him by his ankles as the hapless teacher sought him in vain.

We were lucky in Claddagh Green to be on the edge of Ballyfermot, so the 'backers' – open fields that surrounded our scheme – served as our most exotic playground and the scene of our first sexual adventures. These were innocent encounters, often involving games of Doctors and Nurses with any willing females we could find in our age group; pretty normal stuff for our age.

The backers were a favourite haunt in summer. The fields were bordered by the Dublin to Cork railway line and the Grand Canal. Though we were under strict instructions from my mother not to swim in the canal among the dead dogs, discarded car batteries and abandoned supermarket trolleys, we sometimes did venture in to do the dog paddle.

A local graveyard beside Kavanagh's shop, on the edge of Ballyfermot, was another exotic play area but, given its connotations, it was a rare adventure, as were our trips to the Phoenix Park, even though it was relatively close. When we did take a day trip to the Phoenix Park, we made the fatal mistake of using a washed Chef sauce bottle to carry our milk. The mixture of brown sauce and milk was hideous! We liked the park but, apart from the zoo, which was expensive to visit and too far away to walk to anyway, it seemed a little boring and empty. Nevertheless, we Duffys, the Carrolls and Peter Boylan would sometimes head off, especially during the long summer holidays, to the 'Feeno'.

In August 1969, a man had just landed on the moon, and I was operating my own little travel capsule.

By the time I was thirteen, my summer holidays were devoted to paid work. That year, I got a summer job as a lift boy in the Metropole, with its bar, ballroom, cinema and restaurant, beside the GPO in O'Connell Street. It was one of those old lifts with double, sliding, folding gates. It was controlled by a lever that resembled the chadburn on the bridge of a ship, which had to be manoeuvred so as to 'land' the lift level to the floor so the passengers would not face a step that could trip them up. The skill involved was breathtaking and only came with experience and a steady hand. The work was enjoyable, six days a week, 2 to 10 p.m. and 10 a.m. to 2 p.m. on alternate days, all for the princely sum of £1 10 shillings, equivalent today to about €3 – a full half a crown in excess of my hero Alf Tupper!

I was bullied by one of my co-workers in the Metropole, not because of the bellboy uniform I wore, as my tormentor wore one as well, but simply because I was timid and, in Ballyfermot parlance, a 'cecil' or 'sissy'. The bully bellboy used to collar me in the small room at the front of the Metropole where we kept our cleaning materials and beat the living daylights out of me.

Despite this, I enjoyed working in the main street of the capital. The Metropole's Long Bar was the only bar on O'Connell Street, *Doctor Zhivago* seemed to be permanently playing in the massive cinema and Richie Burbridge and his orchestra performed in the ballroom on the second floor. It was the era of 'dress dances', where companies and their social clubs would host their annual meal and dance for workers and their partners. These dances were a massive part of the social scene in the Dublin of the 1960s. The Metropole and hotels such as the Gresham, Clarence and Wynns dominated the market.

Dress dances were also occasions when this little boy in his uniform might get tips, especially from the slightly inebriated Dublin men. I would squeeze them into the lift to ship them quickly from the dance floor to the Long Bar in the basement for a few extra drinks, unbeknownst to their wives. The wonderful thing about my lift was that passengers could not operate it, so I could order drunken revellers off before I would move. I could be surrounded by big men in black tuxedos, the air in the small lift heavy with alcohol fumes and cigarette smoke, me barely visible beneath them in the corner, dressed in my brass-buttoned, pristine white jacket. Yet I had the power to order some of them off, only relenting if money was proffered, which invariably it was!

But my abiding memories of dress dances were the annual ones attended by my parents, organized by the Glen Abbey social club. My mother would spend the whole day excitedly getting ready: after a trip to the hairdresser's, she would collect her borrowed long dress, with matching shoes, sometimes covered in the same material as the outfit. When she was all dressed up, she would painstakingly apply her make-up. She looked stunning, and still does in the black-and-white photos taken on these special occasions. Yet she was always ready before my father, who only had to don a rented tuxedo but would still be late, usually because he had already consumed a few pints.

These events were memorable for another reason: Jimmy seemed to be in the habit of falling downstairs at them and ending up in hospital with a damaged nose; this happened at least twice within a few years. Mortification, primarily endured by my mother, was inevitable, but I was getting older, and getting used to it.

* * *

I was fourteen when Richard Nixon came to Ireland in 1970. I had been to see JFK seven years earlier, but by this stage my social conscience was growing. We were aware of the horrors of the Vietnam War and were determined to make some form of protest, but part of it was purely the devilment, or delinquency, of a bunch of teenagers. So my brother Peter, Joe and Colm Carroll, Peter Boylan and I walked to the residence of the US ambassador in the Phoenix Park to await the arrival of Tricky Dickie.

After a couple of hours' waiting, the word went around the protesters that Nixon would be skipping the stop because he had been delayed searching for his long-lost relatives in Timahoe, County Kildare. So our 'protest' took the form of a broken matchstick inserted into the air valve of a tyre on an RTÉ TV broadcast van, most likely the same RTÉ Volkswagen I had seen in Dame Street seven years earlier during the visit of JFK.

As the TV van disappeared down the road through the Fifteen Acres, we could see it gradually list to the left as the tyre deflated before grinding to a halt. What a brave group we were: Enid Blyton's Famous Five striking a blow against American imperialism by immiserating the long day of an already overworked RTÉ employee!

I studied hard in school, very hard, driven by the desire to improve myself and my chances of getting a 'good' job. I spent a lot of my after-school time in the local library – a converted shop in nearby Drumfin Avenue. It became my new home. I loved the smell of Mansion floor polish, books and the pipe smoke of the librarian that wafted through this small, dark emporium. The librarian, a tall man who always dressed in a three-piece suit, looked to me uncannily like a bigger version of Leo G. Carroll, the head of intelligence in *The Man from U.N.C.L.E.*

I can still feel the precious library tickets, made from the same cloth-like cardboard I remembered from the registered letters sent from London by my father. You were allowed two tickets, which you would hand in at the desk to borrow a book; its reference card would be inserted into the ticket's blue pocket and filed away until you returned the precious tome.

By the time I got to my Leaving Cert year, I would stay in school after classes finished at 3.50, making the thirty-minute walk home around 6.00 for 'tea' ('dinner' was at lunchtime). After tea, I would head back to the school until 9.30, then be home in time to watch TV with my mother.

By the mid-1970s, 6 Claddagh Green was a house full of teenagers, with the six of us aged between nine and twenty. One of the more bizarre episodes during this period was the refusal of my youngest brother, Aidan, to go to school. He simply would not leave the house. I was delegated each morning to drag him to school, literally, kicking and screaming. Some mornings, his godmother, the wonderful Aileen Carroll, would help me; both of us would return not battered and bruised but none the better for the tearful ordeal. Aidan was normally a placid and calm boy, and never misbehaved, so this daily refusal to go to school was baffling. It's only now that I am convinced that Aidan simply did not want to leave my mother alone at home. He wasn't refusing to go to school; he was refusing to leave my mother.

At this time, James was working in Glen Abbey with my father; Peter, who had gone to the 'tech' in Ballyfermot, and had a lot of 'go' in him, had left school after his Group Cert and started work – also in Glen Abbey. Brendan, with his distinctive blond hair, good looks and bubbly personality, was different.

From an early age, Brendan rebelled against the discipline in the house, and at thirteen was already being difficult, though to us he just seemed a bit more adventurous and bold. My mother's nightly patrols would sweep us all up – except Brendan, who would arrive home an hour later than instructed, but always with a smile and good-natured banter.

Brendan was bright but angry. I remember one Friday night when he went to a works soccer match with my father, but it got messy and, after a few drinks, parents and children clambered into a Glen Abbey van for the journey home. But Brendan's finger got caught in the sliding door and was very badly lacerated, to the point of being nearly severed. It was a nasty incident, and he still bears the botched hospital repair job.

Brendan would leave school at fifteen and start work alongside my father and brothers in Glen Abbey – an explosive cocktail. He was the most difficult to raise every morning. My father had to put the clocks back further and further to dupe Brendan into getting up on time. Then he took up with a local crew who seemed to be sniffing glue; even the thought of it makes me want to vomit. My mother's nightly patrols seemed to focus now on Brendan's capture, but more often than not she returned alone.

Pauline, the only daughter and second youngest of the Duffy children, was – and still is – a bubbly delight. One of my earliest memories is of Pauline's third birthday, for which our mother threw a party. It was a sunny June afternoon, and I can still recall Pauline's beaming smile as she wore the new bracelet she got as a present. Pauline was close to my father but even closer to my mother. She is practical, down-to-earth, very smart and lives in Ballyfermot with her own family, close to my mother, whom she visits daily. More than any of us, Pauline understands Mabel and has much more compassion for my late father's actions than I do. If there is a voice hanging over me as I write about Jimmy, urging me to go easy on him, it would be Pauline's.

I was the first among my extended family to go beyond the Inter Cert, let alone get a Leaving Certificate and go on to university. James had got a summer job with the Swastika Laundry and wanted to stay; he then moved to work in Glen Abbey with my father. Brendan, Peter and Pauline all subsequently got summer jobs there as well. The lads stayed, but Pauline, thankfully, did go back and do her Leaving Cert. I know there were issues with money, but to think that four of my siblings left school around fifteen years of age is distressing, to say the least – mainly because they were all as smart as or smarter than me. But the educational ethos was not there in the late 1960s and early 1970s; school meant costs and income forfeited. It was as simple as that.

Third-level education was never discussed; it was just not part of our lives, another world, light years away. We did not know anybody who had been to university, or anyone who knew anybody who had gone on to third level. UCD and Trinity were not just on a different level but on a different planet, as far as we were concerned.

Even our career guidance teacher in school did not mention third level. He simply handed out blue leaflets for carpentry, plumbing, the lower ranks of the civil service, the army (but not the officer class) or the banks. These leaflets told us, for example, how to become a bank clerk – basically, write to the bank and ask them. Yet we were given to believe that our chances were better than those of our peers in Ballyfermot, because at least we were still in school.

After five years in St John's College, I vividly remember the nervous walk to the school to collect my Leaving Cert results in early August 1973. I was seventeen, and I knew that my mother, in particular, was hoping I would do well. I queued in the corridor where all my classmates had assembled – Barry Cullen, Matthew Russell, Derek Keating, Mick Molloy, Brendan Bartley, Harry Saul, David Delaney, Gerry O'Brien, Brendan Fassnidge and Paddy Flynn.

Looking back, I realize that the results in themselves were of little consequence, because nobody had told us how to apply to third level. But, psychologically, it was wonderful to have completed the exams and hold the certificates in our hands. We all exaggerated the number of honours we got. Having studied hard, I got decent results. While my grades were high, I got three honours and the rest were all pass papers. I got an 'A' pass in maths – but it was the A that mattered!

On that bright summer's morning, we all headed out the gate of St John's for the final time, believing that we would never see each other again. Three years later, I would renew my acquaintance with Barry Cullen, this time as both of us were walking through the grounds of another educational establishment.

I was genuinely thrilled with my own achievement in the Leaving Cert, and my mother was absolutely delighted. 'Joseph, Joseph!' she exclaimed, dropped her tea towel and hugged me. Mabel, once again, was giving me more encouragement to continue in education than she could ever imagine.

For some reason, at that time, I wanted to be an actor. No doubt this was because I imagined it would take me as far away from my life as possible. I remember watching Frank Grimes on *The Late Late Show* after he had scooped the role of St Francis of Assisi in Franco Zeffirelli's *Brother Sun, Sister Moon*, though Grimes and Zeffirelli later fell out and another actor got the role. I was prepared for acting, but of course was a bit worried about the vagaries of the work and the nude scenes! I subsequently took a short course in the Gaiety School of Acting, which would prepare me for the high drama and overacting that was to stand to me in RTÉ. In the end, though, I applied to work in an advertising agency. It was to take me another four years before I even decided to apply for third level.

CHAPTER 9

Mad Men

OF ALL THE PAPERWORK OUR CAREER GUIDANCE teacher gave us in St John's, he missed one important job-seeking document: the *Evening Herald*. That's where the messenger-boy vacancies could be found; I failed miserably at these interviews, mainly because I could not cycle a bike – a Christmas-day fall years earlier from Peter Boylan's new Raleigh still scarred me. But it was also in the *Herald* that I saw the small display advert for a production assistant in Padbury Advertising in Baggot Street.

I had developed an interest in the media and felt I had a creative streak but, mainly, it was the first decent opportunity I had seen, so I applied, was interviewed and joined the advertising world. Within weeks, holed up in the basement of a converted town house off Merrion Square, I was learning the glamorous intricacies and exciting possibilities of hot metal printing. I enjoyed the work, though it was all about making sure the metal blocks with adverts for Dunnes Stores, Leyland cars and JWT Travel were dispatched in time for the various papers – and returned promptly for future use elsewhere.

Within six months, I had secured another job in the same role in the biggest agency in the country at the time, Arks on Harcourt Street. I learned a lot there. The production department was run by a formidable character, Bill Molloy. With a stern military bearing, he sat magisterially at his corner desk in a big Georgian room reading his *Daily Telegraph*. Five of us sat like schoolchildren at desks in the room, the premium seat being the one where Bill couldn't make direct eye contact. Bill was very organized and precise, keeping a rigorous work diary – and checking ours every morning.

We would chase and harass printers and typesetters for the speedy return of work. We also proofread all the typesetting as it returned from 'Repro'. Those were happy days, reading out interminable recipes from the *Stork Cook Book*, which we published for McDonnells, while Bill tried in his own gruff way to spot a mistake. He hated mistakes. In fairness, in my years in Arks, I cannot remember one single typo ever getting into our ads.

I loved working in Arks, especially my regular tours around the 'house' to collect artwork, copy or blocks. This meant I could spend time in the creative departments, which is where I really wanted to be. The visualizers were separate to the 'finishing artists', while the copywriters were located on the top floor, which, in a Georgian house, is of course more an attic than a penthouse. It wasn't exactly *Mad Men*, but it wasn't boring either. With clients like Guinness, Aer Lingus, Fine Gael, CIÉ, ESB, Paddy whiskey, Player Wills and many other top brands, the creatives were important.

Top of the tree (and the house) was the legendary Frank Sheerin. I had already come across his name because he used to write scripts for the topical radio comedy *Get an Earful of This*, which was recorded weekly in the O'Connell Hall, next door to the Catholic Commercial Club where my father once worked. Jimmy once pointed out Frank Sheerin, along with the legendary actors Rosaleen Linehan and Des Keogh, leaving after a recording one Sunday evening in 1968. At the age of twelve, I was awestruck; and now I was working with Frank.

But I was just a jumped-up messenger boy in Arks. I did once submit a 'copy' test for Frank, to little avail. It was around the time that the first ATM machines were coming out, and I proffered an ad with the tag line 'The City within the Wall'. Geddit? I thought it was bright, but Frank wasn't impressed; surprisingly, that brilliant line has never been plagiarized.

There were some great characters in Arks. The building spawned Horslips. Barry Devlin and Eamon Carr were copywriters and Charles O'Connor was a graphic artist in the agency. When music was needed for an ad for six-packs of Harp lager, the three of them decided to provide the sound themselves. Enlisting their talented friends Jim Lockhart and Johnny Fean, they obviously struck a chord. Horslips was born, and Charles, Barry and Eamon were out the door and down the steps of 16 Harcourt Street as quick as you could say 'Dearg Doom'.

The poet Pat Ingoldsby was also a copywriter in Arks. We used to hide in his office, where he would royally entertain us with stories and ideas, and a smoke or two if you puffed. The only disappointment came when, after climbing to the top of the building and reaching Pat's office, you would discover that someone had got there before you. Pat came up with the name for an incredibly small Fiat car – smaller even than the Fiat Uno – which it seemed the Italians could not sell in their homeland and decided to offload in Ireland. Pat came up with the 'Bambino'! He had a bohemian air about him; not only did he dress flamboyantly, always topped off with a fedora, but he was exotic and multi-talented; no surprise then that he went on to become a highly successful children's TV presenter and, subsequently, a fine urban poet.

We had great fun in Arks; it was full of extraordinarily talented and creative people and we *did* have our fair share of 'mad men': good-looking, sexy, feisty, witty and engaging. And the women were gorgeous as well! There was a good social life, too, though it could get out of control.

The most memorable of these nights was, unfortunately, 17 May 1974. The Arks gang headed to the Clarendon Inn, a few hundred yards from the office. We were in full flow when we heard a number of large muffled bangs. Thinking nothing of them, we kept on carousing. But, gradually, word began to filter through that three car bombs had gone off in Dublin, one of them in South Leinster Street.

135

There was very little clarity at that stage as to what had happened. Even though we were less than half a mile from the site, the enormity of the horror had not unfolded, even by midnight. Being quite inebriated at that stage, I was completely unaware that my own family, having heard about the bombings on the news, had been feverishly trying to locate me.

Eventually, with the help of a work colleague, Mick Maxwell, I got a taxi to Ballyfermot. I was so drunk that Mick had to help me up the garden path. He deposited me outside the hall door, banged the knocker and fled back to the taxi, fearing the wrath of my parents. I fully expected to see anger and loathing on my mother's face as she opened the door to find, yet again, a man lying in her garden, crumpled in a drunken heap – except that, this time, it was her beloved son. My fear subsided when I was met with relief that I had made it home safely. I conjured up some excuse for my drunkenness, blaming it on shock at the bombings!

The following day I travelled into the city centre. I can still remember the eerie silence hanging over O'Connell Street. Twenty-six people – including a pregnant woman – had been murdered in one of the worst atrocities of the Troubles, while another seven died in Monaghan. (The survivors' and relatives' battle for adequate compensation would become one of the issues that we dealt with many times on *Liveline*.)

The one downside of Arks was that the weekly wages were not great; I ate every day in what must have been the cheapest restaurant in Dublin, Joe's of Aungier Street: a long queue, long benches, quick service, no menu but great food, and all for fifty pence!

While I was enjoying the new spirit of freedom offered by the world of work, I was continuously seeking to better myself through study and voluntary work, which helped to keep my social conscience alight. The ethos in Arks encouraged me to keep studying. Not a year passed that I didn't take on night classes. I was learning more, but I could also feel my understanding of the world deepening. I became aware that, to get on, I needed more education.

During my first year in Arks, I studied economics and business studies at night in the tech in Ballyfermot, garnering more Leaving Cert grades. I went on to do a course in advertising in the College of Commerce. Twice a week after work I headed from Harcourt Street up to Rathmines, grabbing a bite on the way, for a thoroughly enjoyable course that included copywriting, typography and marketing. My two-year course earned me a certificate in advertising. Arks even refunded the modest fees because I passed the exams.

Then I decided to do a course in printing in Bolton Street College of Technology at night, a fascinating romp through the printing press, linotype, block-making, letterpress and the emerging 'litho' printing, just before they all disappeared off the face of the earth. Later, when I worked in the probation service, I studied intensively at night to become a family therapist, and after three years I had the honour of being among the first group of social workers to add that title to my qualifications.

Where did I stumble across the belief, deeply etched into me, that education, learning and knowledge were the keys to improving myself? Was it something I read, heard, saw, or was it simply a gradual osmosis of tidbits, snatches of conversation or small encouragements? I know that it did not come from home – and that is not a criticism or a grievance, simply a fact. How could it? How could those who did not have the gift or the opportunity of education get a glimpse of its possibilities and its power?

I recall meeting our well-read neighbour Joe Carroll Sr on the number 78 bus in 1976, for instance. As we walked to our adjoining houses, he said to me, 'You could be somebody; you are intelligent. You should try to go to college.' He told me about Martin O'Donoghue, who had risen from working-class Crumlin by working as a waiter, studying at night, and 'bettering himself'. He was then an up-and-coming Trinity professor, and would later become a Fianna Fáil government minister. The fact that this nugget of a conversation with Joe Carroll stays with me, thirty-five years later, says it all.

The impetus for this continuing education did not come primarily from my old school, or indeed my new job, but from the school I hadn't attended – the tech, the second-level VEC school in Ballyfermot. After completing my Leaving Certificate, my neighbour and friend Joe Carroll Jr was still attending the tech.

At the time, it was probably the most progressive school in the country. With teachers such as Jim Shortall,

Janet Ryan, Vincent Sammon, Stephen O'Connor, Áine O'Connor and Larry Masterson – the latter two subsequently carving out successful careers in RTÉ – it was bright and innovative and, above all, encouraging. Through my friendship with Joe Carroll Jr, I got involved in the tech, doing business studies by night for the Leaving Certificate.

Janet Ryan, the German teacher, was organizing a trip to Germany along with a friend who was a teacher in a Ballymun school. So in 1974, a group of lads from Ballyfermot and girls from Ballymun set off on a trip to Oberstdorf. It was a wonderful journey, which had a great impact on my life. I was eighteen, working by day and studying by night, and beginning to realize that if I didn't make a move to improve myself, life would play a trick on me and I would be condemned (in my own eyes) to repeat the life of a generation before me. I was finding a new confidence, taking a stand, conscious of being a little bit older than my contemporaries and friends, Joe Carroll and Liam Maguire. So it seems that while some people talk about 'falling in with the wrong crowd', I happened to fall in with the right, bright crowd.

The group brought together for the German trip were in many ways the best and brightest from Ballyfermot and Ballymun. We were all keen on education, each one of us moving up from our working-class backgrounds – and shackles. At last I felt as though I belonged with a great group of people, people who liked my company and my wit. In turn, I started to like myself; I found a sense of self that had been absent before.

It was a great, mesmeric, liberating trip, the first time most of us had been on holiday, let alone a plane. In fact, it was more than a holiday. The idea of the two groups formalizing our connection arose even before we went to Germany. We prepared for it for months, meeting up with the girls from Ballymun and gradually trying to focus our awkwardness with each other into something productive – apart from the obvious boy-meets-girl stuff!

Every step of the trip was memorable: the flight, the bus trip to Schindelberg, where we stayed in one of the magnificent large wooden chalets so common in that part of the Alps. It was owned by a German trade union, and we struck up some great friendships with the German students from Düsseldorf who were staying there at the same time. We really gelled as a group.

The other thing I discovered in Germany was an interest in women. I had my first ever passionate clinch in the foothills of Bavaria, with a blonde, denim-clad German beauty named Ulla. About time, too; I was eighteen and had never had a girlfriend. It was as if I had suddenly awakened from a long sleep. Within weeks of returning, I was going out with one of the Ballymun girls, Anne, and we were having a ball.

When our group came back we decided to set up a youth club in Ballymun. I came up with the name Tír Na nÓg, and we got premises in a prefab on Shangan Road through the local priests Eoin Cooke and Pat McManus. The idea was simple enough; we would meet each week as a group and run normal club activities like table tennis, but we would also help out in the community. We ran fund-raising events, pantomimes and eventually summer projects for the local kids. We elected a chairman – me. We affiliated with the Catholic Youth Council and got involved in various activities.

It was great fun. We got group membership of An Óige and organized weekends away in their hostels, but we were quickly expelled after the so-called leaders of our group were caught climbing back into a hostel after hours in Baltyboys near Blessington with the so-called members in tow. The two leaders, myself and Anne, were called to An Óige headquarters in Mountjoy Square, where the denizens of the organization quickly realized that the leaders of the Tír Na nÓg youth group were the same age as the members, and equally irresponsible!

Some of the German students we had met in Schindelberg visited Ireland and stayed in our homes, and a gang of us travelled back to Düsseldorf to stay with their families. It was a brilliant, brilliant time. Of course, like me, many of the Ballyfermot boys in Tír Na nÓg did fall off their horses for the beautiful maidens from Ballymun. Relationships blossomed, some endured. Indeed, some marriages eventually came out of the mix, between Ballyfermot and Ballymun, between Dublin and Düsseldorf! There was never any acrimony. I know the whole idea sounds naïve looking back on it, but whenever I meet anyone who was involved, without exception, everyone remembers it as an innocent and joyous experiment.

* * *

In 1976, through the CYC, I was asked to run a children's summer project in the Holy Spirit parish in the Sillogue area of Ballymun. Ballymun had been Ireland's first high-rise housing project. Built in the early 1960s, it was now teeming with young families. The summer project was an instant hit. With local volunteers – powerful women such as Kathleen Maher, Vicki McElligot, Vera Hughes and Mary O'Connor – we managed to run a summer full of great activities.

We would hire a 59-seater bus – at one stage squeezing 169 children on to it – and descend on the zoo. Using the conceit of confusion, we managed to get most of the kids in free. The same bus would head back to Ballymun and bring other kids out to the beach in Portmarnock. Arts and crafts, hip-hop dancing, bingo and discos were the other activities that meant that our prefab headquarters buzzed from early morning to late at night.

For three years, I took eight weeks' unpaid leave from Arks to run these summer projects in Ballymun – and it was this experience that would ultimately propel me to Trinity.

I moved from Ballyfermot to Ballymun in 1976, simply to be closer to the summer project. A local nun, Sister Lena, got me digs in nearby Willow Park in Glasnevin North – near Bono's house! The excitement of moving to a house with my own room and no siblings was intense. Bill and Maureen Purcell became like bright, busy and interesting foster parents to me. Their own grown-up children, Declan and Deirdre, had both left home and were doing well. Declan was in the civil service and would later become chairperson of the Competition Authority; while Deirdre, an Abbey actress, was rearing a young family and beginning her journalistic career in RTÉ, which in turn would lead to great success as a novelist.

To me, Maureen and Bill were so different. I came to admire and intensely like these two wise people. Bill was a senior member of the Civil Service Commission, and I cannot imagine a more decent, honest man for that job. Maureen, an energetic, formidable and busy woman, was a part-time tour guide who had decided to supplement her income with the meagre rent I paid. Theirs was an ordered, quiet, comfortable and welcoming middle-class home. I loved it there; I felt like the only child in a soft, warm house.

In return, I brought them absolutely nothing except chaos, odd hours and the bric-a-brac associated with running a summer project for kids, including posters, T-shirts, cine projectors, tins of coins, tins of paint, tins of coins in paint, and general mayhem. Each morning I would head from Willow Park, climb over the boundary wall and into Sillogue Gardens, where the summer project was located. But the Purcells tolerated my excesses.

Maureen once asked to visit my house in Ballyfermot. She drove me over and met my mother, who I think was intimidated by this formidable, well-spoken matriarch.

This was a fantastic time in my life; I had just turned twenty, had a responsible job running a summer project, and I was meeting lots and lots of new people, mainly through the CYC. Within two years, alongside a young seminarian, Donal Harrington, and Pat Carey, who subsequently became a government minister, I was part of a team of three in overall charge of all summer projects in Dublin.

Through this work I became more involved in CYC, and based myself in their headquarters on Arran Quay. Its progressive director, John Fitzpatrick, asked me to write a few articles for the CYC magazine, *Youthopia*. I remember I got very negative reaction when I wrote a piece in *Youthopia* in 1977 entitled 'The Forgotten 3,000', about Irish children and teenagers then still in 'industrial schools'. I illustrated the piece with an image of a little boy crying – but I was accused of being melodramatic.

In the meantime, my love life had taken another turn. Having broken up with Anne, I started going out with another member of the club. Jackie was one of the Tír Na nÓg girls from Ballymun. All the things you associate with young love, from summer days, pop songs, smells, clothes, I experienced during that sultry summer.

I could not believe my luck the day I first 'got off' with her in early 1976 (before my move to Ballymun). I hopped, skipped and jumped to the 36B bus from Ballymun that night to make the long dash from the terminus in Parnell Square up O'Connell Street to try to catch the last bus to Ballyfermot. I could not wait to tell my best friend Liam Maguire that at last my luck had come in. (Liam made a similar journey every evening to his girlfriend, Linda.)

Over two idyllic summers, Elton John and Kiki Dee sang 'Don't Go Breaking My Heart', Elvis died and Jackie

Left: My great-grandparents, Joseph Ganly and Elizabeth Dowling, in India with their son, Arnold; tragically, both Arnold and Elizabeth would die within a few short years.

Above: My parents, Jimmy and Mabel, with their firstborn, baby James, in Mountjoy Square, 1955.

Above: Myself, James and Peter.

Left: The Duffy family on O'Connell Bridge, 1964: Jimmy, with Pauline in his arms, Mabel, and the boys: myself, Peter, James and Brendan.

On my first holy communion in Palmerstown, wearing shorts and brand-new Little Duke shoes.

Aidan in his pram with next-door neighbour Aileen Carroll.

What a handful: the six Duffy kids with Mabel in 6 Claddagh Green, Ballyfermot, in 1967.

Aidan as a young man.

Left: June, my father Jimmy and Mark Durkan in Great Western Square, 1983, a year before Jimmy's death.

Above: Uncle Bernard, my friend Father Eoin Cooke, Bernard's grandchildren and Mabel in 1984.

Nana Grace Murphy

Left: My USIT card.

Below: Peace in our time: occupying the Junior Common Room at Trinity College Dublin.

Bottom: 'Joe Duffel': addressing a student demo on O'Connell Street.

Expelled: (*left to right*) John Hogan, Mark Wade (TCD worker), Barry Cullen, Paddy Little, Mary Jane O'Brien, Alex White, me, Brian Dowling and Liam Hayes.

Being interviewed by waiting journalists on my release from prison in early 1984.

Professor J. V. Luce (*right*) and another Trinity official eject me during a protest against the removal of medical cards from students in 1984.

My wedding day, the end of June, 1989, with Derek Cunningham, Alex White and David Little, outside Molesworth Street registry office.

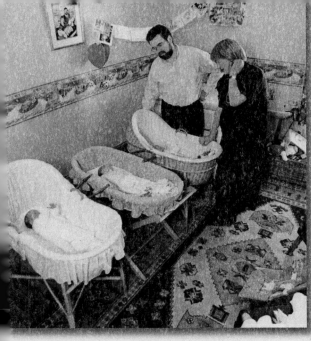

Left: All changed, changed utterly: Sean, Ellen and Ronan arrive home, April 1995.

Below left: On the cover of the *RTÉ Guide*.

Below right: Ronan tells Gay to button his lip, 1996.

IRELAND'S LARGEST-SELLING MAGAZINE

RTE GUIDE

WIN
• 50 TICKETS
FOR ROD STEWART
IN CONCERT
• LUXURY
HOLIDAY IN
AUSTRIA

EXCLUSIVE
JOE,
JUNE
AND
BABIES
MAKE
FIVE!

YOUR 7-DAY MULTI-CHANNEL
GUIDE TO TV PROGRAMMES

Above left: Nana Grace Murphy in 1997 with great-grandson Sean.

Above right: Pirates: (*from the top*) Sean, Ellen and Ronan.

Left: The three amigos on their confirmation day, 2007.

and I conducted a loving but chaste courtship. We even opened an account in a building society to buy a house.

All of these fresh, summery and exciting events – from Germany to Ballymun, from Tír Na nÓg to the thrilling summer projects – were having a deep effect on me. The axis of my life had shifted from my being someone who was going to try to work his way up in an advertising agency to someone who wanted to better himself, get a better job and take a stand in life. I was so determined to do something, be somebody, make a difference, change the world, that nothing – and no one – else mattered.

I was already interested in becoming a social worker, and my stint running summer projects only intensified this desire. I soon realized that I needed to go to university to study social work. Not being old or mature enough to be considered as a mature student, I simply listed all my various Leaving Cert subjects, gained over two separate sittings, on the application form and applied to Trinity College in the centre of Dublin. To my surprise and inestimable pride, I was accepted.

Unfortunately, this huge change in my life would come at the cost of my relationship. Our orbits changed. By the time I reached second year in Trinity and was beginning to get interested in student politics, I told Jackie we would probably be better off apart.

Protest Songs

CHAPTER 10

_____

The Holy and Undivided Trinity

M Y SPELL IN TRINITY COLLEGE, DUBLIN, CHANGED MY life for ever. Upon payment of the fees of £125, I was instructed to attend my first lecture in economic and social studies in Dixon Hall on 11 October 1976. I left Arks on Friday and started in Trinity the following Monday.

Of course, there were difficulties at home. The fees were not the issue; rather, the problem was that I would no longer be handing up my weekly wage. My mother was supportive: indeed, without her support I could never have gone on in education; I presume her own lack of schooling propelled her to encourage me to stay on. However, my father objected and could not see the point in my studying. I don't remember any single conversation about it; family meetings were not done in 6 Claddagh Green. But I have a memory of my mother in the kitchen, when I raised the issue, simply saying to my father, 'If Joseph wants to do it, just let him do it.' So it was settled.

I had no idea what was ahead of me. Simply, none of my peers, at this stage, had been to third-level college. Little did I know that it would change my life. I was so nervous and indecisive about taking the leap. I remember sitting on the 36A bus coming home from Ballymun, tossing the idea around in my head and resolving to let the traffic lights make the decision for me: more greens would be a 'go'; red would keep me in Arks. By the time I got to the terminus in Parnell Square, red had won. But I had made my mind up: education was the key. I broke the lights!

I remember that first morning walking through Front Gate into what was to me the alien world of Trinity. Not knowing where Dixon Hall was, I headed off looking for it around the back of the college grounds. That lonely walk across the cobblestones and down by the cricket pitch in the wonderful bright sunshine is still deeply embedded in my memory.

I bumped into Barry Cullen, a former schoolmate in Ballyfermot. I had lost contact with him, and I thought he was simply taking a short cut through the college – as indeed he thought I was! Ironically, we were heading to the same lectures for the same degree in social work. He told me that he had tried engineering in Trinity the previous year but had now decided to give social work a go instead.

We had not been good friends in secondary school. Barry had been bright and wild, and hung around with the more streetwise lads in the class. It was even rumoured that they were being served in pubs while in fifth year. Of all the people I had hoped to meet in Trinity, I was surprised that the first one I ran into was one of the other two Ballyfermot natives in the enclave at the time. But it was an incredible and fortuitous start. We became firm friends, allies, critics, and still see each other at least twice a week and talk daily.

I cannot tell you how frightened and lonely I was for that first year in TCD. I have never known anything like it.

Having now accumulated enough grades, I was eligible for my first choice: social work. The first year was a general course embracing everything from economics to sociology, mathematics, statistics and political science. There were over two hundred students in my class, and lectures were more like mass meetings than educational gatherings. Bored lecturers would simply deliver the same fifty-minute speech they had undoubtedly delivered the previous year, and with a 'classroom' of that size, there was simply no time or facility for questions. This only added to my fear. But as the year progressed the lectures got smaller and much more interesting.

Having been out of the world of intense day-time study for three years, I was worried sick about not getting through the first year. So I decided I needed to study endlessly. I found a bolthole two floors below the main Berkeley Library, in the 'official publications' section. In this windowless basement, in a dead-end corner with bare concrete walls and low lighting, I hibernated. I would stay there from nine to nine each day, leaving only to attend intermittent lectures. It was so quiet, I could bring a flask of hot tea, corned beef or cheese sandwiches and water without being seen by the librarian. Thus, I could avoid going to the 'Buttery' to eat – or, more to the point, to spend money.

And money was an issue. Despite my father having a low-paid job and my coming from a family of eight, I was not entitled to anything from the state education grants scheme. This was because of the 'four honours' rule: before you could even apply for an educational grant you must have secured four honours in one sitting of the Leaving Cert. Because I had accumulated the grades over two Leaving Certs, I was deemed ineligible. This angered me deeply.

My hermit's life had its severe disadvantages. In May 1977, as I left the library late one Friday evening as usual, I noticed that a lot of lights and marquees had been erected. I thought little of it. On returning to the library the following morning (I came in to study every Saturday), I noticed a lot of rubbish, mainly empty alcohol bottles, strewn around the grounds. It was only the following May that I discovered that I had studied through, and gently tiptoed over, the biggest annual social event in Trinity, if not Dublin: the Trinity Ball. I had heard nothing of it until I was in my second year.

By far the most powerful piece of research I came across in my first few years in Trinity was the work of two UCD academics on the issue of access to third-level education in the Dublin area. Patrick Clancy and Ciaran Benson did a survey in 1976, and they added one very simple graphic: a black-and-white map of Dublin postal districts, with each district accompanied by a number representing the percentage of students from that area who went on to third level. Dublin 10, which is Ballyfermot, came in at 1 per cent, while Dublin 4 came in at 44 per cent.

The Clancy–Benson map was – and still is – etched into my mind. Thanks to the exotic number 18 bus, which was introduced in the late 1960s and crossed the city circuitously from Palmerstown via Ballyfermot to Sandymount, I had been to Dublin 4! So why were the young people in Mount Merrion forty-four times more likely to end up at university than the kids from Ballyfermot? How could this injustice prevail in the same small city, on the same bus route?

Thankfully, things have changed. While I may have been the first of a 'thousand generations' of my family to get to third level – and one of only a handful from Ballyfermot – today, three out of the four houses on my mother's block in Ballyfermot have sent children on to third-level education. It is a mark of how far we have come in such a short time that so many families have gone from one generation barely getting beyond primary school and functional literacy and numeracy to so many today simply assuming that their education should, rightly, continue on to third level.

Looking back on my Leaving Cert class in St John's College in Ballyfermot, I was by no means the brightest, yet, at most, two others from that class of fifty went on to third-level education. I cannot think of one single person in my class who would not have been able for third level. I think of the brain surgeons, lawyers, pilots and businessmen who could have emerged from my peers – there was so much potential there. Neither do I doubt that most of them are living decent lives, like the rest of society, happy and fulfilled. But I cannot get away from this crying chasm of anger about lost opportunities.

I used to rail against middle-class presumptions in ads and the media – the assumption that everyone has a phone, a car, holidays and a happy family. To this day, I bridle at this middle-class obsession of our media, including radio. My annoyance is fuelled by the exclusion this assumption generates.

One of our lecturers proudly announced one morning that we were going on a 'field trip', to one of the biggest, most deprived estates in Western Europe. Twenty minutes later, I was being driven towards my Ballyfermot home! I didn't know whether to laugh or cry when we were bundled into the lecturers' cars and driven out to Dublin 10. Decies Road was described as the longest single suburban road in Western Europe. Thankfully, we did not go near my home.

CHAPTER 11

Joe Duffel

IF OUR LIVES ARE PUNCTUATED BY THE OBVIOUS milestones such as births, deaths, marriages and illnesses, there are other moments that, on reflection, also change our pathways for ever. In what was without doubt one of those pivotal moments, I sent a letter to the *Irish Times* at the beginning of December 1978, two years after I entered Trinity. This letter – its energy, its anger, its sense of injustice, its very publication – determined completely what followed in my life.

The then president, Patrick Hillery, was about to officially open the new arts building in Trinity, which was accessed from Nassau Street. A few weeks earlier, in a supplement in the *Irish Times*, a TCD academic was quoted as saying that the new gate would 'show how Trinity had opened up to the people of Dublin'. (By the way, I couldn't even afford to buy a daily newspaper, so each morning I would arrive in Trinity early and go to the Graduates Memorial Building reading room for a free read of the *Irish Times* and *Independent*.)

I remember standing at the bus stop on the main road in Ballyfermot, angrily composing my letter. The first lines wrote themselves: 'Lest we be totally overwhelmed by the rhetoric that has accompanied the opening of a new gate in Trinity College, permit me to put the situation into perspective.' I quoted the figures from the Clancy–Benson survey, that a child from Mount Merrion was forty-four times more likely to end up in Trinity than his Ballyfermot counterpart. I went on:

Cries of 'new windows on the world' (Christina Murphy, *Irish Times* education correspondent), 'opening up the college to the people of Dublin' (George Dawson, TCD registrar) and 'Trinity now entering the mainstream of Irish life' (Jack Lynch, Taoiseach) fade into absurdity when placed against the facts. The opening of a new gate on Nassau Street does not hide, nor indeed alleviate, the fact that there is not one student in Trinity from the community directly beside it: the Westland Row, City Quay parish. A recent survey carried out by the college revealed that only 10 per cent of the students in Trinity were of working-class backgrounds, which comprises 50 per cent of the population of the country.

That the people of the city can now walk through the grounds by way of a short cut does nothing to alter the fact that a part of the city, Ballyfermot, with a population of 50,000, can only boast 3 students out of 6,000 in these hallowed cloisters. That £5.5 million was spent on the new building – totally financed by the Government – means nothing to the 84 per cent of students who can't get a grant or indeed the other 16 per cent who survive on a pittance. It means nothing to the 90 per cent of young people in this country who will never get to third-level education. It does nothing to change the fact that we spend the smallest proportion of GNP on education in the EEC – and it's dropping! The fact is that Trinity College manifests all that is wrong in Irish society. No amount of door-opening, or window-dressing, will hide the fact that for the vast majority of young people in this country, third-level education in general, and Trinity College in particular, is a closed shop.

The letter was published at the top of the letters page in the *Irish Times* on Friday, 15 December 1978, four days after the building was officially opened. It sparked a further series of letters, including the usual Ku Klux Klan argument that, if I didn't like it, I should just get out! But others wrote in support.

Between the time I sent the letter and its publication, a protest was organized for the official opening of the new building on 11 December to highlight inequality of access to third-level educational institutions such as Trinity. It was here that I met those with whom I was to form friendships for the rest of my life. Alex White, Liam Hayes, Brian Dowling, John Brady, Derek

Cunningham, June Meehan, Pat Tobin, Noelle Spring, Frank Deasy, John Hogan, Mary Corcoran, Michael Cronin and Brid Ingolsby were all there.

The atmosphere at the demo was good-natured but acrimonious – lots of pushing, shoving, milling, laughing, heckling. It was fairly harmless, and it was great fun, but for some reason the college authorities completely panicked and over-reacted. It was not an official 'Students' Union' demo and they were baffled at this new rag-bag grouping, so they erected crash barriers and deployed extra security staff to keep us away from the dignitaries. This heavy-handedness was to become the *modus operandi* when it came to dealing with us over the next two years.

It was all good-humoured until the then junior education minister, Jim Tunney TD, arrived and decided to lecture us on how privileged we were to be in a third-level institution. Not a good idea, as this 'rag bag' of protesters were easily some of the sharpest people I have ever met and, to my horror and subsequent delight, they were afraid of no one. Tunney's condescending attitude enraged the group, who ended up pushing the barriers aside. There were minor scuffles with the security staff, but nothing untoward. Jim Tunney retreated with his signature yellow tulip, which had earned him the nickname 'The Yellow Rose of Finglas', wilting in his lapel. President Paddy Hillery, a former Fianna Fáil minister for education, did not get a much better reception; but he was the president, so our reaction to him was muted. The demo grew more robust when he left.

Of course, if the college authorities had just ignored the demo, things might have died down, but they later decided to bring some of the 'rowdy' protesters before a disciplinary committee. This only served to focus and galvanize us – a mistake Trinity were to make again and again.

Within weeks, Barry Cullen and Frank Deasy had both suggested to me that I stand as a rep in the Students' Union. There was one for each class and, with only twenty-four other trainee social workers now in my group, the only other possible contenders would have been Frank or Barry – so, with their backing, there was no opposition! In many ways, I was an unlikely candidate. I had little confidence and it was only the surprising encouragement of Barry and Frank that pushed me forward.

Between the reaction to my *Irish Times* letter and the intense feeling of community, comradeship and principle that erupted from the Arts Block demo, I had found a cause I passionately believed in. I took the job very seriously. But, from the outset, I was clear about one thing: my main focus would be access to third level.

In Trinity, however, the furthest thing from my mind was to join a political party. It seemed to me that only those whose parents were TDs or who were interested in personal and professional advancement would join one of the two main parties; while, at the time, Labour were embroiled in long, tortuous arguments with their own conscience. I also began a long battle with the

Workers' Party, who, it seemed to me, were simply interested in manipulating groups such as the Students' Union or the national organization, the Union of Students in Ireland (USI), for their own ends. I was always a doer, so the political parties were not for me.

Later that year, a group of us decided to agree on a platform built around access and stand for election to full-time leadership positions in the Trinity College Dublin Students' Union. I cannot begin to tell you how electrifying the campaign was. It was sunny April and early May in 1979. We swept through Trinity like nothing they had ever seen before.

There was such a buzz around the gang of us. We thought we were the Beatles! Myself from Ballyfermot, Alex from Marino and Liam from Limerick were the ideal ticket. I had energy, populism and good oratory; Alex was organized, strategic and could never be beaten in an argument, such was his command of his brief and language; Liam was witty, erudite, waspish and a stunning orator – a genius. Barry Cullen, the fourth Beatle, our wizard of a campaign manager, was tough, mature, totally fearless and ingenious when it came to organizing.

We were young, fresh, energetic, disciplined and organized. Without realizing it, we had tapped into something new, real and different. A combination of the abolition of fees in second-level education – introduced just over a decade earlier – and the lifting of the lunatic 'ban' on Catholics attending Trinity in 1970 had thrown up our group. Nothing would get in our way. Call it naïvety (arrogance it was not), we just went at everything afresh, and it worked. We felt nothing could stop us.

My oratory and passion seemed to strike a chord, so it was decided, almost by consensus, by a small group including Barry, Brian Dowling, Derek Cunningham, Frank Deasy, Alex White and Liam Hayes, that I should stand for president, Alex for deputy president and Liam for education officer, while we would support John Hogan for entertainments officer, which we didn't regard as a political office. We applied to the college authorities for offices for our campaign HQ; much to our surprise, they promptly gave us a room in house number 40, beside the cricket pitch. Little did the board and fellows of Trinity realize what they were unleashing. My years in advertising came in handy, as I was in charge of publicity, posters and leaflets; and I knew a thing or two about printing.

With military precision, Barry prepared a schedule of lectures for us to address. He even made sure each of us was 'chaperoned' by a campaign member whose sole job was to make sure we got to the start of the lecture on time – and to inform Barry on how we had performed! We stormed through college, lecture hall after lecture hall. Out of naïvety, we were impervious to the politics of Trinity. For instance, we didn't know that engineering students were supposed to be a no-go area for any Left-leaning students. We simply ploughed in.

We not only covered the college in Duffy/White/ Hayes posters; we went where no previous student election campaign had ever gone – outside the portals of Trinity. We commandeered the outstretched arm of the statue of Henry Grattan, the eighteenth-century campaigner for an Irish Parliament, which stands opposite the gates of Trinity. He held a daily placard for us, whether he liked it or not. Getting the placard into his hand, thirty feet off the ground, was an extremely difficult task, completed only with the subversive assistance of maintenance staff in Trinity and their ladders.

By this stage, John Walshe, the astute education correspondent of the *Irish Independent*, had spotted the story and promptly ran a piece headlined 'Factory Worker's Son Seeks TCD Student Presidency'; the headline shocked me, but it was true.

Election day arrived. The turnout was the highest ever in the college, and we gathered in the junior common room above the Front Gate of TCD and waited as the results came in. We won by a landslide, getting, on average, 60 per cent of the vote. We hoisted the red flag over Trinity – literally, by climbing through the junior common room on to the roof of TCD facing College Green. The next day the papers proclaimed 'Ballyfermot Student Elected Leader in Trinity.'

Even though I was twenty-three, having worked for nearly four years and studied social work for almost three years, it was an enormous jump. But the sense of comradeship that existed among the Duffy/White/

Hayes group was palpable – and energetic. We were determined to take on the college – and we did.

I was clear that big issues such as access, grants and the ludicrous four-honours barrier were to be my priorities. But I also knew even then that we had to deal with the day-to-day issues, such as running an office, shop and services, with eight staff. As I have always argued, the same people will be interested in better library facilities in Trinity and feeding the starving of the world; these issues are never opposed, they are totally sequential. Charity does indeed begin at home, but that is not where it ends. It's only logical, after all, that those who were marching against apartheid in South Africa would also take a stand against injustice and discrimination at home.

The Students' Union offices were located in house number 6 in Front Square, while the four of us, as elected officers, got 'rooms' in Trinity. In my case, this was a bedsit overlooking the Book of Kells! At this stage, in late May, most of the students had left the college for the summer. So we spent the first few weeks getting to know the staff of the Students' Union.

As for Trinity itself, did I have a visceral hatred of the Anglo-Irish university? No; not of the institution, but of the system it perpetuated. Was I deeply embittered by the class nature of the institution, which seemed to be a closely guarded secret treasure for the children of the rich? Yes; my view on third-level education was formed very early and was simple and straightforward. Third level should be open to all, on merit, not money.

There should be no fees at first-, second- or third-level education. The argument that is trotted out, that students should pay high fees, is fallacious. Graduates earn more and so, in our progressive tax system, pay more to our society – regardless of whether they have children or not – because education is of social value and represents a social good, which should be provided by all and for all. Tax should be paid on the amount of income you earn, not the amount of education you consume. It annoys me that, every time a new minister for education is appointed, they wring their hands in angst, ruminating about 'loans schemes' and 'students paying their way', pitting parts of the education budget against each other.

Because I always wore my trademark green duffel coat throughout my time in Trinity, whatever the weather, I acquired the moniker 'Joe Duffel'. But, believe it or not, the hooded three-quarter-length coats with large pockets and toggles instead of buttons were fashionable at the time. I wasn't the only Trinity student I knew who wore one; so did Brian Dowling . . . and June Meehan.

Indeed, all three of us were wearing our trademark coats on the fateful day beside the new Arts Block in early 1979 when Brian in his beige duffel coat introduced Joe in his green duffel coat to June in her grey duffel coat. June was on her way to a lecture, and Brian and I were canvassing for votes and also on the look-out for more campaigners – preferably not wearing duffel coats. Brian saw June, a fellow psychology student, grabbed me by the arm and hustled me across to meet her. Brian has an enthusiasm and an openness that is un-stoppable, so he simply presumed that June had waited all her life to meet us and get involved in the campaign – no ifs or buts.

'Aw, come on, June, get involved,' Brian cajoled her. He meant with the election, not the candidate, even though I had other ideas. 'We're having a meeting in number 40 at six this evening,' he pleaded.

And so June Meehan, from Mulroy Road in Cabra, met Joe Duffy from Claddagh Green in Ballyfermot. Two duffels, green and grey. You go to Trinity, having read about its students being the children of the wealthiest in the land, and Joe meets and falls for the daughter of a barman from Cabra and a mother who makes donkey jackets. I suppose duffel coats would be out of the question!

I instantly took to June. She was tall, with blonde hair, and had a relaxed, confident air about her. I felt I had met her before as we had so much in common, and indeed it subsequently transpired that she had been involved in youth clubs in Cabra while I was helping to run Tír Na nÓg in Ballymun, and we had attended the same conferences.

It was after I was elected president of Trinity Students' Union – and June had become a linchpin in the whirlwind campaign – that she and I started dating. Gradually, though, destiny did its work and June and I got together. It just felt so natural.

June had rooms in college with her friend Eileen

Dwyer, and after I finished my one-year term in the Students' Union, her rooms became our day centre in the college. Myself and three other social-work students, Barry Cullen, Pat Tobin and Noelle Spring, rented a house in Aberdeen Street near the Phoenix Park, I knuckled back down to my studies and was seeing June every single day.

By 1982, June and I were living together, thanks to the Cupid-like intervention of Mark Durkan. Mark was then a fellow elected officer in the USI and we were sharing a house in Great Western Square in Phibsboro. We needed a third person to pay the rent, and we asked around. It was Mark who suggested that we ask June to take up the extra room – which of course she never did; she simply moved into mine. And we have been together ever since.

CHAPTER 12

The Pope's Child

ONE OF THE FIRST THINGS I DID AFTER THE SUMMER break in 1979 was to speak at the papal mass in Galway in September.

Politics and religion for me have always been intertwined and indeed seemed to grow and complement each other in my life as I got older. I have always been religious; it's in my blood. Each morning at 6.30, my father used to stand in front of the china cabinet in our living room holding our small statue of St Joseph the worker in his right hand, silently intoning his prayers, finishing with a flourish as he blessed himself, with the statue. For Lent, he would go to early-morning mass daily, and I would accompany him. I love getting up early to this day. He would head into work after 7 a.m. mass, and I would head back home, bright eyed and bushy tailed, for a new day. Saturday-morning confessions were a regular event under Canon Troy and Father Daly in Ballyfermot; no exceptions, no excuses, whether we had sinned or not, our mother dragooned us into attending.

In secondary school, some of the stories about the social-justice campaigning of members of the French de la Salle order, along with the founder of the St Vincent de Paul Society, Frédéric Ozanam, must have morphed into my DNA. I subsequently became a member of the 'Vincent de Paul' and was heavily involved in work with the Catholic Youth Council.

In my late teens, I even went through a Jesus Christ – some would say messianic – phase; I took to wearing a beard and a large chocolate-coloured crucifix around my neck. I was genuinely interested in a life of study, reading and contemplation. The priesthood had that calm attraction for me. A group of us from Ballyfermot even took to visiting the Legionnaires of Christ novitiate in Leopardstown, where we were royally entertained, fed on exotic Spanish omelettes and encouraged to sign up. One of the lads eventually joined the Mexican order.

Later, I came across an advert for the Missionaries of the Sacred Heart, answered it and was invited to spend a weekend retreat with them at their headquarters in Western Road, Cork. It was enjoyable, gentle and slow-paced, with no heavy entreaties to join. They had missions in South Africa, Venezuela and the US, which sounded fascinating and inviting. I sometimes think that if the Sacred Missionaries had been as pushy as the Legionnaires of Christ had been a few years earlier in Ballyfermot, I might have joined. Though I was tempted, I decided against it, convinced that, while

I admired the words and actions of Jesus Christ, becoming a celibate priest was not for me.

From my first year in Trinity, I resurrected my religious routines by attending lunchtime mass in college chapel. I saw it as twenty minutes of reflection and quiet. Many people later thought it was bizarre that the quasi-communist leader of the radical Students' Union was a daily communicant, didn't smoke dope and was against abortion. In college, I characterized myself as a 'Christian socialist'. I was never attracted by the ideologues of either left or right. I just couldn't keep up with them; my eyes would glaze over.

I wanted things done, and done now. I hated long meetings and still do. The mention of taking minutes at a meeting is enough to send me to sleep for hours. I was propelled by a great sense of justice, and this was very much based on Christian teachings and principles: fairness, treating people well, everyone deserving a chance – and, above all, the opportunity to better themselves. Every parent's aspiration – that their children should have a better life than they had – was what propelled me. I have lived through a generation that can safely claim that accolade; but of course we now face into one that cannot.

I drew inspiration from the image of Christ as the figure fighting for the powerless, as well as from the contemporary campaigning of Archbishop Oscar Romero in El Salvador and our own Bishop Eamon Casey, Father Feargal O'Connor and Sister Stan working in Ireland. Add to this the writings of Brazilian educationalist Paolo Freire, and I developed a heady mix of idealism, Catholicism and socialism. My paperback copy of *Pedagogy of the Oppressed* was as well-worn, torn, battered and stained as I was!

My religious interests were also furthered by priests such as John Fitzpatrick, the dynamic administrator of the Catholic Youth Council, John Wall, Pat McManus, Arthur O'Neill, Eoin Cooke and Donal Harrington. I had met the latter two through my CYC work in Ballymun, and they became firm friends and strong influences. I had great admiration for the CYC, and I was part of the inner circle. A group of us, Pat Carey, Donal Harrington and myself, wrote a series of information leaflets on different aspects of the Pope's life. I remember concentrating on Pope John Paul's work as a labour organizer in chemical factories and limestone quarries, where he had worked during the Second World War.

In August 1979, I was in the offices of the Students' Union, settling into my new role, when Pat Holmes, the education correspondent of the *Irish Press*, dropped in for one of his regular chats. 'I hear you are going to meet the Pope when he comes next month,' he nonchalantly mentioned.

'That's news to me,' I responded.

Of course, it wasn't news that the Pope was coming; after all, the first ever papal visit to Ireland had been the talk of the country for months. The country was consumed with the details of the visit, down to the provision of foldaway stools for the millions expected to throng venues such as the Phoenix Park, Galway and Limerick.

I thought little of Pat's comment. I was just beginning my stint as president of TCD Students' Union and was up to my eyes preparing for the opening of the college term, working on information booklets and organizing induction meetings for first-years. But my work in CYC had propelled my name to the top of the list to be given some role in the Youth Mass in Galway. So the next time I was up in the CYC offices on Arran Quay, John Fitzpatrick, or 'Fitz', as he was known, asked me if I would be interested in doing a reading at the papal mass in Galway on 30 September.

'No bother,' I said, having already heard the rumour from Pat Holmes.

'Grand,' he replied. 'Just write a Prayer of the Faithful and get up and read it.'

It was as simple as that. I also got involved in organizing the Youth Mass. So, I was president of the student body in Trinity, espousing a radical agenda of access to third-level education for all in a strong Dublin working-class accent, determined to bring the establishment screaming and kicking from the sixteenth into the eighteenth century – and yet I was speaking at the Pope's mass. This led to the hilarious rumour circulating in the hallowed grounds of TCD that I was orchestrating a popish plot to destabilize Ireland's 'Protestant' university!

Like so many, I vividly recall that beautiful September

morning when the Pope arrived, but while over 1.25 million people – the biggest gathering ever in Ireland – were heading to the Phoenix Park, we were heading to Galway to set up camp. A huge tented village had been erected for the massive numbers expected, the plan being that the young people would arrive there to stay on Saturday night and set off at 4 a.m. on Sunday, walking through the night to Ballybrit racecourse four miles away.

There was a brilliant atmosphere in the camp. I shared MC duties with young, energetic priests such as Arthur O'Neill and John Wall. There were few facilities on site, but I remember being not at all bothered by the fact that it was a pretty dishevelled, unwashed and unkempt Joe Duffy that started out in complete darkness, walking into the Sunday dawn. I remember the silence of the night giving way to nervous laughter and the eventual slow-rising tide of singing as we neared Ballybrit through the early fog and chilly sunrise.

Because I would be doing a reading, I was ushered on to the open-air altar. At this stage, the two main organizers of the event were in full flow – the Bishop of Galway, Eamon Casey, and the singing priest, Father Michael Cleary. Their soutanes billowed in the wind as they urged us to sing and clap for the Pope – very patronizingly, I thought. Father Cleary in particular treated us like six-year-olds, kept urging us to sing 'By the Rivers of Babylon', saying, 'Boys and girls, make sure the Holy Father can hear you. Ah come on, you can do better than that!' Jesus, give us a break!

Still, I can see how Eamon Casey and Michael Cleary could have lost the run of themselves that day, gazing out at the 300,000 people present, off the back of the 1.25 million in the Phoenix Park and the 400,000 in Drogheda the previous evening. They must have thought, as clerics, that all their Christmases had come together.

Then, as if from nowhere, the papal helicopter appeared, to be greeted by an enormous roar, and flags, banners and general hysteria. The Prayers of the Faithful come near the beginning of the mass and I queued up to deliver my little contribution. Bearded, hair unkempt, wearing a zip-up blue jacket and big glasses – though I did wear a necktie over an open shirt – I invoked the Holy Spirit to 'give guidance to our leaders in this time of difficulty'.

I was lucky in that, while it was a long mass – with 300,000 people receiving communion – at least I had a bird's-eye view from the raised altar. The reaction by the crowd to Pope John Paul's declaration, 'Young people of Ireland, I love you,' took me by surprise. The cheering response just seemed to increase in wave after wave. It was a simple message, to say the least, but sometimes simplicity works. Looking around, it was clear that most of the congregation, apart from the 800 priests, were younger than me.

The mass finished and everyone slowly melted away. I didn't meet the Pope, and I knew when I saw the throngs on the altar that my chances of a papal blessing were nil. I left the altar and joined friends Eoin

Cooke and Trish Close for a lift home in her Renault 4.

When I spoke to my mother about the experience a few days later, her only response was, 'Joseph, could you not have cut your hair and worn a proper jacket?'

I have learned that, oftentimes, events take on a greater significance the further away you get from them on life's little timeline. So it was with my papal Prayer of the Faithful. Nothing more was said about it – until 2005.

When Pope John Paul II died on the first Saturday in April of that year I was phoned by RTÉ TV News late in the evening and asked to come to studio to recall the papal visit. This I gladly did. Then, as the obsequies unfolded over the coming week, I was asked by a priest friend, Pat O'Donoghue, if I would speak at a 'sunset service of remembrance' to be held at the papal cross in the Phoenix Park on the Friday evening of the funeral. I wrote a short piece for the ceremony, where I mentioned that, since the Pope had stood there, much had happened to diminish people's faith in the Church – but at least we were now talking about it. Not least was the fact that both Father Michael Cleary and Bishop Eamon Casey had fathered children; these revelations in the early 1990s would rock Catholic Ireland to its core.

CHAPTER 13

Walk of Life

I WAS BARELY TOLERATED BY THE POWERS THAT BE IN Trinity College. During the maelstrom we generated, one senior don proclaimed, 'We defeated the rebels in 1916 and by God we will beat them now.' I was a working-class nuisance who no doubt they hoped would go away – the sooner the better.

Despite this, we managed to rouse students about basic issues such as food and libraries. We discovered, after yet another price hike on student meals, that the college was subsidizing food for staff and 'academic fellows'. In effect, this was being paid for by the students. The college was also wasting thousands of pounds on upholding 'free commons', a ritual evening meal for elected fellows and scholars. A boycott of the food facilities led to us setting up our own restaurant. We wanted better food, more input into the catering committee and the abolition of subsidies for academics. A new population of Irish third-level students, less well off than their predecessors, were finding it hard to make ends meet, working part-time jobs and all summer, simply to get by. So prices in college for basics like food were critical.

We also decided to set up our own bar in opposition to the college-run facility in the eating area. There was only one problem: we were not allowed to sell alcohol. The idea of giving away free drink but renting the glasses for the price of a pint came to me after a rep from Murphy's stout had approached me about trying to sell his product in the college; up to then, it was a Guinness closed shop run by the college authorities. I contacted him and asked if he would be willing to supply barrels to TCD Students' Union. He agreed but was anxious about physically getting the product on to the campus. That was easily solved; in a military-style operation, an unmarked truck pulled up, the barrels were abandoned on the street outside Front Gate and eager students simply rolled them through the arch and up the stairs to the junior common room.

This wonderful historic room above the archway that leads into TCD was the venue for the Irish Home Rule convention in 1917 and featured in many lively debates leading to the establishment of the first Dáil. It was now run by the Students' Union, though of course still owned by the college. I had discovered a warren of back corridors from my office on the other side of the building which allowed me to enter the JCR via its historic fireplace; this was to come in handy later on.

Food, drink and printing machines were soon in full

flow in the JCR. The atmosphere was electric. We hung our banners over the Front Gate – a brilliant location. Every morning, just before dawn, a number of students would commandeer college trolleys and head up to the Dublin Corporation fruit and vegetable market behind the Four Courts to buy the ingredients for our canteen. With food and a flourishing bar, our boycott was totally effective. Of course, Trinity is located in the heart of the city centre, so students were also easily finding alternative eateries. The college catering facilities had come to a halt, but the college refused to negotiate.

The Trinity response to us, which backfired, was led by two very different individuals: junior dean J. C. A. Gaskin, straight from a Sherlock Holmes mystery, complete with deerstalker hat and breeches; and a much more enigmatic character, Captain John Martin, the moustachioed, trenchcoat-wearing, walkie-talkie-carrying head of security. Martin was on our case from day one. He augmented security around any event we organized.

But we were on his case too. Barry Cullen and I knew immediately that Captain Martin was a formidable opponent. Barry came up with the novel idea of following him around the campus and shouting out his name – thus alerting all to his presence. It was a simple but extraordinarily effective notion. As Barry's bellowing Ballyfermot accent was heard across the campus, Captain Martin's security perambulations decreased with his rising embarrassment.

On another escapade, when we occupied the accommodation office we found a blacklist drawn up by the college authorities of students who under no circumstances were to be allowed to live in any of the bedsit rooms in Trinity. Guess whose names featured on the list? All of the Duffy/White/Hayes crew. This was totally unheard of, as all students, from second year up, were entitled to apply for accommodation on a first-come, first-served basis.

On the catering side, the boss was Betty Pickering, who was at the front line of the college intransigence against us. Unfortunately, her name easily lent itself to our description of the college stance – petty bickering!

As the boycott dragged on, the college authorities grew more and more agitated. College staff arrived one night and completely removed the massive double doors into the JCR, so we could not occupy the room. In response we simply built a massive barricade, using the fireplace I mentioned earlier as the entrance and exit into the room. We also decided to keep a twenty-four-hour vigil in the room, as the authorities had scurried to the High Court to evict us from it. Within a week, a civil injunction was issued for us to attend the High Court. We ignored it.

A few days later, on 26 February 1980, the Front Gate was fully opened – an unusual occurrence – and Garda vans swept in. A large group of uniformed Gardaí entered the JCR, and I was arrested, along with sixteen other students. I considered this to be a complete overreaction by the college.

We were taken to the Bridewell Garda station before

being brought into the High Court. Justice McWilliams was both bemused and exasperated, and he refused the TCD request to have us imprisoned, urging college authorities to negotiate. In fairness, they did, finally introducing new menus and setting up a new catering committee involving students and a review of the 'commons' subsidy. It was a fairly comprehensive victory.

The manager of the Buttery, Matt, still insists that, when we were celebrating that night in the bar, he asked me if I would ever be satisfied with Trinity, and I jokingly replied, gazing over Front Square, 'Not until the day this is all covered in corporation houses!' I might not have got any corpo houses into Trinity, but at least I managed to get some corporation tenants on to the campus.

One of the things I am most proud of from my year as Students' Union president was when we organized Trinity's first Community Week. It was a brilliant idea, using the grounds and facilities in the best location in the country for local children to enjoy. It was also our way of making a strong point about access to TCD, as we highlighted again and again that a second-level student living beside Trinity has little chance of getting through the gates to study.

We contacted Tom Duffy of Duffy's Circus, who indicated that not only would their famous con-tortionist bend over backwards to help us, so would the rest of the circus troupe! He dubbed the city-centre

Trinity campus the best pitch in the country for a show. We applied to the college for permission to bring the big top, ringmaster, animals, contortionists and clowns on to the campus. Trinity simply hadn't a clue how to deal with this request. Board documents flew around, including one which looked at the implications of wild animals escaping in the Rubrics. Instead of just telling us to get lost, they raged and banned the circus, but they lost the publicity battle.

Community Week became an upfront assault on Trinity Week, the elitist 200-year-old event that consisted of Elizabethan garden parties, cricket matches and back-slapping college get-togethers lubricated by iced Pimms. TCD Students' Union Community Week was a great success and still continues thirty years later.

But the Trinity authorities were not finished with us yet. The academic year comes to an end in late May, so the Students' Union leaders were all surprised when, earlier in the month, we were informed by the Board of Trinity that they were calling us all before the disciplinary committee over the catering boycott, the occupation of the JCR and the running of the restaurant and bar without their permission.

We immediately boycotted the 'D Committee', branding it a kangaroo court. It was essentially a sub-group of the board prosecuting us; they would be the offended party, judge, jury and executioner. We tried to disrupt the proceedings, which were held in the august surroundings of the historic examination hall. The doors were locked as students besieged the building, some trying to get in through the windows. One newspaper called it a mini-riot!

At one stage, as we gathered outside, some members of the college maintenance staff drove up and left a sack beside us; it contained a sledgehammer, which we had requested. The workers, it seems, were equally disaffected by the actions and arrogance of the board and fellows of the college. I lifted the long handle of the massive sledgehammer but quickly abandoned the notion of using it on the door – though I was tempted.

The following night, Thursday, 8 May 1980, the D Committee delivered its verdict, letting it be known what they thought of the ringleaders. I was sitting in the Buttery bar with a large group, including Alex White, Barry Cullen and Liam Hayes, when one of Trinity's security staff handed me a letter informing me that, as from midnight, I and seven other ringleaders were to be expelled from the college for a year. The letter went on to say that 'the Board and Fellows of Trinity College Dublin' would be seeking an injunction from the High Court to ban the eight of us from entering the hallowed grounds of the college until further notice.

True to their word, the following morning the board got yet another High Court injunction, making it illegal for us to enter the cloisters. We decided to hold a protest march at noon.

It was easily the best walk of my life. I led the march through the arch, out the Front Gate, with the clear intention of turning around and parading back in. However, as I proceeded up Dame Street, it was obvious I would have to keep going until the last of the thousands of students behind me had actually exited the campus. I kept looking back in disbelief. The march seemed to be unending.

Eventually, when we reached George's Street corner, we did a U-turn and headed back to Trinity. The only difference was that, when we marched back in, eight of us were now breaking the law.

We took up our regular speaking positions on the dining-hall steps in Front Square, the most invigorating location I have ever spoken from. As I called on the students to stand firm, one of the catering staff appeared in full chef's uniform from the kitchens, grabbed my megaphone and told the gathering that he had been warned by his boss not to show any support for the striking students. He had promptly told them to shove their job. With a flourish, he whipped off his chef's hat and proceeded to dance on it!

It was a dramatic moment, and I knew then, come hell or high water, that we were going to win this dispute. Senator Mary Robinson and Kieran Mulvey, the general secretary of the Irish Federation of University Teachers, offered to mediate. Within three days, the college backed down and we were all readmitted while the college licked its wounds.

The chef, by the way, did not want his job back; but he was our talisman.

* * *

There was an interesting sideshow to these events. Around the time of the march, the Trinity Board revealed that two historic paintings in the college staffroom had been sprayed with red paint, and we were implicated. Damaging paintings was a stupid and crass move; one of the targets was a portrait of the father of the senior dean, J. V. Luce – our nemesis.

I never had a personal animus towards any of the college officers. Luce, as senior dean, was in charge of discipline, and so we had many a battle, but I think he made us out to be a bigger threat than we were. It was simply a clash of cultures, background and worldview. John Victor Luce was every inch the opposite of me. A distinguished professor of classics, his father, a vice-provost of Trinity, had taught him the Greek alphabet when he was five. Prof. Luce always wore the flowing black academic gown and, with his silver hair, classical features and chin curtain beard, he cut a distinguished figure as he rambled around the grey cobblestoned squares, libraries and formidable Rubrics of the 'College of the Holy and Undivided Trinity of Queen Elizabeth near Dublin' like a student in Plato's academy.

When he arrived in the JCR one day during the catering boycott, I greeted him with the words, 'You are not welcome here,' to which he quickly replied, 'I could say the same about you.'

At one point, Prof. Luce even disciplined us for using megaphones; apparently, we had broken another sixteenth-century college bye-law! Still, while he harassed and harried us at our every move, and we gave as good as we got, there was always a civil relationship between us.

Then the defacing of the portrait of his father, Arthur Aston Luce, brought the conflict to another level. But the truth of who damaged the paintings is much more complex. TCD authorities initially blamed the students for the crime, despite the fact that the portrait hung in a part of college only accessible to senior college staff. Little did they know that the vandal was, ironically, one of their number. Within hours, we knew that Peter Mew, the denim-clad philosophy lecturer, who had participated in a number of our occupations, had sprayed the red paint on the two pictures. Of course, we only had his own admission and could not prove it.

It is hard to know why the Trinity College authorities took such a hard stance with us over that twelve months. I believe that they panicked for a number of reasons. We had made it clear that we did not accept their authority, which was a big smack in the face for what had effectively been an independent fiefdom since 1592 – a Vatican-like state in the heart of Dublin.

Of course, Trinity has a history of student upheaval. A full decade earlier, an avowed Maoist (whatever that means), David Vipond, had led an attack on the 'authority' of the state, famously leading a mini-riot when King Baudouin of Belgium visited Trinity in 1968.

One political group on campus was called Revolutionary Struggle, or RS, as we knew them. Their banner appeared at a few of our demos. They were led by a mysterious figure, Mick the Greek, who looked disturbingly like Demis Roussos. He seemed to have a few followers in Trinity, but none of them were keen to get involved in the Students' Union, so I had dismissed them as ideologues. When I first met him, I instantly disliked Mick the Greek, mainly because he began by praising my leadership of the Trinity students and my campaign to 'bring down Trinity College'. Now, whatever about my leadership skills, I never saw myself as bringing Trinity to its knees as part of a worldwide plan to end capitalism. I immediately mistrusted him – and decided in my conspiratorial head that he was probably the archetypal CIA agent, operating as an *agent provocateur*!

But the threat we posed to Trinity was regarded as much more fundamental. We were a group of primarily working-class students who were shocked at the institutionalized privilege we witnessed in Trinity, which went on with little reference to the outside world or the taxpayers who funded the college. At that time, the board of Trinity was a self-perpetuating elite, with no representation from outside the four walls of the college. They had managed swimmingly without outside interference for nearly four hundred years, thank you!

To continue to function in an independent way, they needed internal loyalty and adherence to their code of conduct. When this was challenged, they would run to the Courts, believing that their rules and regulations would be clinically upheld. But by the 1980s, most of their rules were out of date. The ban on Catholics entering Trinity implemented by Archbishop John Charles McQuaid had been lifted in 1970. Of course, before this, Catholics had found ways around the ridiculous rule, but it reinforced the belief among ordinary Catholics that Trinity was a no-go area.

So the college authorities took us very seriously, and their reaction only encouraged us. It was as if we had broken into Trinity and were about to burgle their most precious jewels.

The provost, F. S. L. Lyons, simply could not understand us. While civil, courteous and erudite, he also had the unfortunate and unintentional appearance of looking down on us; he just didn't 'get it'. At best, he seemed angered and baffled by our actions; at worst, uninterested. He resigned in 1981. I vehemently opposed any involvement by the student body in the subsequent election. My argument was that the Trinity board was a self-perpetuating oligarchy with no outside involvement despite massive taxpayer subsidy. At a hustings of Provost candidates, I urged a boycott – the student body had in total three votes – saying that the only difference between the candidates was accent and nationality: 'An English-born provost or an Irish-born one – it makes no difference.'

During my time in student politics, I was at times followed by the Garda Special Branch. I was also told categorically by a senior official in An Post that, during my later presidency of the USI, my mail was being intercepted and read by the Gardaí. I couldn't believe my luck; I was being taken seriously by the state!

A bizarre incident happened in March 1981, nine months after I had finished my term as president of Trinity Students' Union. Geoffrey Armstrong, the chairman of British Leyland and director of the Confederation of British Industry, was giving a lecture in the college when three men wearing balaclavas and combat jackets burst into the lecture hall. They shouted, 'Everybody freeze, no one move! This action is in support of the H-Blocks.' They then savagely shot Mr Armstrong three times in the leg.

As it happened, I was in Kilnacrott Abbey in County Cavan that day with a group of inner-city teenagers as part of my social-work studies. I did not hear about the shooting until I returned to Aberdeen Street that evening. I got a phone call from my father to tell me that two Special Branch officers had been sitting outside the house in Claddagh Green all afternoon in their unmarked 'Avenger' car. One had knocked at the door, but my father had told them I was not living there any more.

The following day, I got a message from Pearse Street Garda station that Detective Jim McHugh wanted to interview me in connection with the shooting. I contacted the Students' Union solicitor, James Hickey, who simply told me to go ahead with the meeting, as he, correctly, presumed I had nothing to hide. So, with some nervousness, I went down to the station, where the very affable and unthreatening Jim McHugh simply asked me if I knew anything about the incident. Given that I was in Kilnacrott Abbey with, among others, a priest and a social worker, I was out of the frame.

No one was ever charged with the Armstrong shooting.

When I subsequently went on to lead USI, I had a lot of contact with the Gardaí through student protests, but it was never aggressive. Just as the security staff in Trinity still thank me for the copious overtime my year as president of the Students' Union generated for them, the Gardaí never displayed any personal animosity.

CHAPTER 14

The Auld Triangle

I HAVE HAD, TO SAY THE LEAST, A WEIRD RELATIONSHIP with prisons: inside, outside, inmate, worker, reporter and visitor – been there, done that, worn the grey jumper and regulation Terylene trousers. I have seen Mountjoy Prison from every angle, having been sent there in 1984 after a long-drawn-out battle with the government of the day over health cuts.

Following my tumultuous year as full-time president of Trinity Students' Union, I had decided to return to my social-work studies in the autumn of 1980. Having started college late, I was now twenty-four, with a full year left on my four-year course. Luckily, my tutors were fully accommodating when it came to my student activities. One staff member, Noreen Kearney, even allowed some of the students to sleep on her floor while they tried to sort out somewhere to live during our brief expulsion from the college. So there was never a problem coming back to the course after taking a year out to work full time in trying to destabilize the college!

As part of the course, I needed to find a work placement. Unfortunately, with my name and reputation, this was proving difficult. Thankfully, Sister Stanislaus Kennedy heard of my plight and offered me work with Kilkenny Social Services, which she was running at the time. So I spent the summer of 1980 in glorious, buzzing Kilkenny, making new friends and learning a lot about dealing with people, often those in severe difficulty. Thanks to the leadership of Bishop Peter Birch, who had invited the Sisters of Charity to initiate social-work services in the diocese, Kilkenny had become a beacon in terms of social work in the country. I really liked the attitude to people in distress that the service encouraged. There was no judgement; people were taken at face value, encouraged to better themselves with help, given a great sense of independence and facilitated in facing up to their own problems.

While I had little money, I managed to squeeze an army camp bed into a small flat opposite the Hibernian bank in the centre of Kilkenny. To one side of me was a fellow social worker; on the other was the brilliant bodhran-playing storyteller Jim Maher, who was determined to let us hear every new story and song he had collected. Never has a bodhran cried out more to be played with a penknife rather than a 'bone'. It was like living with the manic Father Noel Furlong, the Graham Norton character from *Father Ted*.

It was chaotic but totally removed from the pressure

of Dublin, and my so-called reputation as a trouble-maker didn't matter a damn in the marble city.

Having taken a year out, I had to join another class for my final year in Trinity, and I studied as if there was no tomorrow. By the time my final exams came around, in September 1981, I had become a full-time officer in the Union of Students in Ireland, so I combined campaigning work with intensive study. I graduated with an honours degree in social work in December 1981, and I spent the next three years working for USI.

One of the benefits of the campaign in Trinity the previous May, culminating in our expulsions and reinstatement, was the links we established with other colleges around the country, who had all turned out in support. We had already linked up nationally in our common distrust of the USI leadership, which at that time was under the control of members of the Workers' Party, which had vehemently opposed me in Trinity, citing my CYC connections and my prominent role at the 1979 papal mass as signs that I was a puppet of the Catholic Church. Thank God they never saw my big chocolate-coloured crucifix.

USI was affiliated with the International Union of Students; the more we investigated, the more it appeared that the Prague-based IUS was simply a USSR-funded political group, which was neither 'international', nor a 'union', nor run by 'students'. Despite our efforts, we could find out little else about this group, so at the annual congress of USI in Wexford in

January 1980 we put forward a motion that we should leave the IUS. The reaction of the leadership was breathtaking; they simply guillotined our motion to dis-affiliate. We led a walkout.

This made us determined to get them out, so by the time I was back in Trinity the following October we were assembling our plans. We put together another team based around student leaders from north and south on a platform to vote out the Workers' Party influence and focus on national student issues here in Ireland. We were a very mixed bunch, but it worked. Brendan Doris, a forceful, if dogmatic, mature student who was president of Bolton Street Students' Union, was elected president; Liam Whitelaw, an amiable English-born student from the University of Coleraine, was his deputy; and I was elected full-time education officer.

But we had not banked on the wrath of a scorned Workers' Party. It is hard to describe the animosity and vitriol they could generate against their perceived enemies. Mercifully, by the time I joined RTÉ their toxic and secretive influence was waning at the national broadcaster. But they did not give up USI without a fight.

The main battle in my first year was trying to stop colleges leaving – and collecting union fees from around the country. There was a great buzz about the Regional Technical Colleges which had sprung up all over Ireland. They were filled with young, energetic students, deeply appreciative of their third-level opportunities and keen to get involved in the national educational campaigns. The RTCs in Carlow, Cork, Galway, Letterkenny, Waterford, Athlone, Sligo, Tralee and Dundalk were all set up in the early 1970s, and I think they were the powerhouse of our economic growth in the 1990s. My main concern was to push for adequate student funding; luckily, the European Social Fund provided student grants, and these were to become the mainstay of most of the students in the RTCs.

Within months, I had decided to try to stay on in USI for another year, so I stood again and was re-elected easily. Brendan Doris remained as president and Mark Durkan, then at Queens University, came in as his deputy, with my old friend Alex White from Trinity elected as development officer – all of us sharing the one 'platform'. Over my year as education officer, I had built up a great relationship with Northern students such as Jude Whyte, Alex Attwood, Adrian Colton, Ricky O'Rawe, Gerard Cushnahan and Mark Durkan. They were simply the best and the brightest of their generation, and remain so to this day in all walks of life in Northern Ireland, from politics to education.

These were exciting years; we were gradually galvanizing the various student unions to concentrate on local issues such as libraries, grants and keeping college entry fees down. But, of course, political differences emerged during the year. Brendan Doris, who had a bizarre adoration of Enver Hoxha in Albania, could rub people up the wrong way, and after many battles Alex

White resigned prior to the Annual Congress in 1983. Mark Durkan and I had already decided to run as a team for the top posts – which we easily won. At last, as president of USI, with a brilliant team around me, I felt I could strike out on my own and focus totally on issues such as access and expanding the third-level sector.

A few weeks after I took up the presidency, the coalition government decided to have a go at third-level students as part of their cutbacks. It all began very simply; out of the blue, the then minister for health Barry Desmond announced one day in late 1983 that third-level students would no longer be entitled to medical cards in their own right. Up to this, students were regarded as having no income, so they were automatically entitled to free health care, usually provided in the college anyway. Indeed, due to general good health, most students were blissfully unaware that they had medical cards. Trinity had a very good medical centre, but on the few occasions I visited it during my years in the college, I seldom saw a queue of shivering students clamouring for their free bottle of Benylin.

Barry Desmond came out with the tired old line that, because third-level education is expensive, you must be rich to buy it; therefore you should not get any entitlements. I immediately saw the implications: if they whipped the medical card off young, agile students and there was no resistance, who would be next? How could any other vulnerable group put up a fight? I was also of the firm view that third-level students were adults in their own right and should be assessed on their income, not that of their parents.

We immediately sought meetings with the Department of Health, but were initially refused. After pressure, we were granted a meeting with the minister but, a day beforehand, we got a message to say the meeting had been cancelled. This was coming up to Christmas week, so I decided simply to proceed to attend the meeting, ignoring the cancellation.

I informed the media of the meeting, not mentioning the cancellation. They turned up at the Department of Health, then located above Busáras in central Dublin. The receptionist rang up to the minister's office, informing them that the USI and the media were there for the 'meeting'. The minister's secretary arrived in reception and, without batting an eyelid, ushered us to the 'meeting', with cameras and journalists in tow. In the conference room, it was all smiles and handshakes as we met the minister and his team. A cone of silence hung over any discussion about the 'cancellation', and we proceeded as normal.

However, I knew immediately from the laid-back demeanour of the minister's staff that they had no intention of changing their minds. They had all the smugness of knowing that they would not, or could not, be challenged or contradicted. Once the media left, it was clear that the civil servants had no intention of having any discussion. The meeting ended after a very short time, and I informed the minister that we would not be leaving as a protest. This came as a shock, not just to them but to the other student leaders with me, but it turned out they were equally incensed by the department's attitude.

Soon the Gardaí were called from nearby Store Street station and we were arrested and carried out of the building. The writer Joe O'Connor, a UCD student activist at the time, was there in his long overcoat, as good-humoured and good-natured as he is today. Joe always struck me as clear-headed about the issues; he saw the power of education and was keen that everyone should benefit from it, regardless of income. Joe recalls that the Garda in charge reminded us of our in-eligibility for J1 work visas to the US if we ended up in court – which led to the instant melting away of the demo. I have no recollection of that 'threat'; indeed, I have heard that story about every single student protest before and since.

We were arrested and taken to court, where we were defended by an up-and-coming young barrister, George Berminghan, who amazingly – and much to everyone's relief, including, I suspect, the judge and Gardaí – got us all off on a technicality. But I was only hardened by that debacle.

I spent much of December 1983 travelling around Ireland in Tim McStay's red Austin Allegro as we begged the students' unions to pay their annual dues. Tim, the able full-time USI administrator, was a great character, with a deep passion for the issues. He also endured affably all the machinations, politicking and uncertainty that came with working for a voluntary organization that was totally dependent on subscriptions to survive. These subscriptions paid the elected officers a pittance but also, rightly, had to pay the full-time staff a decent wage.

Our ramble in the Allegro took us two weeks and kept the wolf from the door. Unfortunately, given that Tim and I would take turns sleeping between the bed and floor in pokey student flats, I contracted pleurisy after sleeping on a damp mattress in Limerick. I spent that Christmas sick in bed and in severe pain, nursed by June. But in the great tradition of political activists felled by illness, bad luck or circumstances, I was determined to battle on! Also, I saw the need for a medical card, now, more than ever.

And so 1984 began with a resolution by me to move the campaign forward. Meetings had failed; phone calls were useless. We decided to make things as awkward as possible for the Labour and Fine Gael politicians in government over the medical-card cut. We protested wherever Taoiseach Garret Fitzgerald appeared; on one memorable occasion, a Fine Gael meeting in Trinity was completely overwhelmed by the large group of angry students. The meeting was abandoned, as somebody threw an egg and I was carried out by the security staff.

Our next target was the Labour Party headquarters in Gardiner Place. Mark Durkan led the occupation and invented the 'bucket and rope' supply line, which no doubt stood to him when he went on to become leader of the SDLP. Within minutes of beginning this (and every subsequent) occupation, a strategic window was commandeered, a bucket was lowered on a rope and the supply chain began. Efforts by the then general secretary of the Labour Party, Colm Ó Briain, to disrupt the vital supplies by wildly swinging a sweeping brush at the lowering rope were very funny but totally unsuccessful.

These actions were getting us a lot of publicity, but Barry Desmond was not for turning. I then discovered that, in order to remove the medical card from students, the health boards would have to write to every single student to inform them that the medical card they had was invalid. So I had a simple idea: we would occupy the headquarters of the Eastern Health Board in Thomas Street. By our peaceful presence, we could stop the posting of the letters formally withdrawing medical cards from students.

And so it was organized. About twenty of us volunteered to occupy the offices. We would be inside, while a crew outside would manage the logistics, with the ubiquitous bucket and rope system. We were well equipped with food, sleeping bags and my portable typewriter and television.

The occupation itself was very straightforward. I simply walked up to the porter at the main door and told him we wanted to collect forms to invalidate our medical cards. We climbed the stairs, rounded a glass partition and, through my megaphone, I informed the staff that we had no dispute with them but that we would be staying until the work on taking medical cards off students stopped. The staff looked bemused and baffled. It was shortly after four in the afternoon so, on instructions from their bosses, they simply packed their bags and left.

Fred Donoghue, the head of the Eastern Health Board, met me and I told him that we were determined to stay until the government backed down. He was civil but angry, if not slightly embarrassed. He said he would leave two security guards in the building, as he was worried about files. We undertook not to touch anything or allow anyone to interfere with files or look at any documentation – which we adhered to rigidly – and he took us at our word.

We ensured that we had access to windows for communication and supplies, and we used the phones to ring local radio stations – indeed, we had difficulty getting on RTÉ! Around eight o'clock that night, a large group of students turned up. As the smell of burning hops wafted from the Guinness brewery across the street, we lowered our bucket and rope to a group of student helpers led by Maggie O'Kane (who subsequently went on as a journalist to cover much more important struggles). Within minutes it came back filled with food from the local chipper and creamy pints of Guinness covered in cling film for protection. We settled down for our first night.

The next morning, the health board went straight to the High Court, where they secured an injunction against us to vacate the premises, which was served on us within the hour. We made it clear we were not going to leave. So the health board went straight back across the river to the Four Courts to secure an attachment order committing us to prison.

At midnight, we heard heavy footsteps on the fire escape at the back of the premises as the Gardaí arrived. An avuncular sergeant with a lot of paperwork under his arm informed us that he had been instructed by the High Court to take us to Mountjoy Prison for failing to comply with an order of the judge. He was backed up by a large force of Gardaí and a number of Garda vans were waiting, engines running, at the back of the building.

We didn't resist. We simply gathered up our belongings and were ushered into the back of the paddy wagons. We made the short journey across the river, up Church Street and along the North Circular Road, as I balanced my portable TV and typewriter on my lap. The Gardaí were friendly and the banter was good – they asked us if we had informed our parents of our fate! In total darkness, we drove through the gates of Mountjoy and were all signed in. The massive ledgers looked like rejects from a Dickensian clerk's office, Scrivener and Co.

There were only five of us named on the court order, so the Gardaí simply told the others to leave and arrested us. Myself, Eamon O'Doherty and Finbar Cullen from Trinity, Sean McCarthy from UCD and Niall Brennan from Maynooth College spent the first night in one big cell, sleeping on the floor.

The following morning, after a pleasant breakfast of cornflakes, bread and tea, the prison staff rushed around trying to work out where to put us. After about an hour, we were all ushered together and marched out of the main part of the prison. Bizarrely, on the way, we saw two prison officers in the most aggressive verbal tussle I had ever come across behind bars; in the two weeks I spent in Mountjoy, it was the closest I ever came to any sort of violence. We were brought to the training unit, a fairly modern wing of the prison with larger cells. We were put in two spacious cells with a small table and a sink in each, but no loo.

Mountjoy reminded me of Kilmainham jail – with real prisoners. It was – and remains – an image straight from the TV series *Porridge*. Arriving in the corridor of the newer training unit, I met Christy Dunne, a neighbour from around the corner from my mother's house. I don't know what Christy, or 'Git', as we knew him, was in for but he quickly took me aside and gave me a few home truths: 'If you are getting extra visits, don't tell any of the other prisoners. Try to stick together as a group and go around together, but no boasting or going on about what you are in for.' He then told me to ask for a transistor radio – and to 'tell the staff you are all doing exams and get in whatever you need'. It was sound advice.

We kept to ourselves and kept our heads down. We set up a little office, with my orange Brother typewriter on our small table, and began writing to anyone we could think of. Christy was right: within hours, various

TDs came to see us, including Tony Gregory, Brian Lenihan Snr and Paddy Harte, the Fine Gael TD from Donegal, whose son was president of the Students' Union in Letterkenny RTC and a great activist.

But the Labour/Fine Gael coalition refused to budge. A demo was organized for outside the prison, and we got support from the NUS in the UK, whose president, Neil Stewart, flew over. We were at least embarrassing the coalition, with Fianna Fáil TDs reminding them that we were the first students to be sent to Mountjoy since Kevin Barry in 1920. Student protests intensified; four students were arrested for blocking Barry Desmond's state car, while two others ended up in prison for occupying other government offices.

I did interviews from inside Mountjoy. Christina Murphy, the very influential education correspondent of the *Irish Times*, inveigled her way in, claiming she was my aunt. She published an interview in which I vowed to stay in prison as long as needed.

The prison term we had been sentenced to was indefinite and would last until we 'purged' our contempt. After a week had passed, the judge decided that we should be brought before him and offered another opportunity to apologize, purge our contempt and walk free.

Why they decided to handcuff me, and no one else, before transporting us back to the High Court, I do not know. I had already been in prison for a week and had behaved well. As I collected my few belongings from my cell, including my beloved typewriter that had served me so well, I did not know whether I was going to be sent back to prison that day or not.

The prison authorities and most of our fellow prisoners believed the eleven students now incarcerated in Mountjoy would simply give in and be freed. But we were not for turning and refused to give an undertaking to stop the campaign.

Outside the court, students blocked the prison vans taking us back to Mountjoy, until I appealed to them to bring the campaign back to the health boards. At one stage, fifty-two students were brought to the High Court by various health boards – but we had instructed them all to abide by the court's ruling, as we wanted people working on the outside, with only a token few in prison.

When we arrived back in Mountjoy, the other prisoners all rose to their feet and shouted their admiration and support. It was a great feeling.

Prison was not at all as daunting to me as it might have been to others – and it was a lesson to me: never let your fears overwhelm you.

Neither of my parents visited me when I was in prison. My father was embarrassed at my radicalism and involvement in student politics, though at this stage, despite his young age, his health was failing; he had suffered a stroke in 1982 aged fifty-six, which effectively ended his working life. My mother was simply bemused and baffled. It was left to my two wonderful spinster aunts, Rose and Renee – my father's sisters – to visit. I am sure they must have been mortified at the thought of my being in Mountjoy. They brought me a bottle of Lucozade – as if I was in hospital, not jail!

Ironically, it was the Fine Gael backbencher Paddy Harte who applied his skills and set up meetings between Department of Health officials and the USI. It was clear to the government at that stage that we were not going to purge our contempt, so they were keen to end the campaign. A formula of words was agreed on. Minister Barry Desmond agreed that students would be assessed in their own right, leading the *Irish Independent* to declare that the compromise would cost more than the cutbacks were meant to save! We indicated on Saturday that we were willing to purge our contempt, so after two weeks in prison we were brought before the High Court at eight thirty that evening and released to a great reception.

The war of words continued, but the whole campaign had been a great boost to students. By taking a stand on the medical card, we had demonstrated the importance of the issue, not just for students but for others much more vulnerable and much less organized than we were.

Twenty-five years later, the government of the day had another go at removing medical cards – this time for the over-seventies. I am glad I was around for that campaign as well.

Before my term as president of the Union of Students in Ireland ended, I was involved in one more campaign. As a child, I had been brought to wave at JFK on his visit to Ireland; as a teenager, I had made some rather feeble efforts at protesting the visit of Nixon. But by the time of the next visit by a US president, Ronald Reagan, in 1984, I was much more politically active and did my level best to oppose the visit and highlight Reagan's interference in countries such as Nicaragua.

The USI were to the forefront in opposing Reagan's state visit in June. For months beforehand, myself and socialist campaigner Eamon McCann traipsed the country, speaking at public meetings in colleges, trade union halls and outdoor venues, encouraging protests against the visit because of Reagan's arming of the right-wing Contras in Nicaragua, who were trying to depose the democratically elected government. Eamon and I developed quite a double act. I was continually mesmerized by his superb oratorical skills, honed on the streets of Derry in 1969.

Our audiences ranged from around thirty teenagers at a street corner in Cabra to close to a thousand in Connolly Hall in Cork city. Everywhere we went we were met with a rapturous reception. By the time we got to a *Late Late Show* special on the Reagan visit, Eamon's oratorical brilliance got him on to the panel, while my reticence guaranteed me a place in the audience.

The Reagan visit will always be remembered for the massive protests. From his arrival in Shannon on the Friday evening to his departure the following Tuesday, the USI was at the forefront. On the drive to

Shannon, we travelled through the Phoenix Park to express our support for the 'women's peace camp' installed near the residence of the US ambassador. Gerard Cushnahan, a USI official who was driving the car, got a shock in Chapelizod when he was overtaken by a speeding unmarked Avenger car. It was the Special Branch, stopping us to ask why we had supported the women. They eventually let us proceed, but later that night the women were all arrested and held – illegally – for seventy-two hours until Reagan had left.

After our first protest in Shannon airport, we drove to Galway to prepare for the next morning's demo. Reagan was due to get an honorary doctorate from the university. Galway, being the city of social justice campaigners such as Bishop Eamon Casey and Labour TD Michael D. Higgins, added to a heady mix of third-level students, guaranteed a great buzz for the impending demos.

However, I was not destined to make that demo. A large group of us were in a bar in Salthill when word got to me – through the Gardaí, ironically – that my fifty-eight-year-old father had just suffered another stroke and was seriously ill in St James's Hospital in Dublin. I was told he might not survive the night. Gerry Cushnahan drove through the night to get me back to Dublin. By the time we arrived, early on Saturday morning, my father had recovered somewhat, but this being his second stroke, the prognosis was not good.

Having missed the Galway protest, it was back into the centre of Dublin for a massive evening demo. At one stage, as the march made its way from St Stephen's Green to Dublin Castle, a car from the American convoy got caught up in the protest. The occupant was recognized and things looked like they were going to turn very nasty. But realizing that we were winning the propaganda war hands down and that a violent outburst would destroy us, I managed to persuade the protesters to ease off.

As the weekend unfolded in glorious sunshine, the protests got more animated. For the bank-holiday Monday march from Parnell Square to Dáil Éireann, I had bought hundreds of 'Reagan' face masks from Hector Grey's toy wholesalers just off Gardiner Street, where I had also found plastic bags full of cheap whistles. I bought every bag and, on the Monday morning, distributed the whistles among the marchers. As we reached the Dáil, I jumped up on to the back of the truck that was serving as our platform, and urged everyone to blow in unison: 'Let's hear it for the boy!' What a sound! As Reagan's address to both houses of the Oireachtas was broadcast live on RTÉ television, the sombre voice of Brian Farrell was underlaid with the steady whine of thousands of whistles.

After my speech to the protesters, I jumped down off the flatbed truck but, unfortunately, a ring I was wearing got caught in a nail on the back 'H' bar. I swung helplessly, kicking out as the ring embedded itself into my bloody finger, and I also badly sprained my left ankle. Traffic in the city centre was shut down because of the protests so, aided by another speaker, Michael D.

Higgins, Mark Durkan and my partner June Meehan, I hobbled to the Mater Hospital. I limped around for months – another innocent casualty of Ronald Reagan's foreign policy!

CHAPTER 15

Tough Love

Not that he would have been bothered, but my father did make it on to the pages of the *Irish Times*. On the day after he died, I got USI to place an advert on the back page of the paper of record, noting that the offices of USI were closed as a mark of respect for James 'Jimmy' Duffy.

My father's condition deteriorated, and he died on Tuesday, 19 June at the age of fifty-eight, during my final week as president of USI. True to form, he had never been in Trinity while I studied there – nor had my mother – until my graduation ceremony in 1981, when both of them were in their fifties. Born within shouting distance of Trinity College and spending their entire childhood living in the centre of Dublin, both of them must have passed the Front Gate countless times, yet neither of them had ever set foot on the cobblestones of Front Square.

I don't feel I knew my father well. Two years before

he died, after his first stroke, we did start going for a drink at Sunday lunchtime. By that time, he had stopped going to Downey's, so we would ramble down to Nalty's. The conversations were mostly about Dublin in the rare old times, with me prodding him for information about growing up in the heart of Dublin, and he was a great talker, full of memories, images and anecdotes.

As I said earlier, my younger brother Brendan had developed a drug problem as a teenager, and his life had gone steadily downhill. Like so many with addiction problems, Brendan is incredibly bright – easily the sharpest in our family, very artistic and astonishingly good company. But he is crippled, ruined, wrecked by a savage addiction. He has been in prison, robbed innocent people, borrowed and never repaid money from all the family, and God knows who else. Even when I later got a job in the probation service, the first thing I had to do was inform my bosses that my brother was then an inmate in one of our prisons.

As our father lay dying, Brendan was serving a prison sentence for an assault and robbery earlier that year. Brendan and a couple of ne'er-do-wells had travelled by bus out to Blessington, attacked a petrol pump attendant and robbed the takings; in their stupidity, they had boarded a bus heading back to Dublin, which the Gardaí quickly intercepted. To make matters worse, the culprits all gave false names and addresses, implicating a number of our near neighbours. I was fuming, not just about the crime but the cowardice in naming perfectly innocent and law-abiding neighbours as the criminals. Of course the Gardaí visited the homes of the so-called culprits and easily uncovered the lies.

When Brendan appeared in court I accompanied my mother to the proceedings, urging her to stand firm and not pay his bail under any circumstances, which she didn't, despite Brendan's protestations. By then, we were well used to his pleas of being misunderstood and a victim, and my mother's line on him was hardening. His friends were bailed out by their parents, and they encouraged Mabel to do the same, but we stood firm and Brendan was remanded in custody. We desperately wanted to help him to face up to his problems. They were all eventually sentenced to prison for the crime.

All the same, we pleaded with the then minister for justice, Jim Mitchell, who was also our local TD, to allow Brendan to be brought to the hospital from Mountjoy Prison to see his dying father. When I saw the two accompanying prison officers, I hoped they would stick close to him, as I feared he would try to escape.

When my father died I again wrote to Jim Mitchell, urging him to ignore the prison authorities, who also feared Brendan would escape, and allow Brendan out for twenty-four hours for the funeral. I undertook to 'sign' Brendan into my care, to ensure that he would stay in the family home and not consume drink or drugs. Of course, Brendan was full of contrition and promises as we travelled from Mountjoy to Claddagh Green – and he could be very convincing. Even when the priest from the next parish arrived – our local church was unavailable, much to my mother's annoyance – Brendan was full of humility as Father Tony Walsh (later convicted of serious sexual abuse) detailed the plan for the funeral.

That evening, as my father's remains arrived at the Church of the Assumption in Lower Ballyfermot, I noticed some friends of Brendan's in the gathering as James, Peter, Brendan, Aidan and I carried the coffin from the hearse. Just as the priests, Father Michael Cleary and Father Tony Walsh, welcomed the remains, I noticed something being passed to Brendan in the church. I thought that my eyes had deceived me. But as the evening unfolded, I knew things were taking a turn for the worse.

After the removal, mourners returned to our small house in Claddagh Green; soon, even the bedrooms upstairs were full of people. At one stage, James and I were going through the funeral arrangements with the undertaker in our childhood bedroom as the rest of the house heaved with mourners.

About an hour later, a knock came at the door. I recognized the gurrier who had passed the package to Brendan in the church. Brendan got very agitated and tried to leave the house, despite our earlier agreement. James, Liam Maguire and I tried to restrain him but he became even more violent. We eventually managed to get him to an upstairs bedroom, where he proceeded to wreck the place and tried to climb out through an upstairs window.

Most of the other mourners had left at this stage, embarrassed by the unfolding row. My mother and her sisters were now screaming downstairs and barricaded in the front room in fear of Brendan's rampage. I told them calmly that I was going for the police to take Brendan back to prison, which meant he would miss his father's funeral. Mabel immediately agreed, despite protestations from others that it was a cruel blow for a son not to be there when his father's coffin was being lowered into the grave.

I contacted the Gardaí, who promptly arrived in force, ordering us to stay downstairs as they drew batons and headed for the upstairs room. With little resistance, Brendan was taken away, still dressed in his black suit, white shirt and mourning tie, but out of his head on whatever concoction he had been slipped in the church. I accompanied him back to Mountjoy, where I signed the papers to have him readmitted. Asked if I wanted to collect him in the morning for the funeral, I replied, 'No.'

I stood firm on our decision that we should not try to get Brendan to the funeral. It was the easiest option at this stage.

On Good Friday 1988, four years after my father's death, I got a message from my mother's doctor informing me that she was in the surgery, distraught and afraid to go back across to her house. Brendan, her 28-year-old son, had pushed her out and wouldn't let her in. After he had lost another flat due to his drinking and drug dependence, he had moved back into Mabel's house, despite our pleas to her not to allow him to live there. But she loves him as only a mother can, through thick and thin, and when he is well, Brendan is extraordinarily likeable.

I drove to Claddagh Green, got the house key from my mother and walked the short distance from the doctor's surgery across the tarmacked 'green' to our house. I looked in the letterbox and saw Brendan lying prostrate on the floor, obviously drunk. I tried to open the door, but he was lodged against it and wouldn't or couldn't budge. I went to the Carrolls next door and phoned the Gardaí and an ambulance. With help from one of the Carrolls, we pushed in the front door, but this awoke Brendan, and he morphed into the antichrist.

He chased me out on to the street, screaming and shouting. It was broad daylight, nearing three o'clock, and the road was busy with people walking down to the nearby St Matthew's Church for the Good Friday devotions. Brendan flailed around, trying to catch me, with my mother screaming for him to stop. Just as the Garda car arrived, he hit me; bizarrely, when I asked a young policeman why he would not arrest Brendan, even for his own good, he denied seeing him assault me.

An ambulance arrived shortly afterwards, but the paramedics refused to take him in his aggressive state. My mother pleaded with him to get in the ambulance. Eventually, I persuaded a Garda to accompany Brendan in the ambulance and the other Gardaí agreed to escort it to the hospital. We managed to get a still very angry

Brendan into the vehicle. I drove along behind, but the ambulance came to an abrupt halt outside the Church of the Assumption in Ballyfermot. The back doors burst open to reveal another tussle as Brendan tried to get out. The Gardaí were exasperated; a second one got into the ambulance, and it took off again.

At this stage, it seemed to me that the best place for Brendan would be prison; we would know where he was, he would be well fed and looked after medically, and the health services offered no alternatives. Indeed, much more recently, I spoke to a psychiatrist who made it clear to me that she thought that if Brendan's actions were criminal, they should be dealt with by the Gardaí; it's a point of view I have come to see as sensible.

Through Brendan, I became familiar with the Rutland Centre in Dublin, and the excellent work they do, based on the 'Twelve Step' programme of Alcoholics Anonymous, probably the most wonderful helping organization ever founded. I truly believe that anyone who seeks out AA finds great solace in their open, warm, confidential and helping embrace.

The Rutland Centre also helped me to see for the first time that Brendan's problems were his responsibility. He owned his addiction. He made choices, and had made many correct ones, and could again if he wished. With our encouragement, Brendan did find help, and the improvement was long lasting. But he slipped again and, for the last twenty years, it has been an unending nightmare, above all for Brendan himself.

* * *

In the early 1990s, I was contacted by a letting agency who rang RTÉ looking for me. An irate young woman told me that, having gone guarantor on the rental of an apartment in Islandbridge, I was now liable for the outstanding rent and damage to the property. I told her that I had done no such thing; it turned out that Brendan had faked my signature. In the midst of this argument with the letting agent, I got the address and agreed to try to talk to Brendan, who had recently lost his business and his relationship.

We got into the apartment in Islandbridge, again with the help of the Gardaí, where we found Brendan surrounded by empty bottles of spirits. Mabel, James, Peter and I sat with him, trying to persuade him to get help. As we pleaded with him, a taxi driver arrived with a large delivery of spirits – obviously a regular and lucrative run. I won't repeat what I told the driver as I ran him off the complex.

At one point, Brendan ran after me, shouting about my new-found job in RTÉ: 'You think you are Marian Finucane or Gay Byrne, but you are only a waster.' I didn't know whether to laugh or cry.

On another occasion, he embarked on a mad campaign of sending fire engines to our homes. Early one Saturday, my brother Peter rang me from his home in Lucan to say there were two fire engines outside – the third time they had been called that day. As Peter was talking, I heard the sound of sirens and I remarked that there were more fire engines arriving at his house; but then, looking out my own front window, I saw two more screech to a halt. As two firefighters made their way up our front path, one of them wearing breathing apparatus, I realized that it was my turn for Brendan's wrath. He had not only phoned the fire brigade, he had also told them there were children in the house. I thanked the firemen and spent the rest of the day trying to stop them coming again on false errands. The fire service answer every call and don't get into time-wasting debates about whether it's a hoax call or not; regardless of the provenance of the call, they have to come out. Eventually, they agreed to take my phone numbers and said they would send out their normal complement anyway, but would ring the house on the way and turn back if it was a false alarm.

Every now and again, I still get a dreaded call from the Sunday newspapers about Brendan. I will never forget when the World Special Olympics opened on 21 June 2003. I had committed to do some work for it during the fortnight of the Games, and we were supposed to be going to Croke Park for the much-anticipated spectacular opening ceremony. Later, we were to travel to Ballyfermot for my sister's fortieth-birthday party.

But instead my morning began with calls from reporters informing me that Brendan had been jailed the previous day for urinating in public while drunk in Galway. I said nothing; there was nothing I could say. Then a journalist arrived at my front door, and I hid out in the back garden. Eventually, having dispatched June and the kids to her mother's in Cabra, I rang a friend to drive to a lane behind our house. I scurried over a wall and was driven to another friend's house in Glasnevin, where I met up with my family before heading to Croke Park. At this stage, three Sunday newspapers were trying to contact me. I rang my mother, to discover that one journalist had already been to her hall door but, thankfully, Mabel didn't have a clue what she was talking about.

I was agitated and worried, so halfway through the opening ceremony we left and headed to Ballyfermot to be with the rest of my family at the birthday party. Together, our attitude was stoic; we had nothing to be ashamed about. People could make up their own minds about Brendan. My sister Pauline, who has been very good to him and endured an awful lot of torment in return, is brilliant at calming my mother down and took a sensible view of the whole thing, putting everything into context and managing to get us all to relax and not to panic.

A number of newspapers did run with the story the next morning, and the following day. But it passed. We have nothing to fear from the truth.

Our own ability not to wither under Brendan's addictions is primarily due to the 'family days' in the Rutland Centre and my own attendance at meetings for Adult Children of Alcoholics (ACOA). For two years, every Sunday night, I attended a meeting of ACOA in Bray. An offshoot of Alcoholics Anonymous, this gave me a safe weekly forum to listen to others and gradually liberate myself from the guilt I felt about my father and, later, Brendan. I really cannot overstate the worth of AA and all its offshoots; they truly are a magnificent group: confidential, safe, helpful, non-judgemental, humble and generous.

When Brendan is well, he is lucid and insightful. Sober and calm, he displays his immense intelligence, common sense and people skills. But he will not accept any responsibility for his own behaviour. Blaming it on others is OK as far as it goes – but where does it get you? Ultimately people make their own choices – and consequences follow. Here we have a wonderful, bright, handsome man laid low by addiction. He broke free from it before and can do so again, but it is his decision.

Brendan phoned me in work one day in considerable distress. It was around one thirty and I was just about to head into studio. I spoke to him calmly, urging him to seek help. I am sure others who overheard this con-versation in our small open-plan area were baffled by my nonchalance, even coldness. But I was being as straight with him as I could.

People often wonder – and commentators sneer – at my vitriolic distaste for those who urge the legalization of addictive substances such as cannabis or the poisons sold by 'Head Shops'. I have never met a happy drug addict or alcoholic. We don't need more legal drugs.

Brendan still rings my mother every week and visits regularly. She worries dreadfully about him. He is now in his fifties, and Mabel is in her eighties. To her great credit, she stands firm, but in her moments of weakness and blackness she still cries that he is her son, her flesh and blood.

So why write about Brendan now? I have never spoken publicly about him before – but these are my words, unvarnished and truthful, and he is a part of my family, and part of my story. I'm also choosing to speak out now as I believe that more of us need to stand up to addictions and take a harder stance against them. There should be no shame. But the dilemma for us, like for every family, remains: have we done enough to help Brendan? Not a day goes by when I don't ask that question, and each day, I can truthfully say, the answer is different. It's often a choice between brotherly love and tough love.

I am still asked about Brendan often, as he is well known around the centre of Dublin. I don't see him often, but I do see his son, who has grown into a beautiful young man. The main thing is that Brendan is still alive and therefore there is hope.

CHAPTER 16

On Probation

IN THE SUMMER OF 1984, HAVING FINISHED MY TERM IN
USI, I needed work – and quickly. Within nine months
of being a guest of the Irish Department of Justice in
Mountjoy Prison, I was looking for a job with them.
USI did not pay much, so here I was aged twenty-eight,
no money, no savings, living in a rented house and no
income apart from unemployment benefit. I applied for
any social-work jobs advertised.

One of my first interviews was in the Probation and
Welfare Service – and, much to my surprise, I was
offered a full-time, permanent, pensionable job. I knew
my Garda file would have been consulted before I was
offered it. Years later, the then minister for justice
Michael Noonan told me that the decision on whether
or not to employ me had crossed his desk, and he had
okayed it. I had all the qualifications to become a probation officer, including an honours social-work degree.
I also had a couple of advantages: I was male and from

Ballyfermot, and the vast majority of the 'clients' of the probation service were young men from working-class areas.

I was told, along with ten others, to report to the Probation and Welfare Service headquarters in Smithfield in Dublin in October 1984. After an intensive training course, we were called up one by one to the top-floor office of the chief probation officer, Martin Tansey, for our assignments. This was a nerve-wracking experience, as we could be sent anywhere in the country, and this meeting was an opportunity to plead our cases. I wasn't married, so my chances of being dispatched to Tralee or Letterkenny were quite high. I only had one request – that I should not be assigned to Loughan House in Blacklion, County Cavan, as my brother Brendan was a prisoner there at the time. Martin was totally understanding, but as was his wont, he gave no promises. However, I was in little doubt that he would accommodate me.

The probation service was at the time the biggest employer of social workers in the country. In some shape or form, everyone we dealt with had been before a court; many were or had been in prison, while the remainder had 'got off' by being put on probation for a period, usually around two years. I was sent to what was at the time the most glamorous, comfortable location in the country – Anne's Lane, just off Dublin's Grafton Street.

I needed a car, so I had to learn quickly how to drive. June had been driving for years, to get to her job running a community workshop in Finglas South, so she gave me a few lessons. She still regrets it. I remember the day – as I am sure do many other road users – when I first drove the car from Finglas South to the office car park in Anne's Lane. On arriving, I had to prise my now frozen hands off the bent steering wheel, which I had clung on to for dear life on the five-mile journey. I am convinced that, at one stage in the rollercoaster ride, I simply closed my eyes and hoped for the best.

I loved my time in the probation service; my immediate superiors, to a man and a woman, were the best in the business. They were all bright, smart social workers honed by years of dealing with the civil service and tempered by working at the coalface. You learn a lot from dealing with people on probation and are not easily duped. You become a very good judge of character.

To add to the gaiety of the office, we had no bosses; they were all based in the headquarters in Smithfield. As we sat in our dilapidated premises, we could smell the roasting coffee beans from Bewley's Café in Dublin's sexiest street; I know, it just gets better – location, location, location!

Within days of starting in Anne's Lane, I sprang into action. I hauled in my old stalwarts – my orange Brother portable typewriter and my transistor radio – and I immediately got to work . . . setting up a works social committee. Our building had a magnificent rooftop venue which today is home to one of the trendiest nightspots in the capital. The first Anne's Lane rooftop Christmas party was organized, without the big bosses finding out.

Although I was based in the city centre, my first responsibility was as liaison officer to a home for difficult teenage boys in Ballyfermot – located opposite the house my granny had been evicted from twenty-three years earlier. Run by an Italian religious order, the Sons of Divine Providence, Sarsfield House was a hostel for up to thirty 'boys' who were too difficult to handle at home but were thankfully still out of the clutches of the prison system. The Department of Justice provided substantial funding to the hostel, and my job was to liaise with the management and staff. Only about fifteen of the boys were under the probation service's jurisdiction, and demand for places was intense. With good food, excellent facilities and hard-working staff, Sarsfield House did their utmost to get jobs or school places if required for the residents.

As well as visiting Sarsfield House every second day, I organized a weekly outing to ensure I had some time with the residents and could get a good sense of how they were getting on. These outings also allowed me to talk to the lads about life in the hostel without the management present. From ice-skating to visits to local factories, these Tuesday nights became regular and popular events in the hostel calendar. In the main, the lads behaved brilliantly – though we were surrounded once by a number of Garda cars on the Dublin quays when they recognized some of the 'gurriers' in my car and somehow thought I might have been hijacked.

On another occasion, when I organized full-day excursions, we secured a much-coveted tour of the ESB generating station in Turlough Hill in West Wicklow. Built under a mountain with an artificial lake on the summit, this hydro-powered station was a technological and engineering wonder. But of course the first reaction of the lads when we arrived at the gates, in the wilderness of the Wicklow Gap, was 'There are no shops.' After a mile-long drive under the mountain, we exited the tunnel into a scene straight out of a James Bond movie. After a brilliant and informative tour of the magnificent complex, we were brought into the space-age control room, where, following a detailed lecture, the chief engineer asked if the lads had any questions. I held my breath in hope that they wouldn't let me down. After about a minute one of the lads put up his hand and, pointing to a small machine with a spindle handle, confidently asked, 'What does this do in the generating station?' A bemused engineer replied, 'That's the pencil parer.' Tours of Turlough Hill were discontinued shortly afterwards – for security reasons, I am told!

I was also 'attached' to a training workshop, Treble R, aimed at young people of both sexes who could not get steady jobs. Often, as part of their 'probation', the court would instruct the accused to do a six-month training course, and Treble R, with its committed staff, focused not just on mechanical and technical skills but had a major emphasis on the three 'Rs'.

I was subsequently asked to run the probation service resource centre behind Clery's in the centre of Dublin.

Used for meetings, the facility was an ideal city-centre location. We used it for family visits for prisoners with young children, avoiding the massive embarrassment for the adults and children, and also providing a very relaxed setting. The vast majority of 'criminals' do respond well to decent treatment, and the more decently treated they are, the greater the likelihood that they will eventually turn away from crime.

I also started running 'parenting courses' – an opportunity for the hard-pressed parents of the 'delinquents' to meet and swap stories. They were a great success and had the full support of my senior, Marie Sheridan, a wonderful, humane woman who allowed me to bring in great women such as Vicki McElligot, whose own son had been in trouble with the law, to lead the sessions. Indeed, the probation service was blessed with a terrific group of social workers who oozed wisdom and compassion.

In the meantime, I was studying to become a family therapist with the Marriage and Family Institute, which involved an afternoon and two evening sessions each week over a three-year period. It was tough, challenging and innovative, including the use of video and two-way screens during counselling sessions, allowing a team to monitor your therapeutic skills. I found this course creative, liberating and extraordinarily useful in my daily work with families. I was a founding member of the Family Therapy Network of Ireland and for a time edited their magazine, *Feedback*.

Of course, I dealt with more serious criminals as well,

and I always let them know that I was 'wide' to them – I knew what they were up to.

One character I didn't trust was all sweetness and light as he told me on his weekly visit that he was fine, searching hard for a job and coming home on time each night to his very happy mother. Out of devilment, I followed him when he left Anne's Lane. Within minutes, I found him in a nearby shopping centre attacking a security guard with the business end of an industrial sweeping brush. I didn't have powers of arrest, but when he saw me he ran. He knew I would 'breach' him later that day – revoking his probation order and sending him to prison.

The most difficult people I had to deal with during my four years in the Department of Justice were sex offenders; the easiest were murderers. Because those who murder in Ireland invariably get a life sentence – which is, of course, nothing compared with the death sentence of their victims or the life sentence of the victim's family – my job as probation officer was to supervise them on their release, as, technically, they are under 'licence' until their death. They can be returned to prison if the probation service applies to the court.

The few murderers who were sent to me after their prison term had expired were invariably timid, broken, frightened and lonely. My first move was to bar them from returning to anywhere near where the victim's family lived. I made it clear that if they did otherwise, I would have them back in prison that afternoon. They never breached this simple rule. Most of my work with these men involved acquainting them with the world they had re-entered after a long stretch in prison, helping them get accommodation and keeping them busy. As I had now turned thirty, many of my friends were getting married, so I asked them for any unused or unwanted wedding presents, which came in very handy when setting up these ex-criminals in a decent home. Some of them took to coming into my office every day, such was their loneliness. Without exception, they never re-offended.

However, sex offenders do, and they are the most baffling, the most cunning, the most devious of all criminals. In fairness, as I was dealing with offenders in the community, the number of sex offenders was low; but those I dealt with I never trusted.

In cases of incest, I was faced with the obstacle that, for reasons of shame, guilt or fear, the offender's spouse was often reticent in helping me with my inquiries. On one occasion, having insisted that a father could never stay overnight in the family home, as I deemed he was still a risk to his daughter, I was sure that the mother was telling me lies when I would ask about his nocturnal visits, which she denied.

This awful dilemma – who to believe, the issue of collusion and the complexity of the issue – led to a group of us, through our trade union, organizing a series of meetings and a national conference to talk about the challenge of dealing with sex offenders. We were in no doubt that working with them required long-term commitment and resources. Efforts were made to translate what we learned into action, but society's attitudes to these offenders mean none but the bravest politicians or civil servants will ever confront these problems.

The same group of us in the union also looked at another type of crime, which to us had a very simple and effective solution. A 'joyriding' epidemic had overtaken the country in the mid-1980s. Teenagers took to stealing cars, and then would revel in the chase by the Gardaí. A number of children were knocked down and killed by these stolen cars, including two young boys in Ballyfermot. The government reacted quickly; Gardaí were given spiked chains to burst the tyres of the speeding teenagers and, in 1985, they reopened Spike Island in Cork Harbour as a detention centre for these 'thugs'.

A group of us visited a pioneering car project in Belfast that harnessed the young people's interest in cars and speed and used it productively through mechanics, driving courses and literacy classes. It was a brilliant, simple, effective idea. We immediately prepared a detailed proposal for the Department of Justice, complete with costings, but they refused to meet us. They could see only one solution – imprisonment. Spike Island was set on fire by the inmates and eventually closed down. Cars became cheaper and the joyriding epidemic subsided. The government had wasted millions, and another opportunity to look at alternatives to custody had been trashed.

The probation service had only one weak point as far as I was concerned: it was part of the civil service. I could feel the strictures of civil service bureaucracy, conservatism and the innate dislike of change weigh more and more heavily on my work. My colleagues in the probation service were brilliant, my immediate boss was supportive and I liked the challenge of the job, but I gradually discovered that change will only happen if those civil servants and politicians at the top want it to happen, which was seldom. Whenever we came up with new ideas, we knew the decision-making process did not reside in the probation service but in head office in the Department of Justice. The power lay not with a transient government minister but with the permanent staff, who, it seemed to me, were impervious to argument.

In the end, that dead hand was so overwhelming that I seriously started to look for a change – not just of job, but of career. I wanted more freedom, more opportunity to change things and more control over my own life. In early 1988, I saw an advert in the *RTÉ Guide* for a producers' training course and I decided to apply. The idea of becoming a radio producer appealed to me. I had a great interest in politics, current and social affairs – and, above all, radio. I was the only probation officer to have a radio in my office. *The Gay Byrne Show* was essential listening. In 1986, I had even complained to RTÉ about an interview Gay gave to BBC Radio 4 – during his own show – about the state of the country. Gay famously declared that the country was banjaxed and that he would encourage his kids to emigrate. My complaint was not about Gay's language but about the fact that he was both presenter and guest on his own programme. My complaint was roundly rejected by RTÉ.

In preparing for the interview for the course, I tried to find out who else was applying. As expected, it was mostly journalists and seasoned radio staff. I decided to sell them my difference; I believed and argued that I could bring a broader experience to the national broadcaster. With twenty participants, I told the interview panel, they could afford one non-journalist. They accepted my challenge and I was offered a place.

Did I ever think I would actually become a broadcaster? That didn't even enter my 32-year-old head.

Leaving the probation service was a bigger wrench than I thought. A colleague, Frank Moran, left on the same day as me. In keeping with the good humour that had permeated the job, at our going-away party we were both ushered to the front door of our office in Anne's Lane, where a horse-drawn white carriage awaited. It trundled down Grafton Street and around St Stephen's Green, where, to our puzzlement, animated onlookers greeted us and waved enthusiastically. It was only when we alighted that we discovered the 'just married' slogan on the back of the carriage!

Radio Days

CHAPTER 17

In the Producer's Seat

MY FIRST DAY ON THE PRODUCERS' TRAINING COURSE in RTÉ was a nightmare. Filled with doubts, I asked myself why I had given up a permanent, pensionable job with great colleagues to take up a twelve-week training course with no guarantee of a job, and in a craft I knew very little about.

We were all handed antiquated cassette recorders and told to go off and do an interview. I didn't even know how to use the damned thing. The first day is always the worst!

To add to my woes, up galloped my inferiority complex. It was clear within a few days that there were a number of high flyers in the group – and this ex-probation officer was not one of them. Everyone was younger, more experienced, more confident, better talkers and listeners, and would easily make it to the top of the class. I was definitely a donkey among thoroughbreds. We all watched each other like hawks, because we knew that while there were twenty of us on the course, there were only twelve short-term contracts available at the end. It was RTÉ roulette.

The main task on the course was to compile and produce a radio documentary. I decided to make one about the Phoenix Park: its history, the people who live there and famous events. I hit upon the idea of a journey in a horse and carriage through the park. But of course I had not yet learned the first rule of radio: keep it simple. Not content with just a tape recorder and voices – it was the wireless, after all – I set out to beg, steal or borrow a horse and carriage to transport my various interviewees up and down Chesterfield Avenue, the main road in the park. As the horse box arrived early one Sunday morning and the handlers battled to harness the giddy horses to the very fragile carriage, I wondered why I simply hadn't got the sound effects from the vast RTÉ library.

I met some fascinating people while making the documentary (another great aspect of my job), including the extraordinarily knowledgeable park superintendent John McCullen and the gifted arboriculturalist Noel O'Shea. While I was interviewing Noel about the trees in the park he lapsed into an almost mesmeric treatise about how trees were the earth's antennae, giving us not just life but vast amounts of vital information about our planet. He was one hell of an interesting guy, and definitely not out of his tree!

After the interview, Noel said to me, 'I sense you are going to become a household name through your work in RTÉ.' This, of course, came as news to me, as I had not even successfully completed the training course, let alone been offered a contract. I had certainly never entertained any thought of becoming a household name. But Noel believed he had psychic powers and gave me accurate details about things that had happened in my life. Noel could not predict, however, whether or not the programme we were making would be any good. As it turned out, it was not broadcast on RTÉ, but I did get it on the Dublin Millennium station in 1988.

The course itself was very, very good, with lots of practical, hands-on experience and daily lectures from RTÉ staffers such as Seamus Hosey, Michael Johnston, Tom Healy and Micheal Holmes, all brimming with passion and enthusiasm for the medium.

On our final day of training, we were all ushered to an open area at the front of the radio centre. One by one, we were called into Michael Littleton's office. As the twenty of us waited, we realized after five minutes that only the first twelve to be called in would be getting the contracts. The countdown continued. As the tenth person went in, I began to worry, but suddenly I heard my name being called. You cannot imagine the feelings of delight, achievement and relief that overtook me as I was offered a year-long contract. I was going to work for the national broadcaster – what an accolade, an honour and a challenge.

Then my biggest challenge suddenly hit me: if I was number eleven, the person I was detailed to call in would be the last to be offered a contract. So I would be breaking the news to the remaining eight that they were out. I can't remember the name I was asked to call; all I could think of were the brilliant people who would be crestfallen, many having given up good jobs. Indeed, a number of those left high and dry were visibly upset. One of them immediately headed for the door in a fury.

Kathleen O'Connor, the great matriarch of the radio centre, prodded me to follow the distraught trainee. I eventually caught up with her in Donnybrook village and muttered one of my mottoes: 'It will all come around sooner than you think.' While appreciative of my efforts, she was very annoyed, fuming at the cack-handed way in which the offers were made.

Indeed, it did all come around for her, sooner than anyone thought. Helen Shaw was offered a contract a few weeks later after some of the other candidates, pre-dictably, did not take up their job offers. Within nine years, Helen would become a very dynamic head of RTÉ Radio.

If the first day in a new job is the worst day, think about how intimidating the first week is. Thankfully, I already knew some of the producers. Alex White, a close friend from college days, was working in the current affairs department and had encouraged and helped me when I was applying for the RTÉ course. Alex introduced me to the experienced crew, who, it turned out, were all about the same age as myself and were all on the same wave-length – interested in politics, consumed by current affairs and, above all, determined to make programmes with mass appeal.

I was assigned to *Day by Day*, the current affairs programme presented by the learned John Bowman. With producers such as Ed Mulhall, Cathal Goan and Bernadette O'Sullivan, the hour-long programme was the 'must listen' daily dose of current affairs for many people. I had long admired John Bowman, and remembered my father's story of teaching him how to play snooker.

After about a week, I was allowed to take the helm as producer. It was up to me to decide what the 'story of the day' was, to assign reporters to stories, design the running order from beginning to end and co-ordinate the other producers on the programme. I was also in charge in the control room – deciding who goes where and when, whether to add more contributors or let the programme breathe. Every programme requires a different menu, depending on its nature and remit. I can't remember much about the actual content, but Cathal Goan kept his steady hand on my shoulder. It seemed that I was only interested in one thing: would I get my producer credit at the end of my first programme in the studio? Thanks to Cathal, I did.

I spent my first three months working with great producers such as Cathal and Alex, Julian Vignoles, Ronan O'Donoghue, Betty Purcell, Bernadette O'Sullivan and Simon Devilly. I was learning at an enormous rate. Firstly, having come straight from the public service, I could not get over how much responsibility and control

I was given. The team of producers, researchers and presenters run the programme from beginning to end. Making live daily programmes is a pretty difficult task; regardless of what is happening, you have to broadcast at a given time for a certain duration every day, no ifs or buts. Then there is the intense competition, not just between radio stations but among programmes within the station. More often than not, daily programmes are scrambling to beat their colleagues sitting behind the next office divider.

Day by Day was mainly concerned with party politics and, with Charles J. Haughey as Taoiseach at the time, there was a lot of it about. It is hard to portray how powerful a figure Haughey was. He seldom gave interviews and had an animosity towards RTÉ, which seems to be the preserve of politicians. Given that the government has more financial control, through the licence fee, over the national broadcaster than any other semi-state, no wonder the fear is in-built!

Shortly afterwards, John Bowman's *Day by Day* was replaced by the more populist and longer *Pat Kenny Show*. It's hard to know if presenters ever give up shows or if shows give up presenters – or is it simply a case of managers, especially new ones, wanting to make their mark by moving the schedule around? I have yet to meet a presenter who willingly gives up a programme, with the exception of Mike Murphy, who gives ambition a good name. For John Bowman, though, it turned out to be the right move, as it coincided with the start of his 21-year tenure as referee on the brilliant *Questions and Answers* on TV.

In the interim between the end of *Day by Day* and the start of *The Pat Kenny Show*, I did a stint on Andy O'Mahony's summer radio show, produced by, among others, Julian Vignoles and myself. I really like Andy: erudite, gracious, mischievous, devilishly funny and extraordinarily complimentary.

On the Friday before Andy's summer show was due to begin we had organized an interview with Pat Kenny, whom he was replacing. It was meant to be a bit of puff, with Pat asking Andy about his new programme. But Andy's first questions to Pat, who held the dubious accolade at the time as Ireland's most eligible bachelor, were if he was 'still with woman' and how the 'gold lamé' suit he wore into the radio centre was going down in Cork, where Pat was presenting a programme to mark the Michael Jackson concert in Pairc Uí Chaoimh that night! It was a side of Andy I saw subsequently on *The Late Late Show*. As a way of circumventing the awkwardness of the regular host talking about himself, Andy was inveigled into interviewing Deirdre Purcell, who had helped Gay Byrne write his autobiography, *The Time of My Life*. Andy's opening question must have sent thousands scurrying for the back of the couch: 'Did you want to sleep with him?' Deirdre nearly followed her jaw as it hit the floor!

One of the more bizarre off-air moments that summer came when Terry Keane, the journalist and socialite, to my surprise agreed to do an interview with Andy to mark her fiftieth birthday. Just as the interview was about to begin, Terry asked me to check if there was anything for her in radio reception. When I told her no, she muttered some mild expletive. But before the interview was over, a call from reception alerted me to the arrival of a massive bunch of flowers. I bounded up the stairs from our underground studios to collect the bouquet, and I couldn't help noticing that the card on the floral bouquet said it all: 'Happy 50th. Sweetie.'

When I presented her with the flowers, Terry was thrilled and charming. Subsequently, she was a willing and gracious contributor on other programmes I presented, including *Liveline*, where she spoke about her final illness and the reaction to her revelations about her 27-year-long affair with Charlie Haughey – Sweetie.

The end of the summer of 1988 saw the start of the new *Pat Kenny Show* – note the critical decision of management to put the presenter's name in the title. Pat was on the cusp of national fame, presenting *Today Tonight* on TV and moving up quickly to his own chat show, *Kenny Live*. Like any new venture in the schedule, all the best people were dragooned in and put to work on the new radio show. I was appointed as one of the (too many) producers. I enjoyed my stint on the show, learning a lot from the likes of Julian Vignoles, Betty Purcell, Tom Manning, Alex White and Ronan O'Donoghue.

I remember one crazy episode where, after Pat gave one of his many interviews to the *RTÉ Guide*, the final version of the piece gave the distinct impression that Pat did everything himself and was more interested in the TV programme than the daily radio show. A number of his radio producers were severely miffed and decided to confront a crestfallen PK in front of the rest of us. Pat was close to tears, as he felt he was being unfairly criticized for a print interview he obviously did not write. (By the way, I have seen, but not been a party to, the same injustice being visited on Gay Byrne, where a solitary tear did escape.) It was a storm in a teacup, but a lesson for me: beware of print interviews, where you cannot control what ends up on the page. At least on live radio what you say goes out unfiltered and unedited.

I worked on Pat's programme for nearly a year, which coincided with the election of 1989. When the then Taoiseach Charles Haughey came in for the party leader's phone-in during the election campaign, I was in the control room. Haughey was regal, distant, small, immaculately turned out but wearing too much after-shave. He let his guard slip on air when he revealed that he had not been fully aware of the severity of the health cuts until he had gone canvassing. The ubiquit-ous P. J. Mara was standing, even more regally than his boss, in the control room. On hearing Haughey's admission, P. J. let out a shout: 'Holy Jaysus, how will I answer that?'

While PK can turn his hand-held microphone to any topic, this show was primarily a current affairs pro-gramme, with much of the content being determined by the events of the day. It became a hard sell for us to get our ideas on air. On one occasion, I persuaded my sceptical producer colleagues to feature a Chinese author who had endured the calumnies of the Cultural Revolution and had written a stunning book. He was available for interview down the line from London. Luckily, someone suggested that, as we had the luxury of pre-recording items, we should do so on this occasion. Unfortunately, while I had read the book and prepared Pat's questions in English, the author had penned the book in the only language he had ever spoken or read for the ninety years of his life – Mandarin Chinese. His agent had persuaded me that his newfound hero had a good smattering of English. But if my Chinese extends to 'number 49 with sweet and sour sauce', his English stretched to a 'one and one'.

The item was a disaster, in any language. We all had a good laugh, but it was another lesson in radio producing: never suggest anyone or anything before you have at least made one phone call to check availability, interest and, in my case, whether the potential guest has a pulse.

In the meantime, my relationship with June had grown closer and closer and we decided to buy a house, and began saving incredibly hard. It's amazing how much you can save by moving in with friends – Peter Mooney and Mona Somers – and eating your future mother-in-law out of house and home! We were finally able to afford to take out a mortgage, and we moved into a new estate beyond the Phoenix Park in Carpenterstown. Both of us were working full time, we were not married, and the issue of having children simply did not arise at the time.

We had now been living together for five years and I was keen to move closer to the city and the sea. This was embedded in my DNA since my day trips to Dollymount as a child – and indeed one of the things my newfound psychic friend Noel O'Shea had told me in between talking to the trees in the Phoenix Park was that I would move to a house near a famous bridge, on a long street and close to the water. As the GPO was not available, we began looking in Clontarf. Within a year of me joining RTÉ, we came across a terraced house for sale there; at ninety-thousand pounds, it was a big stretch, especially as we were having great difficulty selling our house in Carpenterstown, and eventually let it go for thirty-eight thousand pounds, less than we had paid for it. This was of course before the Celtic Tiger lunacy.

Marriage seemed a logical option for the two of us; we had been together for a decade. We decided to get married on the last day of June 1989. We didn't stick to any of the traditional rituals of getting married in a church followed by a hotel reception. We chose the registry office in Molesworth Street, with a buffet-style reception in the banqueting room – or was it the jockey's weigh room? – at the Phoenix Park racecourse. June led off the speeches. My only gag was recalling the moment I told my future father-in-law, Paddy, that I would be marrying his only daughter: 'He rose slowly from his armchair and replied, "That will be the end of June." I shot back, "End of June, beginning of July – we haven't picked a date yet."' I felt I had once again proved that Ballyfermot wit is far superior to the Cabra version.

It was a beautiful sunny Friday, with a great mixture of relatives, pals from our TCD and USI days, friends of June from the community work constituency, pals from the probation service (one of whom donated his home-made wine, which was alcoholic but awful – the court case is still pending!), and a smattering of colleagues from RTÉ. Andy O'Mahony wrote a hilarious reply to the invite, which was read out in his absence, but Pat Kenny turned up and he was 'with woman': the beautiful Cathy, who soon became Mrs Kenny. Pat, by the way, looked positively radiant in his gold lamé suit – not! The following day we all met up again at a pub in Chapelizod before June and I headed off to drive around France for three weeks.

I don't know if the marriage *was* the end of June – but it was the making of me!

Around this time, I arranged my first full outside broadcast for *The Pat Kenny Show*, a format I would soon become well known for. I had read about the redevelopment of the Sherriff Street area under the aegis of the Custom House Docklands Development Authority. I thought it would be a good idea to do a full two-hour programme from the site, incorporating locals as well as the planners and masters of the universe who were about to oversee the launch of the government-backed International Financial Services Centre.

I remember early on the morning of the show being mesmerized by the vanloads of technical equipment from RTÉ arriving on site – and yes, the ubiquitous Volkswagen van did trundle in, but I was not tempted to let the air out of the tyres, as I had in my Nixon protest days.

It turned out to be a great programme, featuring one of the rare interviews given by Ireland's first big property developer of the Celtic Tiger era and one of Ireland's richest men, Mark Kavanagh. Sadly, Mark's young wife Lynda had recently drowned after a freak riding accident which also claimed the life of their children's nanny, Priscilla Clarke, whose body has never been found. Mark was the height of civility and talked movingly to Pat about the tragedy. The only element of the programme that proved contentious was my decision to give airtime to community activists such as Mick Rafferty and Seanie Lambe, both of whom I had got to know from my Trinity community work days; they were brilliant, despite the reservations of the other side.

Another significant outside broadcast came from London, where Pat chaired a debate among the emigrant Irish. I managed to assemble a great bunch of Tory, Labour and Liberal supporters, who all happened to be born in Ireland, and Pat did his usual brilliant job chairing a lively discussion, which is of course now his forte.

It was these two outside broadcasts which brought me to the attention of the man who was to become my unlikely mentor, supporter and now close friend, Gabriel Mary Byrne.

CHAPTER 18

The Gaybo Show

I HAD THREE DAYS TO ANSWER THE BIGGEST QUESTION OF my radio career. The word went around that Gay Byrne was looking for a male producer to replace Micheal Holmes, the only man in the production team, apart from GB himself. Michael Littleton called me into his office on Friday and asked me to consider moving; I had to make up my mind by Monday.

At that time, moving from *The Pat Kenny Show* to *The Gay Byrne Show* within RTÉ was more dangerous than scaling the Berlin Wall, with a greater likelihood of suffering an injury in the process. While the two programmes were separated by a two-minute news bulletin on the air and an office divider off the air, the current affairs programmes (including Pat's show) were in a separate department to *The Gay Byrne Show*, which was anchoring the entertainment department.

The GB Show was the behemoth in the building, and rightly so. It had a massive audience and was loved by all classes, all ages – a remarkable and very difficult feat. Unlike many of my colleagues in the current affairs department, I had always loved the programme too, and so I visited Micheal Holmes in Phibsboro on Saturday morning to seek his advice. He was adamant: 'Nobody, but nobody, should turn down the opportunity of working and learning with the maestro.' I pointed out that I had been with PK for less than a year, but he reminded me that no opportunity ever knocks at the exact time you would like, so just grab it. By the way, there's another of my new radio mottoes buried in that sentence.

I have always admired Gay Byrne. I remember meeting him for the first time in Moore Street in 1966. He was heading for his car, a Triumph Herald, and clutching his brown zip-up briefcase, which he still has. We had just been to Woolworth's in Henry Street for our annual Christmas outing with my mother and her sisters, and when I spotted Gay I ran up to him, shook his hand and asked for his autograph, which he graciously gave me.

Indeed, my own first tentative experiences of broadcasting involved Gay. When I was president of USI, I was invited on to *The Late Late Show* and his radio show from time to time. My only two memorable contributions on the panel came when Gay suggested that we had a democratic choice between Fianna Fáil, Fine Gael and Labour; I interjected that this was akin to choosing between jumping out the thirteenth, fourteenth or fifteenth storey of a skyscraper.

One morning on the radio show I was asked to defend an episode where students had pelted the then Taoiseach Garret Fitzgerald with eggs over medical-card cutbacks. Lord Henry Mountcharles was leading the charge for Fine Gael. After a lot of high dudgeoning by the eminent lord, I eventually broke in: 'For God's sake, Henry, it was an egg, not a cruise missile.' That line stuck with me throughout my student years.

So, when it came to moving to Gay's show, my mind was made up – and I was seen as a big girl's blouse for defecting to the 'woman's programme'. But I never looked back.

I bumped into Gay on the corridor before I had even joined the team. Gay, of course, was intimidating, direct and pointed as only he can be. 'Oh, I heard you are coming to us,' he said curtly, before adding, 'You did that programme from London with Pat? I want more of that, so when are you going to get out and about?' This frightened the life out of me. I was coming on board as a producer, not a rookie reporter. Apart from being on programmes as a contributor fighting for a cause, no one had ever suggested I should broadcast – or indeed that I might have a voice suitable for audio consumption by an unwitting nation.

For the first few weeks, I simply became one of the five producers on the show. Watching Gay work was a joy – if not a mystery at times. He would arrive into the radio centre at the exact same time every morning, 8.11. He would already have been to *The Late Late Show* office, where he was also producer, and would have opened mail and foostered around, as he would say himself. Arriving in the radio centre, the same worn briefcase under his arm, he would go straight down to Studio 6 and begin prepping for the programme. At eight twenty, the producer of the day would go down to studio with the day file and simply hand it to Gaybo. Apart from a good morning, few words would be exchanged. Even if you had won the Lotto, you did not converse.

But that is the mark of the man: totally focused and determined; the programme came first. That's why some of Gay's stories about his treatment by RTÉ management are at times both hilarious and shocking. He tells the story of how, having morphed gradually from a reporter to a presenter of a daily live programme and then producer and compere of the flagship *Late Late Show*, he eventually got up the courage to seek a meeting with the then director general to seek a wage increase. After a long meeting, an increase was agreed – fifty-two pounds a year!

As he often said, senior RTÉ management – and I suspect a lot of listeners – seem to believe that the likes of Gay, Pat, Marian, Ryan, Miriam, and whoever happens to be up-and-coming at any one time could easily be replaced by simply stopping the next driver at the traffic lights on the Stillorgan Road, persuading them that they were needed urgently, jostling them through the RTÉ security checkpoint into Studio 1 and, after a quick dash of makeup, putting them in front of a TV camera or into a radio studio – and they would be brilliant and household names overnight!

But RTÉ was Gay's life, just as it is for me, Pat, Gerry, Marian, Ryan, Miriam and all the other people on the campus. Indeed, Gay gave more of his life to Montrose than anyone I know in the organization, which is full of dedicated, hard-working 'lifers'. It really is a fantastic place to work, truly one of our great national institutions.

The Gay Byrne Show was simply the biggest audience-getter on the island, day in, day out. It was wonderfully eclectic, with letters, some phone calls, interviews and music, all welded together seamlessly by the maestro.

I have always tried to capitalize on the difference I can bring to a programme or project. When trying to get into RTÉ, I had highlighted my different back-ground, my social-work experience, even playing on my lack of journalistic or broadcasting experience as a positive. Similarly, being the only man on the GB team at the time, I was singled out, especially by Gay, for either a bit more ribbing or encouragement, depending on the day or the mood!

Within weeks, Gay was reminding me that he wanted me to do some reporting, as he wanted an out-and-about sound on the show. Remember, this is the man who dragged a heavy portable recording machine for the great Joe Linnane when he reported on the last journey of the tram up Howth Hill in June 1959.

An opportunity arose a few weeks later; ironically, my first broadcast would also be about transport in Dublin. Complaining about the traffic, a letter writer said he would be quicker cycling in from Malahide to his job in the city centre. We decided to see which was the quickest way of getting into town: car, train, bike, bus or skateboard. I travelled by bus from Malahide, another member of the team got the train, and so on.

I happened to start on *The Gay Byrne Show* just as mobile phones were taking off and so, for my first broadcast, I was going to try out my new phone, complete with powerpack. It was an enormous contraption, heavy, awkward and with limited coverage. But for the type of work I began doing on *The Gay Byrne Show* and since, that wonderful machine has made a huge difference to my career.

I broadcast live from the upper deck of the moving bus as it slowly made its way from Malahide into the capital. I had one crucial piece of revolutionary technology and I made one crucial broadcasting decision. I knew I would never make it as a reporter in RTÉ; my Dublin working-class accent was not exactly the voice of choice with the esteemed national broadcaster. That word 'difference' cropped up in my head again; what's on and how can I be different? I decided to make a virtue out of my difference. I decided to be myself. And it worked.

I spoke to Gay on air the same way I would during the 11 o'clock coffee break. We bantered and laughed, I slagged him and joked that I was getting on my knees as we passed Charles J. Haughey's residence in Kinsealy, out of respect to the then Taoiseach. My first broadcast, complete with my rehearsed 'spontaneous' gags, even made it on to the weekly radio highlights show *Playback*, though such was my obscurity that the presenter, Treasa Davidson, referred to me as Joe Egan!

It suited Gay for me to become a roving reporter. Along with mobile phones, this was another bit of good luck, as Gay was anxious, after over thirty years of a punishing work schedule, to spread the load, and my new role meant at least that *The GB Show* was getting around the country. Soon I was being called Gay Byrne's representative on earth – and I was loving it.

My big break came with the visit of Neil Diamond to Dublin for a week-long series of concerts. He was massive at the time and tickets sold like hotcakes, but the 'Sweet Caroline' singer wasn't so sweet when it came to interviews. He might have liked cracklin' Rosie, but he had an aversion to cracklin' microphones. On the Sunday, I was reading these stories about the reclusive Mr Diamond and I imagined it might be a novel bit of fun to search for him.

The next morning, I landed on Dun Laoghaire pier with a Neil Diamond impressionist, Father Heber McMahon, who duly joined in the search and sang a very passable version of Diamond's 'Red Red Wine'. This whole bit of nonsense escalated by the day; I commandeered the Burlington Hotel, searched bedrooms and somehow ended up (supposedly) in Neil Diamond's wardrobe! I am sure it was funny at the time. We finished up the following day with a live concert outside Neil Diamond's bedroom in the Westbury Hotel, with a slew of Neil Diamond impressionists.

By the end of the week, the search for Neil was the talk of the nation – well, the RTÉ canteen at least – and of course his minders got to hear of it. Given that the concert was sold out, there was no need for publicity, but Anne Walsh, the intrepid producer of the item, managed to secure us a few minutes with the maestro himself. When we arrived at the RDS that night, we were told we could speak to Mr Diamond for a minute as he prepared to go on stage. I am sure my questions weren't exactly Einsteinian in their formulation, but his answers were shorter than the word 'monosyllabic'.

Another lesson in broadcasting, which you can apply to life if you like: sometimes it is all about the journey.

The idea of the live outside broadcast concerts during *The GB Show* had taken off. For the next seven years, we would regularly host these from Clery's on North Earl Street at 10.10 on weekday mornings; from Sonny Knowles, whom we surprised on his birthday and crowned the King of Cabaret, to the talented Vard Sisters, who made their radio debut singing a beautiful version of the Flower Duet from *Lakme* during a heavy rain shower while musicians Eddie Creighton and Paul Finlay struggled manfully to keep their guitar and keyboard from electrocuting them in the downpour.

On another occasion, it had been a particularly long dry spell in the country – it could have been as long as four days – and Dublin City Council told householders not to water their gardens or wash their cars. So, true to form, I had the idea of dancing for rain in the capital. I opened the broadcast by dancing in the 'Floozie in the Jacuzzi', the infamous fountain created by Eamon O'Doherty and paid for by Michael Smurfit to celebrate the Dublin Millennium in 1988 and located in the spot where Nelson's Pillar had been until it was blown up in 1966. The Anna Livia fountain, to give it its formal title, featured a reclining female nude being cascaded by jets of water in her granite bath. During the drought, the 'Floozie' was taken into the dear hearts – and feet and legs – of H_2O-starved Dubliners. I followed their lead and jumped in on air to chant for rain. The rest of the item consisted of members of the public singing in the absence of the rain, aided and abetted by former athlete Noel Carroll, who was the official spokesperson for the city, back in the days when the city burghers let their officials develop a personality.

There was much hype in 1991 when U2 were about to release *Achtung Baby!* It was due out on a Monday morning, but I had managed to get copies of it on the Friday afternoon. I immediately sent them off to various amateur and professional musicians to learn different tracks. Come Monday morning, at my usual time of nine twenty, I proudly told Gay on air that the first live performances of songs from the new U2 album would be broadcast an hour later outside the HMV record store on Grafton Street. Of course I forgot to mention that it would not be the four lads from the northside who would be playing, but whoever I had cajoled over the weekend!

It was a great success, with Anuna, in particular, giving a magnificent rendition of 'Mysterious Ways'. Bono's dad, Bobby, was listening and promptly rang his son, instructing him to participate. Bono came on the phone and acted as judge, as well as proclaiming to the hundreds who had gathered with us that Joe Duffy was mad.

More evidence of madness was forthcoming in my *GB Show* escapades. I jumped at the opportunity to parachute out of a plane. The idea was simple: I would broadcast live from the plane and then Gay would count me down to a jump while I would describe the experience through that new-fangled contraption – the mobile phone. I found willing accomplices in the Irish Parachute Club based in Clonbullogue in Offaly.

Of course, it being Ireland, fog delayed our eight thirty take-off. As the programme slipped by, my chances of broadcasting were diminishing. One of the great strengths of my reports is that we did not reveal or advertise them in advance, so the listener was none the wiser until the broadcast – and sometimes not much wiser afterwards! It looked like this was to be one of those occasions.

Eventually, shortly after ten thirty, the plane was cleared for take-off and the pilot struggled to get his heavy load to a height safe enough for the parachute jump. At ten fifty we were nearly ready to jump, so I dialled the studio number and spoke to Gaybo, setting the scene with my usual limited but sometimes funny vocabulary. Ever conscious of the clock, Gay was urging me to jump, but the pilot was telling me to hang on for dear life as the plane needed to reach a higher altitude.

With about two minutes left before the eleven o'clock end of the programme, I jumped. I was strapped to another parachutist, which allowed me to hold to my ear the grey, brick-like mobile phone, which I had tied around my neck using a length of RTÉ regulation twine. Just as I started to describe the cold, the magnificent scenery and the sensation of floating ever so slowly to earth, I heard the last few bars of 'Tico's Tune', signalling the end of another *Gay Byrne Show*.

I may have been flying without wings, but I was crestfallen. All my effort, risk and bravery to be the first to broadcast while floating unaided across the centre of Ireland had come to naught. But then, within a minute, while I still floated, the phone rang; it was my old pal Julian Vignoles, the producer of *The Pat Kenny Show*, who had had the bright idea of continuing the broadcast. Within seconds, I was yapping to Pat, who brought me safely down to earth with a slight bang. It was great fun. I had jumped off Gay Byrne's shoulders and landed in Pat Kenny's lap. What an image!

I also had a video camera strapped to my head, so Gay's TV team melded the radio broadcast and the pictures and put together a hilarious package for that night's *Late Late Show*. I think it may have been the first time PK was on the *Late Late*, but not the last.

* * *

I regard myself as first and foremost a producer, somebody who comes up with ideas. I singlehandedly introduced that great British institution 'Workers' Playtime' into Irish broadcasting. This began in canteens throughout the UK in 1941, and was a mixture of morale-boosting comedy and music presented by the employees of a firm from their workplace and broadcast nationally, hence the inordinately original title, which we adopted.

The moment I mentioned the idea, Gay was enthusiastic. He remembered the original BBC programme, having lived through the 'Emergency' and made his First Holy Communion in May 1941, the week of the North Strand bombings. As soon as he went public with the idea, we were inundated with offers, and off we went.

Such was the array of talent that filtering through the auditions for 'Workers' Playtime' turned out to be a workers' nightmare! We began in one of Ireland's oldest firms, Jacobs biscuit factory in Tallaght. It was brilliant talking to people who lived their lives through work in the 'mallow house' or on the 'chocolate line'. The greatest achievement of that day – and probably of my radio career – was that, while reminiscing about long-gone biscuits, an intense demand for the re-emergence of the defunct Chocolate Kimberley emerged across the airwaves. Jacobs at the time had a young, bright marketing manager, Michael Dwyer, who jumped on the idea and had tins of Chocolate Kimberley in the shops for Christmas. They have been selling like hot-cakes, so to speak, ever since.

Another memorable 'Workers' Playtime' was broadcast live from the magnificent Tayto crisp factory in Coolock. Not only did it have great music, but some of the stories by the older members of staff, who remembered working in the original two-roomed 'factory' behind Moore Street in central Dublin, gave an indication of how the legendary Joe 'Spud' Murphy not only invented 'cheese and onion' flavour snackfoods but got it all going from little or nothing. Once, on being summoned to court to answer a charge that a customer had found a foreign and potentially dangerous object in a bag of crisps – a mouse's tail – Joe denied that such a thing could happen and asked the plaintiff's solicitor to produce said object, which Joe promptly popped into his mouth, chewed intently and swallowed. He won the case and lived to tell the tale.

Soon companies were clamouring to get the 'Workers' Playtime' cavalcade to their canteen. From Avonmore Agricultural Co-op in Ballyragget, Kilkenny, who claimed they were the cream, to firefighters in Dublin's Tara Street station singing a beautiful version of 'Love Me Tender', the shows were a hit, and a remarkable publicity vehicle for RTÉ before the local stations took hold.

In late 1990, we were contacted by an irate listener who told us that the age-old Christmas tradition of mechanical gnomes in Switzers' window was to be abandoned. At that stage, Switzers had been bought over by Brown Thomas and a new management regime wanted to 'update' their Christmas display. For 'update', read 'going forward', and for going forward, read bland, clinical, surreal black-and-silver displays of mannequins with loads of empty space and 'meaning'.

I was having none of it. I was determined to get the gnomes back home. The following morning I organized a picket of out-of-work gnomes on Grafton Street. I enlisted two great stalwarts of the programme at the time, Eamonn Hunt and Jack Lynch, who raided the RTÉ wardrobe department and arrived as the funniest-looking little men ever seen on Grafton Street – a remarkable achievement in itself. The crowd gathered, the band arrived and we led off the protest.

Diminutive pantomime legend Maureen Potter added her support and each day the campaign grew; but each day the Brown Thomas management grew more recalcitrant. A few moles – or was it gnomes? – within the shop told us that the new manager was from Germany and was not for turning.

Luckily, the protest coincided with the inauguration of Mary Robinson as President of Ireland, so the children had the day off, which meant we had a massive crowd. But still the gnomes had no homes to go to. In Dublin Castle, our new president was encouraging Mná na hÉireann to rock the nation, while a mile away we were encouraging g-nome na hÉireann to rock the conglomerate.

A bizarre thing happened around five o'clock on the Friday when I got a phone message, ostensibly from *The Late Late Show*, inviting the gnomes to appear in a live broadcast from Bewley's on Grafton Street that night. I immediately contacted Eamonn Hunt and Jack Lynch and by 8 p.m. the three of us were slipping into our gnome outfits in Anne's Lane, right outside my old office in the probation service. How far I'd come!

We hoisted our placards and marched around to Bewley's, to be met by a bemused *Late Late Show* team who informed us that we had not been invited and there was no place or cause for us to be on the programme. Being ever anxious to get on telly, I was crestfallen, embarrassed and looking pretty stupid in green ladies' tights, yellow bib, red bow and slumped gnome hat – you know the type.

But I didn't admit defeat. Ever resourceful, I discovered that the opening shot of the outside broadcast would be a 'walk-in' by the reporter Kieran Fitzgerald, who told us he did not object to us standing in the crowd as he walked by; he knew three fools when he saw them. So there we stood, the unhappy gnomes, not just booted out of Switzers' window but turfed off the *Late Late Show* by a cruel hoax. I later discovered that radio producer Ronan Kelly had made the hoax call, presuming we would get the gag. He had underestimated my desire to get on TV. Gay, of course, was mortified by our unscheduled appearance.

Brown Thomas relented the following week and repatriated the working gnomes to their Grafton Street window. It was a win-win solution!

* * *

If truth be told, on my radio inserts I always tried to mortify Gay a bit. In April 1993, he interviewed the mother of Bishop Eamon Casey's 'love child', Annie Murphy, on *The Late Late Show*. Gay had ended the icy interview with the comment: 'Well, if Peter is half the man his father is, he will be fine.' Annie had sharply retorted that the boy's mother 'isn't half bad either'.

Five days later, we were bidding farewell to the last 'Guinness ship' as it set sail from Dublin Port. These were bulk liquid containers that shipped the sloshing brew from St James's Gate to Liverpool for barrelling and bottling. Technology now meant that tankers pulled by trucks would simply use the roll-on, roll-off container ships – so Guinness were bidding adieu to the last of their ships.

I did the outside broadcast and, of course, all the locals turned up. Some of them began reminiscing about Eddie Byrne, Gay's father, who worked the Guinness barges plying the Liffey from the brewery to the port. As one of them waxed lyrical, I asked her if Gay was half the man his father was. Maybe I shouldn't have used the quote against the master but, hey, Gay seemed to appreciate when I acted like his bold son.

My reporting work for Gay continued apace; I was also a producer on the show at the same time. I would do my two days in the studio and then head off around the country trying to rustle up ideas. Along with sharp producers such as Anne Farrell, Ronan Kelly, Anne Walsh and Alice O'Sullivan, we usually came up with the goods, ranging from a birthday party for the oldest cow in Ireland to live broadcasts from inside Irish prisons, mental hospitals and drug rehabilitation centres.

I had heard about Bertha the cow while listening to BBC Radio 4. She was born to Jerome O'Leary – not her real father – in Sneem, County Kerry, on St Patrick's Day 1944, so we organized a forty-ninth birthday party for her on 16 March 1993, in the local pub. It being the eve of our national holiday, we had great craic, with tales of breeding and cattle-rearing interspersed with jokes and music – and a bit of milking of some of Bertha's 39 Friesian offspring. We succeeded in getting her into the *Guinness Book of Records*, and acquiring a Jacob's Award for me from the radio critics. Sadly, Bertha never did hit the half century, as she passed away the following New Year's Eve. After a short illness, bravely borne, and fortified with whiskey, she headed peacefully to the big milking parlour in the sky.

By 1994, the almost daily outside broadcasts were my bread and butter, and I loved them. I would do a brief insert shortly after the programme started, to get a crowd to the location for the broadcast an hour later. The public adored these broadcasts. Gay liked them, too, because they gave him a twenty-minute break during the two-hour show. The Sawdoctors made their first national appearance during an outside broadcast from the centre of Galway, and they blew the place apart, not just with their energetic, manic music but with their affable personalities.

We eventually spread our wings further afield: from

Sydney with emigrants at Christmas; to Moscow for St Patrick's Day, which was uneventful except for the GB banner being stolen and shots fired; to China for an Irish walk along the Great Wall; and to New York for the 1994 World Cup, where a certain local teacher named Frank McCourt came out to meet me in the middle of the night to talk about James Joyce, and mentioned that he was trying to find a publisher for a book about his mother, Angela. I travelled to Romania to see their horrific orphanages; the awful smell stayed with me for weeks. I visited Ethiopia to report on the work of Bóthar the Irish 'farm' charity; Toronto for a family reunion surprise; and the Bahamas for a 'divorced' couple's reunion. I can truly claim to have seen the world with *The GB Show*.

During the summer of 1991, I was presenting a fill-in summer programme in the *Liveline* slot. We tried to get out and about for the daily show. For the last week in August, I pushed the idea of taking one of my heroes, singer Christie Hennessey, back to his home town of Tralee to visit his old neighbours and then perform live at the Siamsa Tíre for our programme on Wednesday. It was the week of the Rose of Tralee festival and the town would be buzzing.

I called to my mother's house on 25 August, as I often do for Sunday lunch, and as usual my brother Aidan was there. He had recently moved into a house in Clondalkin with his girlfriend. He had done well for himself; even though he had left school early, he was

265

never without work, had completed a few night courses and was always busy. Aidan was always interested in music – we had both gone to Howth in 1986 for Phil Lynott's funeral – so I told him about the upcoming programme with Christie. He told me that he had written to one of his heroes, Arlo Guthrie, and was thrilled not only to receive a handwritten reply but a signed copy of his album.

Aidan and I headed off at the same time. He showed me his old red Peugeot estate company van. He kicked the tyres, telling me he was finally to get a new van the following Monday.

I headed off to Tralee after Tuesday's programme, and the following morning I met Christie. We rambled with a tape recorder around the Rock Street area of the town and met some of Christie's old neighbours. It was a joyous, sunny day, and Christie was in sparkling form at the Siamsa Tíre, lacing his songs with laconic, moving and funny memories. I headed back to Dublin after the programme.

As I was walking into studio around one thirty on Thursday, I heard a snatch of the news headlines about a horrific car crash at noon in Maynooth, which had left two people dead and many injured. I remarked to the sound operator about how dreadful the accident sounded. One hour later, when the programme finished, I returned to my desk, to be met by a colleague, Noel Coughlan, and the RTÉ chaplain, Father Romauld Dodd. They told me what I already knew, that there had been a terrible crash in Maynooth. As I sat looking up at this priest dressed in grey, it dawned on me in a split second that horror was awaiting its visitation. Names flashed through my head: James, Peter, Brendan or Aidan? (Pauline didn't drive.) Then Noel told me that my brother Aidan had been killed.

Aidan the baby, Aidan the innocent, the hard worker, trying to better himself. Aidan, who had been sickly as a child, confirmed in his cot in Clonskeagh Hospital for fear he was going to die. Aidan, who I had pushed around Claddagh Green in his pram. Aidan, who had had to be literally dragged screaming and kicking from my mother's side to school every morning.

My first reaction was: 'How am I going to tell my mother? This will kill her.'

I rang our next-door neighbour's house, and Deirdre Carroll told me that my mother was sitting outside in the back garden, enjoying the August sun. I could picture her on her wooden kitchen chair. June, my wife, arrived from work, and she drove me to Ballyfermot. It was the longest journey of my life. I knew that image of my mother relaxing in the sun was gone for ever.

As she opened the door, I simply said to her, 'Mabel, I have some very bad news. Aidan has been killed in a car crash.' She collapsed on the floor, screaming, fighting the news. The disbelief, the anger, the pain. It was the beginning of a nightmare. James arrived, and we desperately tried to contact Peter, whose job as a sales rep involved constant driving. It transpired that Peter had passed Aidan on the road that morning and they had hailed each other.

I then set about ringing other relations: my mother's sisters, my father's siblings and Nana Murphy. Within an hour, James, Peter and Pauline were lined up on the front couch with my mother, all bereft and wailing. I was in the other room punching the wall and screaming with anger and pain. My mother's sisters, Monica, Patsy and Agnes, arrived and began consoling Mabel. Brendan arrived; I was worried how he would react. He was doing well in life at that time. He had given up the drink a couple of years earlier, had a loving partner, was about to start a family and was running his own early-morning milk delivery business. He was so shocked he was silenced beyond belief. Our baby brother, dead at twenty-five.

Nana Murphy arrived, pleading with God to take her instead of Aidan. She said it in such a gentle way, I know she was prepared to offer her life for his. It was an astonishing glimpse of her humanity. I can't imagine what the death of the youngest in our family was dragging up for her from the recesses of her memories of her Indian childhood, the tragic death of her own young brother Arnold and her own subsequent miscarriages.

I began to make the funeral arrangements. James, his wife Cynthia, my sister Pauline, June and I travelled to Blanchardstown hospital to identify Aidan's remains. It was a fool's errand; Aidan's injuries had been so horrendous that his head was bandaged like a mummy. The image haunts me to this day. The only decision I made was to ensure that the coffin was sealed for the removal the next day.

The following morning, a group of friends travelled with me to the scene of the tragedy in Maynooth. Aidan's front wheel had collapsed, his company van had careered under an oncoming truck, which in turn had crashed into a bus full of Spanish students travelling behind his van, killing one of their teachers and demolishing a wall on Carton House. The demolished wall was the only reminder of the crash; Aidan's car had been taken to a nearby garage. It was an unmerciful wreck, still covered in blood and, unbelievably, small slivers of skin.

I asked musician friends Paddy Glackin and Sean Potts to play at the funeral mass in St Matthew's church, beside our house. I wrote a eulogy for Aidan, but I was in no condition to deliver it, so June read it from the altar. Aidan was buried alongside my father in Palmerstown cemetery, just a mile from the house where he had been born. Afterwards, we all retired to a nearby club. I was so demoralized, overwhelmed with hurt, pain and anger, that I left after an hour and went home.

I often wonder if my memories of Aidan are so clear because I so vividly recall his birth at home on 19 January 1966, a week before my tenth birthday. I always associate my birthday with his birth – and now, of course, with his untimely passing. When I hit fifty, Aidan, dear Aidan, would have been celebrating his fortieth birthday.

There was a poignant postscript to Aidan's death. We were dumbfounded a year later to discover his name spelt incorrectly on his headstone – it read 'Aiden', with an 'e' where the second 'a' should be. An irate phone call to the stonemason elicited the information that he had written down the details on a piece of paper, which he had shown to my mother, who in her grief-stricken, upset state, had not noticed the misspelling. We eventually changed the headstone to the correct spelling, but close examination still reveals the scar of the rogue 'e'.

CHAPTER 19

Behind Closed Doors

HAVING WORKED AS A PROBATION OFFICER FOR OVER four years, I was very keen to give a glimpse of life inside prison to the public. Radio is the ideal medium, and live radio is even better, as it allows interaction between the listening public and prisoners.

I know my inserts into *The Gay Byrne Show* were often characterized by my acting the eejit, but I was keen that we should also do serious programmes. I tried to aim them at Gay's own interests; he was especially consumed by crime. Like most of the country, he believed criminals should be treated harshly and he articulated this daily. So we did the only live broadcasts from inside Irish prisons, including Mountjoy, Arbour Hill, Cloverhill and the women's detention centre Dóchas. They were daring, challenging and ultimately uplifting broadcasts.

My first foray into prison issues on *The GB Show* came when I suggested we feature the ongoing campaign to free the Birmingham Six. I had campaigned for the release of Nicky Kelly when I was president of USI and have always taken a keen interest in miscarriages of justice. So I headed off to Birmingham to meet the family of Dick McIlkenny, who were to the forefront of the campaign to free the six men who had been sentenced to life imprisonment in 1975, having been wrongly convicted of the Birmingham pub bombings which killed twenty-one people and savagely injured 162 others.

Kate McIlkenny and her daughter – also called Kate – were very keen on my idea of doing a live broadcast from their house, but not before I had visited Dick in prison. I returned to England the following week, this time with another campaigner in tow, the singer Brush Shiels. Travelling by bus, train and taxi, we eventually reached the prison.

While the security was tight, it was not overwhelming. The only inconvenience came when Brush Shiels was asked to remove his ubiquitous trademark beret. We were led into a big open room with tables, armchairs and tea urns. Dick and Paddy Joe Hill were like two children on Christmas morning. Dick was over the moon when Brush arrived and soon a sing-song began. Paddy was especially grateful that Kate junior had come along, as the 20-year-old was especially gorgeous.

It was a great afternoon, relaxed and informative. Later, as we stood on a nearby lonely railway platform, Brush and I turned to Kate and both promised we would up our efforts to raise awareness of the injustice.

Brush went on with Gay the next morning and, in his own inimitable way, brought the story and the ultimate injustice home.

The following week, with the help of a bemused BBC outside broadcast unit, who brightened up visibly when I presented them with a few bottles of Irish whiskey, we did another memorable broadcast from Kate McIlkenny's kitchen. Gay back in the studio in Dublin was his usual brilliant self with Kate, whose life had been blighted by the miscarriage of justice: her husband had been badly beaten by the British police and sentenced to life in prison, and she was left to rear six children on little money and much opprobrium from the residents of Birmingham where she lived, who were still reeling from one of the greatest atrocities of the 1970s.

The programme followed the court appeals over the course of the next year. On 14 March 1991, I was in the Courts of Justice in London to hear the appeal being granted and, in the last minutes of that morning's *Gay Byrne Show*, I was first to broadcast the news that the men were to be freed.

I loved the idea of Gay Byrne talking live from the studio to prisoners behind bars, and letting listeners do the same. After a lot of negotiation, I managed to secure a live outside broadcast from inside Arbour Hill Prison, home to many sex offenders. I usually managed to find a 'hook' to get into the prisons. On this occasion, a number of offenders were running a marathon inside the prison walls for charity.

It was a difficult project, and not without its opponents, both within the Department of Justice and on the *Gay Byrne Show* production team. But I knew who held the power within the prisons from my probation days: Governor John Lonergan was the key to the Mountjoy broadcasts, while the chaplains in Arbour Hill were instrumental in getting me and the outside broadcast crew through the prison gates.

It was a moving and troubling programme, but worthwhile. One of the eeriest and most disturbing moments was listening to a contrite sex offender sing 'Every Time We Say Goodbye' in his melodic but high-pitched voice.

On another occasion, as we prepared for a broadcast from Mountjoy Prison, one of the inmates approached me and asked, 'Are you the Joe Duffy who used to be a probation officer?' When I admitted it was indeed me, he replied, 'You're not a bad broadcaster, but you were a brutal probation officer – look at me!' I couldn't remember him being on my 'books' in probation, but if he was he wouldn't have been the first to graduate to prison despite – or maybe because of – my efforts!

I had no fear or worry about going into prisons, though I suspect today it is different, with inhuman overcrowding and a harsher regime.

As *The GB Show* often dealt with victims, I decided to try to get some victims of crime to come into Mountjoy. I concentrated on those who had been robbed or mugged, and I quickly assembled six citizens who were willing to come inside the prison gates and sit in a room with those who had committed similar crimes. I broached the idea with Governor John Lonergan, who advised me on how to approach the Department of Justice: slowly, and with sparse information. Right to the bitter end, the department simply would not give an answer. Reluctantly, on the eve of the broadcast, they gave a weary nod.

We got a fascinating glimpse into crime and punishment. The prisoners were genuinely gobsmacked at the depths of despair and punishment they had inflicted on decent people, often neighbours, with their random crimes. The victims got an insight into the spiral of pointlessness and powerlessness of young men who chose robbery over reason.

On New Year's Eve 1999, I did a live TV broadcast from Mountjoy to mark the beginning of the new millennium. It was probably the lightest of the pieces I did from inside the walls, mainly because New Year's Eve is a great day in prisons. The turning of the year means that the end of everyone's sentence has taken a gigantic leap forward, and midnight is marked by whooping, shouting and general merrymaking.

I was genuinely keen on these prison broadcasts and I do believe they made a difference to public and prisoner attitudes to the causes and effects of crime. The success of the broadcasts encouraged me to approach another 'enclosed' institution for a glimpse of life inside. To my surprise, I was invited to visit the Poor Clares in Ennis, County Clare, to discuss the idea. We took to each other immediately.

Just before Christmas 1995, we broadcast the first live programme from inside an enclosed religious order in the Poor Clare convent. It was a serene, joyous and revealing experience. They had no access to television and very limited knowledge of newspapers and radio. The twenty nuns never leave the convent, depending on the local community for food and support. Above all, they find joy in living the Gospel in the spirit of St Clare and St Francis of Assisi. With vows of poverty, chastity, obedience and enclosure, and strict daily prayer and work rituals, they struck me as deeply intelligent, encouraging, communal, fulfilled and hopeful.

I especially enjoyed their stories, such as having to ring a bell to let the town know they were running out of food. They refused offers of Christmas turkeys, as they were strict vegetarians. They also held a draw each year to decide who should go where on their annual holidays. This is not as exotic as it sounds; first prize was the seat under the tree at the corner of the garden, followed by the suntrap near the kitchen door or the spot near the oratory window. For a fortnight every year, routine was thrown to the summer wind as the nuns enjoyed their holidays, still enclosed in their cloister.

I then wanted to broadcast from another closed institution, St Patrick's psychiatric hospital in Dublin, so I wrote to the then medical director, Professor Anthony Clare, who agreed to meet me. To say that I was in awe of Tony Clare would be an understatement;

his radio programmes on the BBC, where he literally sat his guest 'in the psychiatrist's chair', were illuminating and intimate. He had thoroughly blended his training and experience into a non-exploitative form of broadcasting, something that has inspired me ever since.

Anthony Clare was very open to asking patients if they wished to participate in a live broadcast. At the end of our first meeting he offered to take me on a tour of the hospital. To his credit, he did not attempt to hide any of it, bringing me through the older part of the hospital, founded from a bequest from Jonathan Swift following his death in 1745. Swift penned the immortal lines: 'He gave the little wealth he had, to build a house for fools and mad, and showed by one satiric touch, no nation needed it so much!'

Tony Clare went up even more in my estimation when he brought me through the locked wards, and it is no exaggeration to say that 'bedlam' is exactly what I saw that day: men and women screaming, wandering aimlessly, rocking incessantly back and forward. Even though I had visited the hospital before and attended lectures there while studying social work, it was still a shock.

During our walkabout, one middle-aged woman stood up from her bed and bellowed at Tony: 'Anthony Clare, you are only a fraud! On the radio, making a name for yourself, the big psychiatrist. Get me out of here!' Tony did not blink, hide her or brush off the incident; neither did he attempt to placate the woman. Instead, he spoke to her calmly and moved on, showing no regard for any damage to his ego in front of a stranger.

Thanks to the staff and patients of the hospital, the programme was superb. Explaining his manic depression, one patient tried to put it as simply as possible: 'Even if I won the Lotto today it would make no difference.'

I kept up some contact with Tony Clare subsequently; he was particularly helpful and honest when I subsequently spoke to him about my brother Brendan. Tony Clare, to me the picture of good health, died suddenly in October 2007. He was only sixty-four. I believe the enormity of his loss for medicine and broadcasting is still not fully appreciated.

From the moment I first heard about the crimes of Father Brendan Smyth, the convicted sex offender, I wanted to interview him. I could not believe my luck when Smyth, then a prisoner in Magilligan, agreed to meet me. I was the only journalist ever to interview the notorious paedophile cleric. Like so many things, my scoop came about through a series of circumstances – a combination of brass neck, knowing how the prison system worked, Smyth's own desire to tell his side of the story and bad weather!

I had visited Kilnacrott, where Smyth lived, in 1982. It was a warm, welcoming place, even giving some of its facilities free for holiday homes for community groups from Dublin's north inner city. The members of the Norbertine order were at that time open and hospitable.

In early 1994, I was contacted by a friend from Belfast from my USI days who asked me to interview a family whose children had been abused by a long-standing family friend, Father Brendan Smyth. Within minutes of meeting the family at home in Belfast, it became obvious that Smyth was a serious career paedophile.

When we broadcast the interview on the then most popular radio programme in the country, there was an instant reaction, with other victims from many parts of Ireland coming forward. Over the next few months, Father Brendan Smyth became a household name as his actions and his superiors' inactions convulsed the nation. His botched extradition from the south eventually led to the downfall of the then Fianna Fáil/Labour government.

I wanted to confront this sex offender directly to find out how he had evaded justice for four decades. I had long dealt in my mind with the moral dilemma of giving sex offenders or prisoners a voice, believing firmly that allowing them to be heard in the privacy of a listener's home damaged neither person, indeed only increased understanding.

One Friday morning in November 1994 I happened to be in the North for a feature on *The Gay Byrne Show*. After the show, I drove up to the gates of Magilligan Prison in Derry, where Smyth had recently begun his first sentence for child abuse. I didn't expect that the most notorious prisoner on the island would accept a visit from me. After all, during his 40-year reign of child abuse, he had never co-operated with any investigation, despite numerous requests from his superiors, police and journalists.

Having run through howling wind and teeming rain from the prison car park to the visitors' area, I was ushered in out of the storm and asked to fill out a form to be given to the prisoner I wished to visit. I was surprised a few minutes later when the prison officer returned to say Smyth was willing to see me. Within seconds, I was sitting in front of Smyth in a spacious open room with armchairs and coffee tables, and the 67-year-old cleric was offering me tea.

No recording equipment was allowed, so I took notes. Smyth knew who I was. He told me he was glad he had been caught. He wanted me to communicate to other victims to come forward in the south, as he expected to be charged upon his release from Magilligan and wanted everything dealt with in one go. One of the reasons he had agreed to see me was that he had not received any visits since his imprisonment. He told me that he had been attacked by another prisoner wielding a snooker ball in a sock, but he was getting used to the routine of the prison, even managing to celebrate a daily 'dry mass' in his cell.

When I asked him about his crimes he tried to mitigate his actions, claiming he did not abuse children he did not know! He was at pains to point out that he didn't hang around public parks picking up children to abuse. Incredibly, he even protested that 80 per cent of his physical interaction with children was not harmful.

He listened avidly to radio, but was not interested in politics, describing himself as a de Valera republican who also liked Charles Haughey and Albert Reynolds. He didn't care about all the political fuss in the Republic, and revealed that even when there was an RUC extradition warrant sitting in the attorney general's office in Dublin he was travelling freely across the border. The question arose as to why the RUC did not arrest him when he travelled north. Smyth had given himself up at Grosvenor Road police station in Belfast some months earlier. He was annoyed that his name had become such common currency in the country at the time and angry that his extradition warrant was being used in a political battle in the south. He was adamant in his belief that Labour leader Dick Spring was intent on bringing down the coalition and was only using his case as an excuse.

Smyth was not a physically repulsive character when I met him face to face. He came across as relaxed and, at times, smug. But it was obvious within minutes that this man was a seriously deluded criminal, without any remorse for his victims, feeling sorry for himself and hoping to get everything over with as quickly as possible. In my previous life as a probation officer, I had met murderers who were more likeable than Smyth. I have no doubt that, if anyone in authority had confronted him over the previous forty years – which, we are told, many did – they would have realized that he was a serious criminal, who admitted his abuse of children but did not see the full harm in it.

The visit ended after an hour. As I left Magilligan, a prison officer ran after me to say that if I wrote to Smyth I would get another visit within ten days.

However, after I revealed on air the details of what Smyth had to say, especially about how he had travelled freely through police checkpoints when he was a wanted man, the political situation in the south deteriorated and Smyth became even more notorious.

Other victims in the Republic came forward after the broadcast, and Smyth was sentenced to prison in the south on his release from Magilligan in 1997. However, a month into his second sentence, he dropped dead on a sunny Friday afternoon in August 1997 in the Curragh Prison (nicknamed the Vatican by prison officers because of the number of clerics incarcerated there).

In parallel to my radio career, I have also for the past twenty years been writing a weekly column for different newspapers, beginning with the *Star* and moving on to *Ireland on Sunday*, which became the *Irish Mail on Sunday*.

In 1989, shortly after I started doing reports on *The Gay Byrne Show*, which began to generate media coverage, I was approached by James Dunne, news editor of the *Star*. He asked me if I would be interested in writing a weekly column. The *Star* was the country's newest and most energetic newspaper. I jumped at the idea.

Given my role in RTÉ, I have always tried – I think

successfully – to steer clear of turning the column into a forum for attacking people. I have kept a fairly complete file of columns, and it struck me recently that there are some consistent themes, many of which would later emerge on *Liveline* – prison conditions, rehab for drug users, the curse of illiteracy, rip-off companies, pyramid scams, depression, powerlessness and abuse of public money. I invariably took up issues for the underdog, and I am proud of the themes that have run through the ink. As far back as 1992, I also called for the abolition of the Seanad – my God, that really frightened them!

On Monday, 21 February 1994, the Blood Transfusion Service Board called a press conference where they revealed that a link had been discovered between the Hepatitis C virus and Anti-D, a product they had given to some women at childbirth. In my weekly column I revealed that a PR company had set themselves up in the radio canteen the following morning, where they waylaid us as we walked by. The PR man told us the contamination story was 'blown out of all proportion'.

I knew Gay would champion this cause. He was fearless; back in 1990, when the then minister for communications Ray Burke announced plans to shut down 2FM, turn it into an 'educational channel' and cap RTÉ advertising, I received an early-morning call from a senior RTÉ executive instructing me, as the producer, to tell Gay he was not to refer to the proposal in any shape or form on the programme. Gay laughed when I told him this and went on to open the programme with a stunning attack on Ray Burke. He didn't exactly say that he was corrupt and was attacking RTÉ to help the commercial sector, but he came close enough – and, as we know, Gay was subsequently proved right.

I immediately wrote a script for Gay about the blood scandal. Women who had received the controversial Anti-D started to phone the programme. It was the beginning of our extended coverage of the scandal and the campaign for justice and compensation. The victims, both haemophiliacs and the women who had been poisoned while pregnant, were given a platform on *The GB Show*.

There was a very personal angle to the Hepatitis C scandal for me. A friend of mine and a very close one of June's, Benny McEvoy, was a haemophiliac, one of the two groups given contaminated blood by the Blood Transfusion Service Board. Benny had died in February 1991, and it subsequently emerged that it was because of the blood given to him for his condition. We had visited Benny often as he lay in Cherry Orchard Hospital in Ballyfermot, watching as his life ebbed away. We had attended his wedding weeks before he died and through him got to know many of the people in the haemophiliac community, who were suffering greatly.

The BTSB, a state agency, was found to have been negligent in how it had made the Anti-D product. It was potentially poisonous to those who received a transfusion of the product. Despite this, the Board simply covered up what had happened and ploughed ahead, hoping, it would appear, that it would somehow right itself. There was no money involved in the decision, just what seems to have been arrogance, indolence and disregard for the health of the 'little people'.

It was a case of such obvious and clear injustice, yet the initial reaction of the government was to defend the state agency and put up an expensive legal defence against the victims who tried to get justice, including the infamous case of Bridget McCole from Donegal, who was threatened with legal action while on her state-induced deathbed.

A compensation tribunal for the thousand people affected (although many had died) was set up, costing €800 million, a lot of which went in legal fees, and a tribunal of inquiry effectively blamed two members of staff, neither of whom was ever prosecuted. A criminal charge was eventually brought against one of them, but later withdrawn by the DPP.

There was one simple lesson for all of us from the blood bank scandal: when you make a mistake, face up to it and accept the consequences.

In early 1994, Gay mentioned to me that he was feeling a bit 'mousy'. For a man with a very healthy lifestyle, both the phrase and the revelation shocked me. But Gay was clear: he wanted to cut down his workload. In his own words, 'I have yet to hear the graveside lament, "His one regret was not spending more time at the office."'

Gay never missed a day's work through illness, or anything else for that matter, and swore by his daily routine and Rubex. But just before he was due to present the Rose of Tralee festival in September 1995, the shock announcement came that he had been admitted to hospital for a prostate operation. Now, there is no one I know who has a greater dislike, indeed fear, of hospitals and everything associated with them. On the day of his release from the Blackrock Clinic, I met Gay. He told me that if he had known what he was facing into in hospital, he would have 'walked off Howth pier'.

A year before this, RTÉ management had not been keen to let Gay go from the radio, so a compromise was agreed; from September 1994, Gay would continue presenting *The Late Late Show* but would only do the radio show on Wednesdays, Thursdays and Fridays. This gave Gay four days off each week, but left RTÉ in a real quandary about what to do on Monday and Tuesday. The situation was getting critical as we finished the season in June 1994, and it came as a surprise to me when I got a call from the *Sunday Press* to inform me that management had announced that I would be presenting on Monday and Tuesday, and would still be a reporter and producer on the show for the rest of the week.

When I was informed of the decision a week later, management made no secret of their lack of enthusiasm for the idea. It was clear that I had got the gig almost by default. They were unsure whether the odd arrangement would work or not and indicated this by their reluctance to advertise the change.

The producers were in a real dilemma, having to put together programmes for both myself and Gay for the week. We kicked off to a lot of fanfare in the first week of September, Gay's traditional return date. On reflection, this was a mistake; Gay should have done the initial few weeks and then eased off. On my first Monday, all the newspapers covered 'Gay's replacement'. My first guest, after a lot of effort, was Mandy Smith, the 24-year-old model whose main claim to fame was sleeping with Rolling Stone Bill Wyman when she was fourteen and he was forty-seven! Strange stuff indeed – and unsuitable for my first interview.

But in terms of content, the programme was never found wanting, thanks to a great team, including Anne Farrell, Ronan O'Donoghue, Eithne Hand and Alex White. From my point of view, my most memorable interviews as presenter on *The Gay Byrne Show* were with Gary O'Toole, Andrew Madden and Phyllis Hamilton, and they set the agenda for topics that were to crop up time and again in years to come, especially on *Liveline*. These remain three of the most deeply impressive interviewees I have ever been lucky enough to face in the studio. It was former Olympic swimmer Gary's first broadcast interview since outing his former trainer George Gibney as a serial sex abuser. Likewise with Andrew Madden, who had been abused by Father Ivan Payne, who received a loan from the Dublin diocese to try to silence Andrew. And it was Phyllis

Hamilton who had had two children by Father Michael Cleary. With the power of radio, interviews such as these sparked others to tell their harrowing stories, leading to subsequent public inquiries into abuse and other scandals in the Irish Catholic Church and in swimming.

However, despite the best efforts of the production team, I never managed to find my own 'voice' presenting *The Gay Byrne Show*, and it would all end in tears in 1996.

CHAPTER 20

Good News Comes in Threes

NOT LONG AFTER WE GOT MARRIED IN 1989, JUNE AND I began trying to start a family. It took some time!

June discovered she was pregnant a couple of weeks before we were due to drive to France on holiday. It was June 1994, and France was celebrating the fiftieth anniversary of D-Day and the liberation by the Allies. But June was in severe pain at night and we contemplated returning home. We phoned the hospital and were told there was no need to worry, as long as she was not coming home by plane!

Once home, we attended Dr Paul Byrne in the Rotunda. He was the picture of calm and kept a close eye on June – but she did most of it herself. A light drinker and a non-smoker, she always minds herself. Thankfully, all went well for the rest of 1994. Then June had a scan in September and, lo and behold, we discovered she was pregnant with triplets. I know; like the 78 bus from Ballyfermot, you wait for a long time for one to come along and then three arrive together.

In early January 1995, on a routine check-up, Paul insisted on admitting June to the Rotunda there and then, as he was concerned that she was going to go into labour, despite being only twenty-seven weeks' pregnant. I remember crying in his office with worry, but June just bit the bullet and got organized. Paul's idea was that June should stay completely rested for the next few months, and the only way he felt he could achieve that was to confine her to hospital. So she became a resident in the Rotunda until the children were born. After begging Paul for remission for good behaviour, we were allowed a couple of three-hour forays to nearby restaurants and the Gate Theatre – but that was the height of it.

June was just getting bigger and bigger, but she was very healthy and was determined to hold out as long as possible, and she did. But by St Patrick's Day, problems were arising with three babies fighting for space in one womb, so June was now being monitored on the hour.

On Monday, 27 March, when the pregnancy was at thirty-six weeks, Paul Byrne decided it was time for the babies to be delivered. He got a team together to perform a Caesarean delivery the next morning. Of course I would be there, but first I needed the time off. Because I was presenting the *Gay Byrne Show* each Monday and Tuesday, the great man had to be contacted to come in prematurely. Once I had assured him that I would do the same for him when the occasion arose, he was more than happy to oblige.

We were all nervous, but it was a beautiful sunny morning and June was, as usual, the calmest. The anaesthetist arrived early to explain the epidural, while Paul Byrne told us that there would be three teams in the delivery room. Each would take a newborn baby and immediately head for the intensive care unit. At that stage, we still did not know the gender of the babies.

I was allowed into the theatre only after they had performed the incision. Then, Paul simply delivered each child: 'Child number one – female.' He quickly showed each baby to June and myself before two other medics took each new arrival, placed him or her in a small glass cot on a trolley and immediately headed off. This system worked like clockwork, beginning shortly after nine and finishing within minutes. Ellen weighed in first at 5lbs 4oz, Ronan was next at the same weight, and Sean was born a minute later, weighing 4lbs 2oz. Miraculously, only one of them, Sean, had to be kept in an incubator for any length of time. Ellen and Ronan were brought to June's room within forty-eight hours.

I rang the grannies, who of course immediately wanted to come in. Once all close relatives had been informed, and knowing that there might be some media interest, I rang the programme and Gay announced the three arrivals just before the end of the show. June was very sore and tired, and the hospital staff were anxious that visits be tightly regulated, so shortly after Gay made the announcement I was called to the foyer of the Rotunda, to be greeted by reporters.

*   *   *

The next few days were a haze. I had prepared a room in the house with the help of June's brother Terence, and following the expert advice of a former colleague, Nuala O'Connor, who had given birth to triplets a few years earlier. She instructed me to get the room ready and not to buy a triple buggy. So while June was in the Rotunda I had organized one bedroom with three Moses baskets, running water, a sink, a fridge, armchairs and three diaries, which I tied to the end of each cot for the imminent arrival of the three amigos. The diaries were critical, and simple. When friends called, we simply told them to go to the room and, if a nappy needed to be changed or a feed was due, they would know from the diary, which they would fill in. It was a good system. But those early days and nights were punishing. I would have crumbled under it without June's skills and energy, and the combined help of relatives and friends.

For the first year after the triplets were born, even though June was at home full time and her mother was a great help, we were run off our feet. But the biggest killer was lack of sleep. We discovered a brilliant child-minder in Anne Conroy, who became indispensable; her husband Mick was a great help too – and he came free! Friends such as Myrna Russell, Mona Somers and Pauline Doyle were also generous and invaluable.

Taking care of three babies was unrelenting, unstoppable, all-consuming. I knew we were in trouble when I discovered one Friday that the previous Monday had been a bank holiday but we hadn't noticed the difference. The saying 'It's a seven-day-a-week job' doesn't adequately explain the amount of work involved for every parent; it's seven days a week, plus the next week and the following weeks, months and years.

Thankfully, all the children have remained fine and healthy. I did have a few nights on the floor of Temple Street Hospital as Ronan recovered from bronchiolitis; and we saw in New Year's Day 1998 in Wexford General Hospital with a sick child. But overall, thank God, we have been blessed with good health.

And it's great fun. Sean, Ellen and Ronan are a great gift, no ifs or buts. If you want proof that there is a God, the granting of three children at the same time to June Meehan was a decision so wise that it could only have been made in heaven. If anyone can handle children, it is June. She is organized, energetic, very affectionate and sensible – a trait she brings to all aspects of her life, from home to work. It's a joy to watch her love up the three teenagers who have now taken over our house. I know of no one more suited, more able and more wanting of three children the same age than the woman from Cabra born of a strong, hard-working mother – just like Mabel – and a bartender soccer-loving father. In that respect, she is every inch her own mother, Maureen, who also had two boys and a girl.

It's weird really; there you are, pottering along, the house is yours to ramble free as you please. You can display your precious model fire engines wherever you want; your music is safe no matter where you leave it; you can come and go when and where you want. Then these three interlopers arrive, have a quick look around your property and promptly take it over, falling just short of pushing you out the front door. It's a coup d'état which you have planned, organized, marshalled and paid for – but you are the deposed leader!

Don't mention fire stations to my three children. One of the great joys of having children is not simply the moments of earthly joy as you watch them grow and develop, accompanied by glimpses of transcendent luminosity as they light up your life. Forget that; they provide great camouflage if you want to visit fire stations, as I frequently do. 'Would you mind if the children look at the fire engines?' I ask as they kick the back of my legs.

In truth, I am obsessed with the big red machines. I have a collection of nearly two hundred models – *not* toys – from all over the world, and numerous 'fire brigade' books and magazines. Don't ask me where this obsession came from; I reckon my mother was frightened by a Dennis F60 from Dolphin's Barn fire station when she was carrying me in the womb!

Moments of madness, stress? Want some distraction? Get down the bi-monthly magazine of the Fire Brigade Society and lose yourself in the new Scania 'command and control' unit purchased by Dublin Fire Brigade. Go on, ask me anything about the vehicle fleet of the DFB and I will leave you speechless – and bored!

It's not just fire stations; I am fanatical about public buildings in general. I can't believe they are free to enter, so I gorge on them. Public libraries? Love them. I'd be there all day, every day, if I could. The smell of the books, the rows and rows of excitement, learning, knowledge. I am insatiable.

I love art galleries, anywhere, any time; from the wonderful National and Municipal Galleries in Dublin, to the private galleries on Molesworth and South Frederick Street, the Crawford in Cork, the Hunt and Municipal in Limerick. My idea of capturing small sublime moments of intense relaxation is quick visits, when I can manage, to view a painting.

I date my interest in all things artistic to my four-year stint in advertising. To this day, I am still fascinated by fonts and typefaces, graphics, design, branding and art. I even started going to weekly art classes ten years ago. When I rang the artist Brian McCarthy and told him I would like to paint, he replied, 'What's stopping you?'

As a stress-buster I cannot recommend it highly enough. I paint in oils, which simply means you can wipe out mistakes, again and again – just like the sculptor who created an elephant out of a block of granite, declaring that he did so simply by removing all the bits of the block that didn't look like an elephant. Oils can be like that. And I have something to show for it; at least once a year I paint a new piece to be used as a 'thank you' card for people who participate in *Liveline* – God, the rewards people get for baring their souls on national radio!

CHAPTER 21

Trouble Ahead

B Y 1996, TROUBLE WAS BREWING FOR ME AT RTÉ. I should have seen the warning signs.

My weekly newspaper columns have never received a negative reaction within RTÉ, save for one bizarre incident. In 1995, I started to write a light column for the *Sunday Express*, a sister paper of the *Star* which wanted to beef up its Irish content. It was at the height of the controversy surrounding allegations by the then minister for transport, energy and communications Michael Lowry that he was being followed by someone in a white van. I wrote something fairly innocuous about him and the issue in the *Express* column.

I was summoned by the then director general, Joe Barry, whom I had never met before, to his imposing office on the top floor of the administration building. To my surprise, the director of radio, Kevin Healy, was also present. The DG told me I must terminate my column in the *Express* as there had been 'traffic' about it. He wouldn't tell me what the exact nature of the complaint was, but he was adamant that I give it up. He said he was unaware that I had been writing it and that I had not gone through the correct channels in seeking permission.

I was in shock. I had just had my three children in March and was being paid a modest amount on top of my producer's salary for presenting, so I was keen to keep up the column. I timidly pointed out that I often used the column to promote RTÉ programmes, but he was not interested. The following day, Kevin Healy told me that if I wrote a letter of apology to the director general, I would probably be allowed to continue the column – but I would have to be careful. I was grateful that Kevin Healy had done me a good turn, and I was able to keep writing the columns.

We were just blowing out the candles on the cakes for the kids' first birthday party in our house in Clontarf on 28 March 1996 when the phone rang. It was Louis Hogan, the former director of 2FM, who on his retirement had offered to represent me in meetings with RTÉ management. Above the singing of 'Happy Birthday' for the third time, he informed me that Kevin Healy had just told him that I was finished filling in for Gay Byrne on Mondays and Tuesdays – and my reporting and producing role for the other days was to be terminated.

I was so distracted by the party, and the fact that one of my children was sitting on Gay's lap at the time, that I didn't take the message seriously. I simply presumed I had misheard it in the mêlée. There had been no indication that the news was coming – and surely they would give it a few more months before they made such a definite decision?

Nothing further was said at the time. I continued presenting, producing and working on *The Gay Byrne Show*, with not a word from management about what was happening.

I was presenting the show when Veronica Guerin was assassinated in June 1996. We were all deeply shocked. I had spoken to Veronica only a couple of weeks earlier. She had had a conversation with 'The Monk', Gerry Hutch, who lived in Clontarf, and who was upset about something I had said on the programme about him. As with the other times Veronica and I had met, it was friendly, and she knew I admired her unending courage and instincts.

The day after she was killed, with people's anger rising at the savagery of the murder and looking to the government to act against the drugs gangs, I suggested that people place flowers or mementos on the railings of the Dáil. Over the next few days, a massive shrine was constructed, flower by flower, photo by photo, in Kildare Street.

I thought I was doing great radio. Around that time, I covered the poignant eviction of Joan Cunningham in Blanchardstown as a reporter on the show. I happened to be in her house when the bailiffs arrived, broadcasting live as they pushed me aside to remove all and sundry. I felt as if I was back in my social-work days.

Listeners reacted, as did the neighbours, by banding together to pay some of the outstanding rent for Joan and the young children she was rearing alone. Joan was doing her best, but it was chaos. I remember her clutching her young children, who were getting ready for school as the bailiffs arrived. Sadly, one of those young children, Eddie, was shot dead in his bed in 2008, apparently a victim of a gangland assassination.

Nevertheless, despite the fact that the figures for that time have never been bettered, when the newspapers announced in June that 2FM DJ Gareth O'Callaghan would be my replacement as presenter, it became clear that my days working with Gabriel Mary Byrne were nearing an end. I asked for a meeting with Kevin Healy, at which he told me that the 'perception' of me wasn't good. I know my Dublin working-class accent doesn't go down well at D4 dinner parties, but I reminded him in a heated exchange that RTÉ gets more licence-fee money from Ballyfermot than from Ballsbridge. It was galling to read about my professional demise in the papers. All through the summer of 1996 I waited for RTÉ to decide my future role. I vainly tried to fight back with a series of interviews. This was a lesson in itself: when RTÉ management decides you are out, for whatever reason, that's the end of it.

During that awful summer, Kevin Healy, under fire for the schedule changes, wrote a long piece for the *Irish Times* in which he referred to all the talent available to him in RTÉ, including Bibi Baskin, Carrie Crowley and Richard Crowley. My stomach churned as I read the article and the grim reality hit me as I reached the last paragraph that he had mentioned nearly everyone in the RTÉ internal phone directory – except me. It was a reminder that those of us who have an exaggerated view of our own importance always look for the missing names, especially if it's our own. I was standing up when I read it and nearly retched, but I was quickly brought back to earth, with the three babies bawling in the background.

Not knowing my fate or even if I would have a job, I frantically submitted new proposals and ideas, ranging from a nightly current affairs programme at 10 p.m. to a resurrection of a summer weekend programme I had presented two years earlier each Saturday and Sunday from eleven to one. Both ideas were in fact taken up – but without me at the helm or microphone. I was determined to take any work available. I remember meeting Gerry Ryan in Clontarf Castle over that awful summer and he advised me to simply stay in the building and do anything I was offered – even cutting the grass!

I went on holiday in Rosslare that July with my family. On a drive to visit the Wexford slobs, I bought the *Cork Examiner* to read about the new RTÉ Radio autumn schedule – in which of course I did not feature. However, the reporter asked what was going to happen to Joe Duffy, who up to a few weeks earlier had been presenting the station's flagship show? Tom Manning, the then head of Radio 1, revealed that I would probably be a reporter on the evening news programme, *5-7 Live*. The *Examiner*, first with the news to me – about me!

I found a phone box in the car park of the wildlife sanctuary and rang RTÉ to find out more. It sounded as if I was simply being put somewhere out of the way. I was told not to worry; just to show up when the new programme started in early September. I was given little other information. The increase they had given me for presenting *The Gay Byrne Show* was also withdrawn by a manager who disappeared up the ranks. When I returned from my holiday, I even had to 'sneak' into the radio centre on a Sunday evening to see if I could locate a desk where I might sit. Another one of my little mottos: always confront your fears by rehearsing!

It also looked as if my weekly columns were to suffer because of the decision to drop me from *The Gay Byrne Show*. Gerry O'Regan, then editor of the *Star*, and James Dunne asked to meet me at short notice in the Yacht pub in Clontarf, where they informed me that the column was finished. Gerry cited 'the high cost of sourcing the greyhound results' as the main reason why they could not continue to pay me the weekly fee. I was shocked – but hey, that's showbusiness.

I could see that Jim Dunne did not agree with the decision – but to me it was a sharp and quick reminder that I work in a fickle business. After the way I was treated by RTÉ management when Gaybo went part-time, I was getting used to the insecurity.

Luckily, my work on *5-7 Live* involved being out of the office most of the time, so the grinding embarrassment of being kicked off *The GB Show* was not visited on me daily. Meanwhile, Gay's show had a new shorter time slot, as he and Pat Kenny flipped spots; Gareth O'Callaghan did indeed step into my shoes as the new fill-in presenter.

Still, I enjoyed my time on *5-7 Live*, presented by the wonderful, multi-talented Myles Dungan, another man who gives ambition a good name. The editor, Pat Brennan, asked me to head to London for daily coverage of the Albert Reynolds libel trial. The former Taoiseach was suing the *Sunday Times*, believing they had libelled him in an article shortly after his coalition government fell in 1994.

I reluctantly agreed to go, as it would entail heading off to London each Sunday evening and returning hot-foot each Friday – but I did not think the trial would last for six weeks! The children were 18 months old when it started. But Pat Brennan's instincts, as usual, were bang on, and I managed to turn the trial into a daily soap opera. I always sat through the full proceedings and it afforded me the opportunity to work and socialize with some of the greats of Irish journalism, such as Miriam Lord, Ann Marie Hourihane, Jerome Reilly, Jody Corcoran and Emily O'Reilly.

As luck would have it, I managed to get the scoop on the verdict by broadcasting it first on *Liveline*, then presented by Marian Finucane. Mr Reynolds was awarded one penny in damages by the jury. I also got the actual penny; James Price, QC for the *Sunday Times,* handed me one in court and asked me to give it to a crestfallen Albert Reynolds, who told me to keep it. He also gave me his copy of the offending article, which he had used during the trial.

I won a National Media Award for my marathon endeavours in London, and this began a series of court reports, primarily around high-profile Irish criminal and libel cases. I covered a number of trials associated with the murder of Veronica Guerin, for instance.

Sleeping in my car in the grounds of Stormont for a week during the negotiations for the Good Friday Agreement in 1998 was another glamorous assignment for *5-7 Live*, but I loved it. It was history in the making. I reported into all the main programmes during that week, and it was an education. Mark Durkan, my former flatmate and my deputy when I was president of USI, was cosseted full time in the building, crafting and negotiating on behalf of the SDLP. The Sinn Féin delegation seemed to spend most of their time buttering up the media, while Alastair Campbell, Tony Blair's über-confident press officer, arrogantly let us know that he was the boss and we were mere hacks feeding off scraps. Ironically, when the week finished, the *Sunday Independent* wrote a strong piece commending my work. I subsequently met and became good friends with the writer, Jonathan Philbin Bowman. I felt Jonathan and I had an unusual bond, our fathers having met in the 1950s, though not as equals. Jonathan always wrote about me favourably and we began to meet for coffee regularly – right up to a week prior to his untimely and tragic death in March 2000.

CHAPTER 22

Adventures in TV Land

FROM 1992 ON, I BEGAN GETTING A FEW BREAKS IN TV land, despite my stunning radio looks. I have long given up on my desire to make it 'big' on TV. But if opportunities arose I would invariably take them. I frame TV opportunities like auditions for a play – just because you don't get the gig doesn't mean you are useless; you are simply not the right person for the part at that time. For TV audiences, that often means I am the wrong sex and age – but, hey, you can't have all the gifts.

At one stage in 1991 I stood in at short notice for Shay Healy, the amiable presenter of the hugely popular and avant garde *Nighthawks*, who had taken ill unexpectedly. In one sense, this was a great way to get a gig; no advance notice, no worries, just get in and do it. The *Nighthawks* concept was relaxed, to say the least, and the crew simply assumed that I knew how to do it. I don't think my few stints were up to much, but it was no disaster – that comes only after intense preparation!

Philip Kampf, the creative genius who had pre-dated me as a producer on *The Gay Byrne Show*, had pioneered the 'survival' programmes made infamous by Gerry Ryan's 'Lambo' escapade – surely the true precursor of the *I'm a Celebrity, Get Me Out of Here* genre. In 1992, Philip came up with an idea for a magazine programme called *Summer Journeys*. I jumped at the notion of travelling around the country and meeting people, using a different mode of transport each week.

When I arrived in Dingle to do the Ring of Kerry, Philip presented me with a bicycle. I didn't have the guts to tell him that cycling was not one of my talents. Indeed, since that embarrassing fall off Peter Boylan's gleaming new bike on Christmas Day 1970, I had never dared get into the saddle again. Within minutes, it must have been obvious to Philip that I was totally un-balanced as I careered down the side of a mountain near Annascaul. I wanted to kick myself for not taking cycling lessons, but a kick would have propelled me into the furze.

Philip came to my rescue when he agreed to long shots and lots of scenes of me on foot scouring grave-yards and mountaintops for interesting items. At one point Philip ran along the road shouting at sheep to get them to turn their heads for a 'cutaway'. The sheep did make it into the programme, giving the impression that they were craning their necks to see this lunatic on two wheels careering towards an early demise.

The following week, I climbed Carrantouhil, to be

greeted on the summit by fellow climbers, who revelled in the RTÉ figure actually having the stamina to climb the 3,400 feet to the top. However, they needed all their stamina to run away as a helicopter landed to whisk me to base camp at Kate Kearney's cottage in nearby Beaufort. Nearby if you are in a helicopter, that is.

Further episodes included a visit to Tom Crean's grave and South Pole Inn in Annascaul, igniting my interest in this great Arctic explorer; and a rather un-poetic trek by horse through Yeats country. Despite being from Ballyfermot, where some locals have been known to present themselves at the local bar on horse-back, I have no equine abilities whatsoever and was terrified for my twelve hours filming in the saddle. I tried wobbly surfing in Enniscrone with Eurovision winner Charlie McGettigan; and travelled by noisy vin-tage car through the locations for *The Quiet Man*.

I enjoyed the ten-week series, which was intended as an antidote to the wall-to-wall coverage of the Barcelona Olympics. While Michael Carruth and Wayne McCullough brought home gold and silver medals respectively, Ireland did not feature in the medals for either cycling or showjumping, me being otherwise engaged and unavailable.

After the broadcast of *Summer Journeys*, I was told in no uncertain terms that one senior TV manager in par-ticular had taken a scunder against my accent.

I know my Ballyfermot accent was initially a hindrance to me, both on TV and radio. I used to regularly receive well-written, anonymous letters from someone else who claimed to be an RTÉ manager, berating my accent and asking what the national broadcaster had come to, allowing me on air. Gay advised me to tear up such letters. I think my voice can be harsh and nasal, but it's the only one I have and I do try to soften it.

Once, I got a particularly nasty (but true) comment after I had referred to Cardinal Cathal Daly on air as a very good 'tinker', rather than a 'thinker'. I finally decided then to do something about using my tongue properly. Having been unable to afford the weekly sixpence for elocution lessons in national school, I was doomed forever to speak like Brendan Behan – but not to write like him, unfortunately. But I vowed to improve my diction and clarity; after all, I reckoned that clarity was the least I could aspire to, as silence was not an option. Quietly, I went to a series of speech coaches. I received great help from the in-house RTÉ voice coach Poll Moussiledes. Today, I do pronounce my 'th's, and insist my three children do as well.

When *Nob Nation*, *Gift Grub* or *Après Match* imitate me, I cringe; when they mimic others in the public eye, I remark how accurate they are!

In 1993, Gerry Ryan persuaded me to do a turn on his madcap *Secrets* TV adventure. So desperate was I for any outings on the box that I readily agreed to do a Gary Glitter impression. (This was a time when Gary Glitter could be impersonated without fear of criminal charges.) After numerous dance lessons, I strutted out on our TV screens in silver platform boots, winged one-piece jumpsuit and coiffed hair, looking to all intents and purposes like a female member of Abba (the one with the beard) and making an unholy show of myself.

I will do anything to get on telly.

This was reinforced the following summer when I agreed to be the reporter on another twice-weekly summer TV magazine filler, *Gortnaclune*. With a stellar cast led by Pauline McLynn, Jon Kenny and Pat O'Mahony, and with a wonderful production team, this summer variety show set in the fictional village of Gortnaclune and featuring top guests surely could not go wrong. Could it?

At the same time, I was reporting on the escapades of the Irish team in the World Cup, USA 1994. (Remember Saturday, 18 June 1994, when Ireland beat Italy 1–0 in the Giants Stadium? That's me in the crowd with a funny hat and leprechaun suit – seriously. Check out the limited edition Opel souvenir poster.) As soon as I got back to Ireland, I had to head straight to a circus to do my first 'live' report into *Gortnaclune*, which involved me and a young Mexican human cannonball. I know it worked for him when he got into the US from his home-land, but the show simply didn't take off in Ireland. To be honest, I couldn't revisit the trauma now; nor, I sus-pect, could many viewers, judging by the critics.

In fairness, though, with Pauline, Jon and Pat fronting the whole affair in the studio, it did get good ratings, which, I came to learn, is very, very important in TV land.

When Gay Byrne decided, after thirty-seven years, to give up *The Late Late Show*, a special four-hour programme was planned for his final night on 21 May 1999. Gay suggested that I interview him on his final *Late Late*. Of course I said yes. When I eventually got to sit down with Gaybo a few days before the broadcast, he was a bit tetchy. He was keen that I would not bring up Russell Murphy, Gaybo's former friend and accountant who had ripped him off. Gay wasn't censoring the interview; he was simply wearing his 'producer's hat' and thought viewers would be bored with the retelling of an old tale.

So on Gay's final *Late Late*, after Larry and Bono of U2 had surprised him with a gift of a Harley Davidson, I was plucked from the celebrity audience and proceeded to interview him. Remembering that Gay had once reduced Nuala O'Faolain to tears of frustration when she had interviewed him at the time his autobiography was published, I had thought out my questions carefully beforehand. I had also asked listeners to *Liveline* to submit questions; at least I could blame them for any inane queries.

It was tough to sit there with interviewers of great skill such as Gay sitting in front of me and the likes of Mike Murphy in the audience, so I was nervous and got off to a bad start. I jumped in with a question about the 'scoop' on the previous week's *Late Late* when Terry Keane revealed that she had had a long-running extramarital affair with former Taoiseach Charles Haughey. I wondered if Gay felt any sympathy for Charlie; I understood that they were friends. Gay bit the nose off me: 'He had the affair, I didn't,' he snapped. I don't think I or the interview recovered.

I should have known better; if there is one thing I have learned from the master it is that the programme comes first, no ifs or buts. As those who work with me know, it is my motto to this day. Why would Gay let anything get in the way of the *Late Late*? If Terry Keane was willing to provide such a scoop, stand back! By the way, Gay much preferred the previous week's show, with Terry Keane's bombshell, rather than the back-slapping final programme.

Exactly ten years later – almost to the day – I was invited back to contribute to Pat Kenny's final *Late Late Show* on 29 May 2009. I think Pat was a great presenter of the show; the mix of heavy and light melded brilliantly under his baton and I firmly believe that he left the programme way before his time was up.

Dragging a broken leg behind me (about which more later) for the show, I presented him with a cake and said a few heartfelt words about his time before introducing a video compilation of great moments from his tenure. Some of Pat's family were upset that his stint on the *Late Late* had finished, and they were especially hurt by the totally unfair descriptions of him as dry and wooden by some critics. Of course, Pat bounced back and has thundered on to great TV success with *Frontline*.

By the way, yes, I have told Ryan Tubridy that I am available for his final *Late Late* – if I live that long!

Another big foray into television for me came in 2006, again thanks to Philip Kampf. I had over the intervening years put my name to various TV proposals, but they all came to nought. Indeed, some of the ideas were bang on. After covering the rip-off culture in Ireland incessantly on *Liveline*, a number of us pitched an idea on the subject to RTÉ TV in 2004, but it got nowhere. When Eddie Hobbs launched a similar (and, in fairness, excellent) TV programme a year later, it worked wonders.

In television you need a mentor, somebody who believes in you. Philip came up with another idea, melding the 'rip-off' notion and churning it into a game show. *Highly Recommended* was an independent production, but Philip somehow managed to get an eight-week run of the 'consumer game show', in which punters would pitch money-saving ideas to a *Dragon's Den*-like panel. The best idea would win a modest prize.

We recorded eight programmes over a few days in the National Dog Show centre in Swords, a cavernous hangar so large that the TV trucks were able to park inside the building. I thoroughly enjoyed that show. Though working on a tight budget, it got a great slot at eight thirty on a Sunday night. Despite the added zest of Ben Dunne and Conor Pope on the judging panel, I wondered if a comedy programme or soap opera might be a better fit for that slot. Ben and Conor were brilliant but, like all shows with a consumer bent in RTÉ, it had a lot of legal problems so, while being well received by viewers and critics, it lasted just one series.

Television came knocking again in 2008 when Roger Childs, the newly appointed head of religious affairs in RTÉ, asked me to front a religious magazine programme on a Sunday morning. Roger was more enthusiastic about me than I was, so I agreed, and that's how *Spirit Level* was born.

Over the years, like so many, I have become a 'collapsed Catholic'. Two of my closest friends from my CYC days, Donal Harrington and Eoin Cooke, were wonderful priests. We regularly holidayed together back then, and we would take turns reading the daily priestly 'office' aloud. Donal left the priesthood in 1997, while Eoin died after a battle with oesophagal cancer in 2001, aged fifty-four. While my faith had taken a battering since those days, *Spirit Level* appealed to my spiritually questing side.

I was knocked back a bit during the first series after I was knocked down, but I managed only to miss two programmes, doing the remainder of the series firmly seated! The second series of *Spirit Level* was even better, because it was going to be 'live'. I jumped at the idea; obviously, it has a particular niche following, but live at five on a Sunday for twelve weeks in November, December and January during the GAA closed season was a great learning experience for me – though I am not forgetting that it has to be primarily a good experience for the viewer! I love *Spirit Level*; it hits my curiosity button right on the head. I am learning about live television and talking about topics that I don't normally broach. Of course, that sometimes leads to tension; I want to be more topical, but the programme comes from the religious affairs department – so I need to read my own book and remind myself about focusing and exploiting difference! Guests have varied from the inspiring Rose Callely, whose daughter Rachel O'Reilly was brutally murdered by her husband in 2004, to Tyrone football manager Mickey Harte and my wonderfully talented neighbour from Ballyfermot, Mary Byrne, all of whom spoke about the power of religion in their lives.

People ask me if I would like to do more telly. I have never believed that simply because I am doing a daily radio programme I should somehow be entitled to a TV gig. My attitude has always been, if you are offered an opportunity, take it. Very few programmes are born of presenters proffering their hitherto hidden talent to baying TV executives. I simply get on with my daily radio work, which I have always loved. If television happens for me, so be it; but TV likes young, slim, good-looking, yummy, blonde, vivacious, bubbly presenters – and that's just the fellas!

'Talk to Joe'

CHAPTER 23

Liveline

THE ORIGINS OF *LIVELINE* ARE STILL SOMETHING OF A mystery. Looking back from where the programme now resides, one can see *Women Today*, undoubtedly the mother of the show. But to get from there to here, you have to clearly see the thousands of listeners and callers who are its creators; they took it and, like a popular army, twisted, pushed and turned it into the programme we know today. More so than any other RTÉ programme, *Liveline* is owned by the listeners, who, with the willing co-operation of a creative, open team, have transformed an afternoon 'graveyard' slot into a daily listenership peak which is now only surpassed by the breakfast-time news programme *Morning Ireland*.

If 1979 was a hectic year in my life, taking on the college authorities as president of Trinity Students' Union, it was an equally tumultuous year of great change in RTÉ. Nowadays, we forget that it was only in

1968, forty-three years after the station was established, that RTÉ daytime radio actually began; up to then, the only radio station in the country shut down after the nine o'clock morning news, reopened for ninety minutes at lunchtime and began again at five, continuing until midnight – I kid you not!

The 1970s were probably the period of greatest change in broadcasting since the foundation of the state. Raidió Na Gaeltachta, the Irish-language station, opened in Connemara in 1972, and Gay Byrne got his first daily show on radio in 1973 when the RTÉ studios moved from the GPO in the centre of Dublin to the new radio centre in Donnybrook; but the biggest changes were to come to RTÉ at the end of the decade.

A second national television channel, RTÉ 2, was launched in November 1978. Six months later, on 31 May 1979, another national radio station went on air, RTÉ Radio 2 (later 2FM), as a response to the massive blossoming of pirate radio stations. Across on Radio 1, as it was now called, *The Gay Byrne Show* was extended to two hours. On the same day that Radio 2 was launched, Marian Finucane got her big break with the start of a new 30-minute daily programme on RTÉ Radio 1.

Earlier that year, RTÉ had set up an internal working party to investigate representation of women in news reporting. Their report found that 'a lone Martian orbiting the earth who happened to tune into some hours of Irish radio or television might well conclude that humankind was divided into two sexes in proportions six to one.' Producer Clare Duignan suggested the idea for *Women Today* to Michael Littleton, the visionary head of radio at the time, to redress this imbalance. *Women Today* did exactly what it said on the tin. A mixture of reports, interviews, music and studio discussions, it was an instant success.

Marian Finucane was a qualified architect when she became a continuity announcer in RTÉ in 1974. Her warm voice and sharp intellect ensured that she would soon get free rein on the radio. She was also involved in the fledgling Irish women's movement in the 1970s, so she was the obvious choice as presenter of *Women Today*. Marian temporarily left the programme after two years to edit *Status* magazine, again aimed primarily at women, and Doireann ní Bhriain and Hilary Orpen continued presenting *Women Today*, with Patrick Farrelly and Micheal Holmes producing.

Extended to one hour in 1985 and renamed *Liveline* – a title dreamt up by Hilary Orpen and Ed Mulhall – the 2–3 p.m. slot kept many of the elements and staff of *Women Today*, and with Marian Finucane back as presenter, it was given a much broader remit. In the early days of *Liveline*, it was mainly a magazine programme with an emphasis on the empowerment of women.

One new feature of *Liveline* was a Friday panel discussion where callers were allowed to interact with experts in the studio. Gradually, the phone element gathered ground on *Liveline*, but only on the basis of the response of listeners to the issues under discussion;

reports, inserts and studio guests were slowly phased out as the production team saw the power of listeners phoning in. This was no doubt aided by the modernization of communications in Ireland, the overhaul of the then Telecom Éireann under the dynamic minister Albert Reynolds in the late 1970s and the massive increase in domestic phones in the country.

Julian Vignoles, a producer during that period, pinpoints the moment in 1990 when *Liveline* as we know it – a live phone-in show – emerged fully evolved. A woman who had walked out of mass in Dingle in protest at a right-wing sermon contacted the programme to explain her actions; the phones lit up, the priest replied and the following sixty minutes was the first time the show was completely dominated by callers. The listeners had taken over! After that, there was no turning the clock back.

One other shadow which may have delayed the introduction of a live phone-in show was Section 31, introduced in 1971, which banned all Sinn Féin members from talking on the airwaves about anything, but this was lifted totally by minister Michael D. Higgins in 1993.

Marian Finucane and her brilliant production teams established *Liveline* at the centre of Irish life and at the heart of our national discussion over the next decade.

I filled in as presenter of *Liveline* for twelve weeks while Marian Finucane was away in 1998. Much of the success of this three-month summer run was due to the

With June after I won the Jacobs Award for my work on *The Gay Byrne Show*, 1994.

Above: Amongst women: the *GB Show* team (*back, left to right*), Mary Farrell, Julie Parsons, Lorelei Harris, Gay, me, Fiona Guilfoyle, Anne Walsh; (*front*) Mary Martin, Alice O'Sullivan and Máire ní Chadhain.

Above: Dressed to impress: broadcasting from Grafton Street for a Christmas Eve *GB Show*.

Right: The world's oldest cow, 49-year-old Bertha (*third from left*) was an early guest on *The Gay Byrne Show*.

Left: What's that on your head, Joe? Outside broadcast from North Earl Street.

Below: Come fly with me: the lengths (and heights) I went to for Gay Byrne!

Bottom: Visiting the Birmingham Six, with Brush Shiels and Kate McIlkenny.

Above: The outside broadcasts for *The Gay Byrne Show* roamed far and wide; carrying a water container in Ethiopia, 1995.

Left: With Sonny Knowles on his sixtieth birthday.

Below: Duetting with Maureen Potter at the opening of the Smithfield chimney viewing tower in 1997.

Left: In studio on my first day as fill-in presenter on *The Gay Byrne Show*, 1994.

Below: My least favourite interviewee – Fergie . . .

Bottom: . . . and one of my favourites, Norman Wisdom.

Left: With my friend and mentor, Gay Byrne.

Below: One more thing: reporting for *5–7 Live*.

Bottom: Reporting for *5–7 Live* from Hillsborough Castle following the Good Friday Agreement in 1998, with John Hume and RTÉ crew members Kevin Fowley and Donie Stritch.

Above: The success of *Liveline* is down to the listeners and staff, such as our campaign to supply Portacabins for the Mater Hospital, seen here with the donors and recipients.

Susie Long's moving and heartfelt letter to *Liveline* in January 2007 highlighted the crisis in the health service and became one of the most powerful moments on the programme. Susie died in October that year.

Breaking my leg in April 2009 was an unexpected setback.

Above: Happier days: launching the autumn radio schedules in September 2009 with Eibhlín Ní Chonghaile, Gerry Ryan and Miriam O'Callaghan. Within eight months, Gerry's death would come as a great shock.

Left: Paying tribute to Gerry on *The Late Late Show* with Ryan Tubridy, Gay Byrne and Pat Kenny.

Below: Rehearsing the spontaneous gags for Funny Friday: (*seated, left to right*) Sil Fox, Packie O'Callaghan, Brendan 'Doc' Savage; (*standing*) Uncle Bob Carley and musician Yann O'Brien.

fantastic work of the small team of Anne Farrell, Kevin Reynolds and Frank Reidy.

It was a feverish time in Northern Ireland, with the infamous Drumcree standoff over the disputed right of Orangemen to parade along the Garvaghy Road in Portadown. On 12 July, three young children, Jason, Mark and Richard Quinn, were burnt to death when their house was firebombed by loyalist supporters. I remember being totally bereft at our daily morning meeting. The only thing I could think of was to ask Cardinal Cathal Daly to come on *Liveline*, which he did, making an impassioned plea for peace, finishing with a powerful prayer in memory of the three dead children.

We left no stone unturned to ensure that *Liveline* was on top of the daily story, using all our instincts and experience to provide a national platform for that tumultuous summer's discourse, culminating in two weeks of powerful programmes after the horrific Omagh bombing on Saturday, 15 August 1998 which killed twenty-nine people, including one woman pregnant with twins. I drove to Omagh with the series producer, Anne Farrell, early the next morning, and the human devastation had to be seen to be believed. Driving back to Dublin that evening, I knew that this horror demanded that *Liveline* cover it, non-stop, from every conceivable angle, which we did.

We spoke to survivors, the relatives of victims, the heroes who helped in the carnage. We also persuaded Bernadette Sands McKevitt to give her only interview.

Along with her husband Michael McKevitt, she was a spokesperson for the 32-County Sovereignty Movement, considered to be the political wing of the Real IRA, which carried out the bombing. In the interview, she rejected the widespread media speculation at the time that their organization was ambivalent about the atrocity. In 2003, Michael McKevitt was convicted on a charge of directing terrorism between 1999 and 2001 and being a member of the Real IRA.

I was asked to travel back to Omagh on the Saturday after the bombing to anchor the RTÉ radio coverage of the memorial ceremony in the centre of the devastated town.

It was the arrival of Helen Shaw – yes, the same trainee producer who was rejected so ineptly at the end of our training course less than ten years previously – as head of RTÉ Radio in 1997 that set in motion the series of changes that would see Marian effectively replace Gay Byrne in the morning and me slip into her seat on *Liveline*. Helen had become a producer in RTÉ shortly after the training course in 1988, and was soon afterwards snapped up as news editor of BBC Northern Ireland in Belfast, where she remained until returning to the mother ship as head of RTÉ Radio.

Helen was determined to clear up the 'Gay Byrne issue' which, by 1997, was descending into farce. Gay was by now presenting a mid-morning music show three days a week, with the Monday and Tuesday slots held variously by Des Cahill and Gareth O'Callaghan.

Of course, I cannot be objective here, given my upset after I was sacked from the slot. The situation was exacerbated by the decision of RTÉ at the time to launch a massive outdoor poster campaign promoting Gareth O'Callaghan as the new presenter, something they had pointedly refused to do when I originally started presenting the show.

At this point, I was presenting a weekly media programme, *Soundbyte*, and when Helen Shaw was appointed MD of radio she gave her first interview to me, where she made it clear that the two-day slot had become something of a poisoned chalice – it didn't work for me, Des Cahill or Gareth O'Callaghan. It was Helen who amicably agreed on a retirement date with Gay, and the final *Gay Byrne Show* was broadcast live from Grafton Street on Christmas Eve, 1998.

With *The Gay Byrne Show* now gone, Marian would begin her new fifty-three-minute daily programme at 9.07, while Pat Kenny's two-hour show was being moved to a new starting time at ten, leaving the *Liveline* slot wide open. Newspapers speculated that the front-runners were either Emily O'Reilly, who was then a very successful journalist and broadcaster and is the current ombudsman, or Richard Crowley, the talented reporter whom Helen had favoured for some high-profile 'fill-ins' during her first year.

When Helen almost nonchalantly offered me the *Liveline* job, I have no doubt that my own summer stints on the programme were a big influence. When she made the offer, Helen advised me not to get obsessed with keeping Marian Finucane's listenership figures in the short term. Marian would still be on air, at a more popular time, so some slippage was inevitable. As for me, I was determined not to repeat the mistakes of five years previously when I took over the Monday and Tuesday *Gay Byrne Show*.

There were a couple of other distinct differences and advantages this time. I got to present *Liveline* for the final few weeks of December, before the new schedule changes kicked in fully at the start of January 1999, so I was at least somewhat settled when the New Year began. It also helped that the media focus was on the new *Marian Finucane Show* after nine rather than Joe Duffy presenting *Liveline*.

The first few weeks of the new schedule generated reaction, mainly around the decision to drop the popular 'It says in the papers' slot after the nine o'clock news. At the time, Helen Shaw took the criticism, arguing that people's lifestyles were changing, that they were getting up earlier – and wasn't she right!

So, when it came to replacing Marian Finucane on *Liveline*, it was all about timing and chance.

CHAPTER 24

Scams and Schemes

A LMOST FROM THE GET-GO, *LIVELINE* – THE JOE DUFFY version – seemed to land in the middle of convulsive changes in Irish life. Not only were we witnessing the roar of the Celtic Tiger, but the massive growth in the use and availability of mobile phones, texting, emails and other social media contributed enormously to the programme's success.

Over the first two years I gradually found my feet and, more importantly, my voice. I saw *Liveline* as totally falling within the remit of public service broadcasting, offering a platform for the 'underdog'. I thrived on issues where the powerless took on the powerful, be it politicians, local authorities, the Church, banks, courts or big corporations – including RTÉ. We were always keen to get both sides of the argument on air in an animated conversation. Propelled by the callers, we chased dodgy builders, banks, car dealers, model agencies and holiday-home providers. More often than not, we got results, as well as warning people to be vigilant.

Public issues such as political and judicial decisions were played out daily on *Liveline*. When second-level teachers went on strike demanding a 30 per cent wage increase, for example, our phones went crazy with irate parents. Taxi drivers and bus companies fought over the lucrative trade at the burgeoning Dublin Airport, and charity collectors complained about being pushed too hard to sign up direct-debit donations on Dublin's Grafton Street.

But the stories that have often enthralled *Liveline* listeners more so than most are the scams, rip-offs and double-dealing that became such a feature of the last decade. When I was a prisoner in Mountjoy, the most intriguing criminals were the con artists. Their stories of sheer brass neck, derring-do and incredible acting fascinated me for hours. These were invariably bright lags who had ripped off shops, hotels, car dealers and, often, their neighbours. Their argument – that insurance companies invariably footed the bill – seemed to render their activities, in their wide eyes, victimless crimes. You would, as the old saying goes, never be up to them!

On *Liveline*, among the first and funniest 'scam' stories was the tale of one of the slickest, wiliest confidence tricksters of all, 'Tom the Con' – Tom McLaughlin, a former prison officer – who came to our attention in 1999. His scam involved defrauding unsuspecting B&B owners, usually female, of any property he could slip away with. The first call described how Tom had skipped from one guesthouse with unpaid bills, a chequebook, some jewellery and a car. By the end of the programme, we had located the car in Rossaveal in Galway. Had Tom headed for the Aran Islands?

To me it was reminiscent of my hunt for Neil Diamond on *The Gay Byrne Show* a decade earlier, and I was determined to milk it. Tom re-emerged in Dublin's Parkgate Street, again in a guesthouse. But he was a slippery one. The nationwide sightings turned the hunt into a cat-and-mouse game, with Tom almost urging us to 'catch me if you can'. He disappeared for months, only to turn up in Northern Ireland, where callers told us their tales of woe. But the RUC, as it was at the time, acted, and nabbed him. He received a short prison sentence in the North and was arrested by the Gardaí on his release, serving another, no doubt embarrassed about being 'minded' by his former colleagues. As soon as he was released, he was off on another rampage. He even rang me in the office and asked to meet me in the Burlington Hotel, but of course Tom the Con fooled me and never turned up.

I have always had a good eye for spotting things that sound too good to be true. So when I saw the full-page newspaper ads for 'Trilogy', a 'three-day tennis, music and fashion extravaganza' to be held in the RDS in December 2002, I instinctively felt something did not fit. The ads were expensive, but the detail was slim, as were the graphics.

I asked the *Liveline* team to put in a call to the

organizers, who immediately referred us to a respected PR company. This, I thought, was a bit odd. Surely the organizers would jump at the opportunity of free publicity? But I suspect they knew that we were sceptical, which is the natural reaction of most organizations when *Liveline* calls!

When they refused to come on, hoping that this would scupper the item on *Liveline*, we started to contact some of the other groups mentioned in this 'unprecedented event' which would see the 'top female tennis stars from the US pitted against their European counterparts in a Ryder-cup style event'. There would also be a rock concert featuring one of the biggest (unnamed) bands in the world, while the third leg of the bizarre project would be a fashion show featuring some of the most famous supermodels in the world.

The Chernobyl Children's Project was invoked as the beneficiary of some of the proceeds. When we contacted Adi Roche's charity, they were baffled, but anxious not to damage the prospect of getting some much-needed funds. They knew nothing about the details of the event and demurred from comment, which in retrospect was a pity.

Sean Collins McCarthy was extraordinarily shy for someone who was organizing such a flamboyant event. He refused repeatedly to come on *Liveline*. Within days, more sceptical callers were raising serious questions. But *Liveline* was quickly accused of being a spoilsport and trying to destroy a great effort. It was the height of the Celtic Tiger, and money could buy you anything, so the *Liveline* scepticism simply ran out of steam within a couple of weeks. Even the RTÉ website a week before the event was advertising the €100 tickets, with a long, positive blurb that did not once mention the controversy that had been generated on *Liveline*.

In fairness, Anna Kournikova and other tennis and fashion stars did participate in the event in good faith. The rock concert had been dropped, so the trilogy was now being described as a duology – and was descending rapidly into codology! Taoiseach Bertie Ahern even turned up to present Kournikova with the 'Collins' award – named after the 23-year-old founder of the tournament, not the founder of the state.

But soon afterwards it emerged that few people had been paid and there were massive bills outstanding to many small companies. Ultimately, the company set up to run the event went bust, reportedly owing investors and creditors €3.6 million. Collins left the country a short time afterwards.

It was a prime example of how Establishment Ireland could rally around a bizarre scheme and decry anyone who dared say that the emperor had no clothes. My early scepticism had paid off, a trend that was to continue as we exposed conmen, pyramid schemes, rip-off 'holiday clubs' that sold dud holiday homes in places such as Bulgaria, and various scams thrown up during the bogus Celtic Tiger.

My attitude and approach to pyramid schemes is a good example of how I see *Liveline* working. The minute we got a call about these schemes, I took the attitude that this was not simply a two-sided debate about an issue, with pros and cons. As far as I was concerned, these schemes were immoral and it was right to expose them so that good people could be saved from financial ruin.

Pyramid schemes are a scam, nothing surer. Nothing is made, produced, distilled, brewed, bought or sold. People are led to believe that if they simply 'gift' money to someone, it in turn will magically mushroom and they will be rewarded in spades – provided they bring other people, invariably their friends, into the scheme. In 2005 and 2006, as our listeners testified, there was a lot of spare cash sloshing around the economy.

Pyramid schemes can often be the hardest to crack, mainly because those sucked in live in fear of being the last to join, which means that they will not get any return. For a pyramid scheme to work, it perpetually needs more suckers to join. Once it stops, as it invariably will, the whole scheme collapses, a small number of people (usually those who started it) get a lot of money, while many others are left high and dry. It takes a brave person to break ranks, as he or she will be accused of bringing the house of cards down.

Once we would get one call on a pyramid scheme, we would be on red alert, determined to give it coverage. Of course, the next callers would be those desperately trying to keep the scheme going. *Liveline* was listening to ordinary people screaming at each other as these schemes drove friends, families, neighbourhoods and villages apart. *Liveline* itself is accused of collapsing the schemes. How proud I am of that allegation.

From Dublin to Cork, there have been some bizarre pyramid schemes exposed over the years. They call themselves different things, sometimes 'gifting', or the 'golden egg'. Crazy stories emerged: one pyramid scheme meeting in a house in South Dublin was held up by a bunch of thugs and all the money stolen; while in another lunatic scheme, the money had to be delivered weekly from Cork to Germany. Despite these stories, people still signed up and were ultimately devastated. The government eventually brought in legislation in 2007 to outlaw pyramid schemes.

Of course, as the phones crackled with these stories, little did we know that the whole country had become one big pyramid scheme that would collapse around us within a few years.

Some of the most notorious and dangerous fraudsters can be those offering wonder cures; it's a conceit as old as the world itself. While listeners use the programme to highlight doctors', dentists', consultants' and lawyers' fees, they have also warned against quacks and fraudulent cures.

I will never forget the tearful word picture painted on the programme by a grieving father as he described bringing his teenage son, who was dying of cancer, to a doctor who prescribed tablets and banned the child from eating McDonald's. The bereft father described finding the hoard of revolting tablets under the dead child's bed and regretted that he had denied his son a few little pleasures in his last days. I am surprised when good people pay out good money for 'miracle cures', but then, when it comes to your health or that of your children, you will try anything, no matter how bizarre, ludicrous and unworkable these 'cures' sound. From gastric banding to cosmetic surgery, the listeners' stories have been harrowing. But I firmly believe that hearing those stories has prevented others from falling into the same trap.

Liveline is constantly getting phone calls about rip-off tarmac merchants, roofers and gutter specialists. There have been vivid stories about sinking driveways, leaking gutters and old people being frog-marched to ATM machines to shell out vast amounts of cash to these fly-by-nights. The modus operandi of the fake tarmac merchants was to coat a driveway with a superficial covering of tar, not the layered surfaces that you need and pay for. On one occasion, a tradesman told us how, when he spotted such a scam on his own driveway, he refused to pay, but the bogus builders got their retribution by stealing his van and tools a few weeks later.

Of course, *Liveline* has to keep listeners, and there are only so many times you can do the one story. But one Friday afternoon it was different. The 'magic call' came in around one o'clock – I pray for one of these every day. A group of these rip-off 'tarmac merchants' had marched an elderly victim to the local ATM for cash payment, but an eagle-eyed neighbour had managed to get the registration number of the Transit van they sped off in, and he called *Liveline*.

I decided to give out the details on air. Within minutes, thanks to mobile phones, listeners had spotted the van in the Navan Road area. Another listener came on air as he followed the van towards the M50. As he gave chase, it was clear that the conmen were also listening, as they managed to lose the *Liveline* listener. We then got a fleeting sighting on the M50 and, just before the programme ended, a flurry of calls located the van in the car park of a supermarket in Greystones. Surrounded by irate 1850-715-815 callers, the van was cornered and the Gardaí arrived.

These guys are wily operators, and while the Gardaí might not always be able to convict them, I do believe that these dramatic stories put conmen out of business and listeners on their guard. They also show public service radio at its best: the community freely coming together to warn and prevent others suffering the same fate. The public space and forum that *Liveline* provides is good for democracy in Ireland.

I always argue against the notion that 'public service' broadcasting is a niche area; from my point of view, for *Liveline* to be effective we need a large, nationwide audience. The more people listening around the country, the better we are able to serve them and search out ne'er-do-wells. *Liveline* is still the only national public phone-in show with a high daily audience. In recent years, it has gone from number seven in the top ten national daily programmes to number two, after *Morning Ireland* – a fantastic achievement for a programme that starts at one forty-five!

CHAPTER 25

'It Will Be Remembered as the Day that Changed the World'

As the *Liveline* signature tune rolled out on Tuesday, 11 September 2001, we launched into a continuing story about certain Bulgarian customs officials extorting money from Irish holidaymakers as they boarded their homeward flights from Bourgos Airport. Little did I know that, within thirty minutes, the world would be changed, changed utterly, by four planes in the United States.

While the calls about the Bulgarian story unfolded in the first fifteen minutes of the programme, we began to realize, through live footage on Sky News, that a minute after *Liveline* had begun, a plane had flown into the World Trade Center. Just after two o'clock, I called in Niall O'Dowd from New York, telling listeners that something major was happening, but the line failed. I called a break, after which I immediately went back to Niall, who reported that in the space of the previous seventeen minutes, two planes had crashed into the Twin Towers.

It is a reflection of the speed of communications and the mass media that within twenty minutes of the first attack in New York and five minutes of the second, we were talking on *Liveline* about 'kamikaze bombers', 'terrorist attacks', 'Middle Eastern connections' and a 'Pakistan-based terrorist leader'. By the time the programme ended at two forty-five, we had reported the attack on the Pentagon, and the dying moments of the programme were taken up with a live statement from President George W. Bush, promising that 'terrorism against our nation will not stand . . . we will hunt down those folks who committed this act'.

Within the space of those sixty minutes, more carnage, terror and unimaginable horror had been unleashed than anyone ever thought possible in such a short space of time. I said on the radio that day that September 11th would be remembered as the day that changed the world, but even then I had no idea of the enormity and historical significance of what had happened.

When the programme ended, it was followed by the daily pre-recorded fifteen-minute book reading. I went straight to Helen Shaw's office and urged her to abandon the pre-recorded programmes. Shortly after three, *Rattle Bag*, the daily arts show presented by Myles Dungan, came on air as usual but quickly morphed into a news programme as the tragedy unfolded. I offered to go back on air. Helen informed me that she was going to keep a news schedule rolling, but I was to go back on air that evening for a two-hour *Liveline* special. I stayed in RTÉ as we all watched the

Twin Towers collapsing, almost in slow motion, on to a busy city, as thousands fled, chased by clouds of white dust from the horror that had already claimed almost three thousand lives.

By the time I went back on air at six thirty that evening, America and the world were in turmoil. It became apparent that four passenger airplanes had been hijacked and crashed, the Twin Towers had collapsed, thousands had been killed, airports all over the world were in chaos and North American airspace was closed. We spoke to a lot of Americans, many of them stranded in Shannon Airport, and Irish people trying to contact relatives in New York and Washington.

For the next two weeks, *Liveline* each day was devoted to the tragedy. By Thursday, the government had announced a national day of mourning – the only country in the world to do so. Friday's *Liveline* was broadcast live from outside the American embassy in Ballsbridge as thousands converged to sign books of condolence. One of the most moving scenes that afternoon was the Dublin Fire Brigade Pipe Band, heads bowed, their instruments silent as they marched slowly towards the embassy to pay their respects to the 343 New York firefighters killed when they responded to the attacks.

Helen Shaw wanted us to travel to New York to cover the aftermath and to be there as the world marked the exact moment of the conflagration one week after the event. So, by Sunday morning, myself, Philip Boucher Hayes, John McMahon and Margaret Curley were on one of the first Aer Lingus flights to New York since the disaster five days previously. Sitting in the taxi from Newark Airport on Sunday evening, we could still see the smoke smouldering from the ruins of the Twin Towers ten miles away in Manhattan.

We did a week of programmes live every day at one forty-five Irish time, eight forty-five a.m. in New York. We would head out each day to collate interviews and word pictures of the search for the dead. One of my first impressions was reading through the names of the firefighters who had died. As I remarked on air that day, it was like reading an Irish telephone directory: Ahearn, Allen, Barnes, Barry, Bates, Boyle, Bracken, Brennan, Brown, Burke, Burns, Butler, Callahan, Carroll, Cawley, Clarke, Coakley, Coleman, Collins, Coyle, Crawford, Cullen, Devlin, Donnelly, Fanning, Farrell, Farrelly, Feehan, Foley, Geraghty, Halloran, Hamilton, Hanley, Hannafin, Hannon, Healey, Hefferan, Hickey, Higgins, Holohan, Hynes, Kane, Keating, Kelly, Kennedy, Kerwin, Leavy, Linnane, Lynch, McAleese, McAvoy, McCann, McGinn, McGovern, McHugh, McMahon, McPadden, McShane, McSweeney, McWilliams, Miller, Mitchell, Moody, Muldowney, Mullan, Mulligan, Murphy, O'Callaghan, O'Hagan, O'Keefe, O'Rourke, Phelan, Regan, Russell, Ryan, Stack, Sullivan, Sweeney, Tallon, Waters and Whelan all featured, some three times, many twice. This just gives us a glimpse of the enormity of the tragedy.

We travelled to Ground Zero. The exclusion zone still covered a significant part of Lower Manhattan, but we managed to interview Irish workers still desperately digging in the ruins and, of course, local hospitals were a rich source of Irish staff willing to talk about the awful tragedy. I was particularly struck by the countless hoardings with photocopied pleas for information about missing family members and friends. Others simply wrote their own stories and pasted them up for all to read. One story has stayed with me, and I often quote it when asked to speak to voluntary groups. A firefighter found himself trapped under a three-storey-high pile of rubble from the fallen towers. He thought all was lost; hope was draining. Then suddenly he saw a sliver of dusty sunlight breaking through. He knew there and then that he would be saved. As he said, it was not the amount of light he saw that mattered but rather the ink-black darkness it replaced that made the difference and rekindled hope.

There's a message in there for all of us: our efforts should not be measured by being the biggest, the brightest or the best, but rather on the difference our deeds make. One narrow sliver of light in itself is pretty meaningless, but when it is replacing darkness, it's a miracle.

CHAPTER 26

The Great Hurt

THERE WERE A LOT OF THINGS WE HAD TO PUT UP WITH as children in Ballyfermot, but the worst was the threat that we would be sent to Artane, Letterfrack or Daingean. These were prison-like industrial schools supposedly for 'delinquents', who often came from places like Ballyfermot, or even lower down the ladder. But it seemed to us it was family difficulties that determined their fate, rather than delinquency. We heard the horrific stories of some kids being 'kidnapped' by the 'cruelty man' – the local ISPCC man – and sent to these 'gulags', simply because their fathers had disappeared or died, or for the most trivial misdemeanours, such as non-attendance at school or mitching. We had no idea what these industrial schools looked like or how to get there – except under duress and court order. And, of course, be in no doubt that, just as most clerical sexual abuse took place in working-class parishes like Ballyfermot, most of the inmates of these gulags were working-class kids from different parts of the country.

On one occasion in October 2001, my neurotic monitoring of all things print and broadcast led me to stumble across a piece in *Magill* magazine by John Waters about the government's Laffoy Commission, where victims of abuse in industrial schools were being heard. John wrote that many 'alleged victims' of abuse 'will have been young offenders with all the baggage and possible motivation that this might imply'. He went on to say that 'these were people who, as adolescents at least, had a history of disturbance or even criminal activity'.

I knew this to be nonsense, having written a long article in the mid-1970s for the CYC's *Youthopia* magazine about the 'Forgotten 3,000', the young people still in industrial schools and Magdalene laundries. I reckoned at that time that there were about three thousand still in various 'care homes' around the country. Of those sent to Artane, Letterfrack or Daingean, only 6 per cent were for so-called criminal activity – some for such heinous crimes as robbing orchards.

On reading John Waters's article, I immediately asked the producer to put this argument to some of the previous callers who had contacted us on the issue. Michael O'Brien had called us before on the topic; we tried to fax the article to him, and when he read it he was incandescent. Michael O'Brien's reaction to the article sent the phones into meltdown, unleashing numerous other stories about life in industrial schools,

340

many of which we were to hear in greater detail years later when the Ryan Report was issued. Many of the great campaigners about the horrific abuses in industrial schools, who had been working relentlessly for justice for years, participated in the *Liveline* discussion over those few weeks in 2001. 'There but for the Grace of God go I' was the mantra I kept intoning to myself.

Liveline was giving a platform to the voiceless – and an increasingly powerful one.

Of all of the topics we've covered over the years, this issue of sexual or physical abuse, whether by industrial schools, by clergy, or by families or other individuals, has revealed a world of hurt and pain. It has cropped up regularly over the years, most recently after the publication of the Murphy, Ryan and Cloyne reports.

The fact that the programme had always been available to victims of abuse is one of the reasons why we were contacted again in October 2005. This time the issue was another example of abuse of vulnerable people, but the perpetrators were members of the legal profession. Some of the self-same victims of abuse in industrial schools contacted *Liveline* when they realized that they were being double-charged by their solicitors for bringing their cases before the Residential Institutions Redress Board.

The controversy began with a phone call from a spokesperson for a Cork victims' group, who alleged that, despite the Redress Board assuring victims that their legal fees would be covered, they were still getting 'extra' bills from their legal representatives in addition to the twelve thousand five hundred Euro fees they got from the Board. (Lawyers received a total of almost one-hundred million Euros in fees from the Redress Board.)

Within minutes, other victims were on the phone. Remember, those going before the Redress Board did so as individuals and, bizarrely, had to swear on oath not to talk publicly about their award or the process. But the number of complaints and allegations of double-charging flowed in by the hundreds. Some of the stories were shameful beyond belief, with decent, vulnerable people being hoodwinked, browbeaten and deliberately confused by their so-called 'betters'.

The Law Society – the society representing solicitors, which has added government power of discipline and regulation – immediately went on the defensive. Ken Murphy, the normally affable director of the Law Society, initially refused to come on. But by the end of the week he did admit that there was a problem, and the Law Society took the decision to set up their own 'helpline'.

After a lot of asking, we were subsequently told that 158 complaints had been received on the helpline, with 75 per cent of them being dismissed. But at least some of the fifteen thousand survivors of the industrial schools felt they had a public platform on *Liveline*.

By the way, when one solicitor was caught bang to rights 'double-charging', he was ordered to pay five thousand Euros by the Law Society to their own 'compensation fund' and given a rap on the knuckles.

Little did we know that this glimpse of greed by some members of the legal profession would be only the tip of the iceberg, as we realized after the crash of 2008–9 that some lawyers were up to their necks in the property bubble.

We received a call in October 2003 from a listener in the US, Imelda Murphy, who had just heard of the death of a woman called Maggie Bullen. In previous years, we had provided a platform for women who had survived the notorious Magdalene laundries, many of them young women who found themselves pregnant and unmarried in the Ireland of the mid-twentieth century. Imelda had lived in the High Park Magdalene laundry run by the Sisters of Our Lady of Charity and simply wanted to commemorate Maggie's life. Imelda was angry, as she felt Maggie had been given a pauper's funeral, despite a lifetime of service to the nuns. Maggie had been in care since she was two and remained so until the day she died aged fifty-one. While in care, she gave birth in 1972 to twins, who were taken off her, and another child four years later, who was also put up for adoption. Imelda was especially upset at the fact that Maggie had been buried in a communal grave in Glasnevin cemetery.

Incredibly, by the end of the programme Maggie's twin daughters had contacted us to reveal that they were unaware of their mother's passing. Through their adoptive parents, they had kept in touch with Maggie over the years and were baffled as to why they had not been informed of her death.

We made efforts to get a response from the religious order in charge of High Park, but they referred us to a public relations company they had retained; the Broadcasting Complaints Commission subsequently said we did not try hard enough. The nuns also told us, through their PR company, that they had tried to contact Maggie's twin daughters, but that they had been unable to find up-to-date contact information for the adoptive family.

As with many *Liveline* issues, this story continued over the next few days, with many moving anecdotes of Maggie Bullen's life being told. One subsequent caller, who used the name 'Elizabeth' to keep her anonymity, was extraordinarily bitter and upset about the nuns, calling the plot in Glasnevin a 'mass grave'. The following day, producer Anne Marie Power and I travelled to Glasnevin to see for ourselves. It wasn't a 'mass grave', with all its awful connotations; rather, a communal grave, about the size of a suburban living room, with no individual markings but a single headstone with a list of names, nothing else. There was no date of birth or death for Maggie, or the fact that she was a beloved mother.

The nuns subsequently took severe umbrage at these stories, and they made an official submission to the Broadcasting Complaints Commission. Amongst other things, they had singled out the use of the phrase 'mass grave' as, rightly, being unfair. Now, let me be clear:

RTÉ, more so I think than any other organization, takes complaints very seriously. If a listener or viewer writes to the director general, their missive hits the organization like a steel ball in a pinball machine. We immediately get copies and are instructed to reply within twenty-four hours. For live daily radio programmes, already stretched with the complex task of preparing the next programme, this can be an onerous task, but the organization is very strict about this ethos. The licence-fee payer foots the bill, so they deserve proper public service. One of the reasons I believe RTÉ is the most trusted institution on the island is that people believe they can participate in our programmes, complain if necessary, seek redress if needed and ultimately influence the output.

The nuns' complaint against *Liveline* to the BCC was upheld. They objected especially to the contribution of 'Elizabeth' – Kathy O'Beirne – whom I had admittedly allowed to run rampant in her florid language about the nuns. My only, feeble, excuse was that she was reiterating what I had heard over the previous two days. I was still in shock over the news that Maggie's daughters had only learned of her death through *Liveline* a day previously.

There was a bizarre twist in the tale. Two years later, I spotted that a book, *Kathy's Story*, was number 2 in the UK bestsellers. The blurb said it was a true story of horrific abuse in an Irish Magdalene laundry and it had sold 400,000 copies – a publishing phenomenon. Now,

I consider myself to be fairly on top of what is happening in Ireland, but I had never heard of this book, nor indeed heard the author being interviewed. So on Monday morning I suggested to the producer that we interview her. It turned out that Kathy O'Beirne was 'Elizabeth', who had intervened so dramatically in the Maggie Bullen discussion two years previously.

But from the get-go that afternoon, when Kathy started talking on the programme, I was suspicious. I pride myself on my ability to spot inconsistencies, and my antennae were up. During the interview, I began to ask her hard questions to try to lead her to substantiate her claims. The more I questioned her, the more annoyed she got, and the more doubtful I became.

Within minutes, members of her family contacted us to refute some of the claims that she had put forward, alleging that many of Kathy's stories were untrue. This led to an almighty row. Soon, certain commentators who, as far as I'm concerned, had agendas, jumped on the bandwagon and saw this as a chance to debunk all the accusations against the Church, offering Kathy's story as an example of how people will exaggerate – and some suggesting we shouldn't be surprised; sure wasn't that why they were locked up anyway!

If one positive thing came out of the sorry mess of the 'Kathy' story, it was that it showed the power of radio: two people – in this case from the same family – disputing what had gone on, putting polar opposite stories forward. Throughout the uproar surrounding the subsequent Ryan and Murphy reports, victims found they could participate without leaving their homes or being intimidated by legalese – and, above all, they could maintain their anonymity. Of course, the publication of the Murphy Report into clerical sexual abuse in the Dublin diocese, and how it was treated by the hierarchy, had an extra poignancy for me, as I knew some of the accused priests who had ministered and molested in Ballyfermot.

CHAPTER 27

The Health of the Nation

IT WAS A SIMPLE IDEA. AFTER A HARROWING SERIES OF calls to the programme about overcrowding in accident and emergency units revealed that at times patients could not even get a chair to sit on, I asked one day in the office, 'Why don't we simply give them the chairs and space they need?' It was one o'clock, only forty-five minutes to air. Luckily, the producers were amenable, so I expanded on the idea: let's get the price of three state-of-the-art Portacabins and equip them.

The signs that things were not all well below the surface of the Celtic Tiger had been there for all to see. In late 2004, *Liveline* had received an inordinate number of calls about overcrowding in A&E departments. By the beginning of 2005, the calls about people on trolleys in the Mater Hospital in Dublin were overwhelming.

I began to ask questions on and off air, such as why

we got very few complaints about the busy A&E Department in St James's Hospital, or indeed Temple Street Children's Hospital. For whatever reason, the A&E units in both these hospitals seemed to function better, though they all complained about lack of resources. The consultant in St James's, Pat Plunkett, had been a near-neighbour of mine from Spiddal Road in Ballyfermot. I vividly remember the Plunkett family, not just because their father had a Henkel 'Bubble car' but also because every week the family could be seen walking, almost in formation, in their pristine black-and-white St John's Ambulance uniforms, to their first-aid classes. I always knew Pat Plunkett was destined for great things, and in turn he was an inspiration to me.

Eventually, the Mater A&E debacle got to me. Firstly, the hospital simply never responded to our queries. We were always referred to a public relations company, which I presume was paid out of the hospital budget. Their attitude veered between disbelief, disdain and annoyance upon receiving the dreaded query on behalf of the patients via *Liveline* producers. But, in fairness, they were only doing their job.

I also had in the back of my mind the whole debacle over the Mater Private Hospital. Members of the Private Hospital's management had bought the building from the Sisters of Mercy in 2000 for forty-two million Euros – the bargain of the century. The modern private hospital sat next to the overcrowded public area. I drove by on a regular basis, and the dichotomy between public squalor and private wealth annoyed me to hell. The sign on the wall of the new building on the corner of Dorset Street and Eccles Street says it all: the word 'private' is in bigger lettering than 'hospital'!

The next step for *Liveline* in the Mater Hospital saga was simply to do what, it seemed, the hospital couldn't: to get the space, somewhere, anywhere – and quickly.

So, having raised the idea of buying Portacabins, I asked one of the producers to ring businessman Ben Dunne, who I knew would give an immediate and straight answer. Live on air, he offered thirty thousand Euros. Within minutes of the programme starting, another businessman, Ronan Lamb, had donated the same amount and other companies were barrelling in with chairs, hygiene equipment, cleaning gear, crockery. By the end of the week, *Liveline* had three fully equipped state-of-the-art hospital waiting areas ready to be shipped up to the Mater.

As the week went on, the Portacabin campaign caught the imagination of the public. In the meantime, the PR company representing the 'impoverished' hospital was ignoring our offer, as was every health bureaucrat, from minister Mary Harney down. By this stage, between listening to callers tell their 'trolley' stories and hearing the deafening silence from the Mater management, I wanted to drive the three Portacabins to the Mater and simply leave them in the big open space beside the A&E unit on the North Circular Road; but wiser counsel prevailed.

By Thursday's programme, we had to decide what

to do: lose the offer, or do something else with the Portacabins. We reluctantly offered them to charities, which, in their droves, jumped on board. We eventually narrowed it down to three groups and, on Friday's programme, the three massive cabins arrived in the RTÉ car park. We handed over the keys and all the equipment to the three grateful charities in Carlow, Wicklow and Dublin. To answer those who dismissed the idea as a gimmick, Ben Dunne refused to be photographed with the Portacabins. He argued that he did not want to hog the limelight, as many other people had contributed relatively more than he had.

While the Portacabins are still working away, more horrific stories have emerged from the country's A&E units. The managers who bought the private hospital in 2000 for forty-two million Euros sold part of their stake seven years later, at which point the hospital was valued at €350 million, and they went on to win further contracts to manage other private hospitals that were popping up all over the country – the legacy of the boom years.

In 2006, on a *Late Late Show* St Patrick's night special on the health crisis, actor Brendan Gleeson launched a controlled explosion. He quoted from *Liveline* and from his own mother's experience to paint a devastating picture of the state of the health service. Sitting in the *Late Late* audience, I said that the actor's eloquence would resonate until the next general election.

When I saw the letter from Susie Long in January 2007, I had two reactions. My initial response was: is this just another A&E story? But after reading the powerful letter, I knew that this was different. I had recently finished a book about Martin Luther King and was struck by the power of his letters, especially the ones he wrote from places such as Birmingham City Jail; I have no doubt that Susie's letter had a similar power.

Dear Joe,

Today I had my twelfth session of chemo. I got to talking to the partner of a man who was also getting chemo. She told me that when her partner's GP requested a colonoscopy for him he was put on the waiting list. She then phoned the hospital and told them he had private health insurance and he was seen three days later. He had bowel cancer that was advanced, but had not broken through the bowel wall and spread to other organs. She said the tumour was the size of a fist and what made him go to the doctor (apart from her nagging) was he started to lose weight rapidly. Thank goodness they got it in time and he's going to recover.

I then came home, flicked on the TV and got into bed. The first ad on the TV was from the government telling people that bowel cancer can kill, but not if caught in time. If Bertie Ahern or Mary Harney or Michael McDowell were within reach I would have killed them. Literally. I'm not joking.

I don't have private health insurance. It's a long story, so I'll start at the beginning.

I've suffered from digestive complaints for years. It started out with being unable to eat in the mornings or when my stomach felt tense. I'd feel too queasy. Then I got heartburn after just about everything I ate. I lived on Rennies. Then, in 2005, I got a lot of diarrhoea and after a few months it became constant and blood accompanied some of my bowel movements. I went to my GP clinic in the summer of 2005. Probably about two months after the blood started appearing. I look back now and feel stupid for delaying for two months, but I wasn't sure if the blood was caused by piles, which my late mother suffered from. I was 39 years old and had read in books and heard a doctor say on TV that bowel cancer doesn't affect people under 50. Anyway, my normal GP was on holiday, but I saw his colleague, and she immediately sent a letter to the local hospital requesting a sonogram and a colonoscopy. Within weeks I was called for a sonogram and was diagnosed with gallstones. That explained the queasiness and the heartburn. I expected to soon be called for the colonoscopy. I waited through the autumn, then through the start of winter. No word on the colonoscopy and no word on when my gall bladder would be removed.

In November I started to get serious lower abdominal pain after eating. I phoned the consultant's secretary and asked if I was on the waiting list. She assured me I was and would be called soon. In December I started to rapidly lose weight. This

definitely wasn't like me! I love my food, Joe. I
phoned the hospital again after Christmas. Again I
was told that I was still on the list and would
definitely be called soon. (I later found out that that
consultant had retired and they had just hired a new
one.) Joe, from November to the end of February I
was in agony. Apart from the pain and diarrhoea I
was tired all the time. I'd literally get out of bed to
go to work at 4.30 in the afternoon. Came home
around 10.30 p.m., ate my dinner (I couldn't eat
before work because it'd make me too sick to do
my job), tidied the kitchen and went to bed again. I
was miserable.

Finally, on 28 February 2006, four days after I
turned 40, I was called for a colonoscopy.

I woke up in the middle of the procedure and saw
on a large screen them probing a blob on my colon.
They were taking a biopsy. But I didn't have to wait
for the results. I knew what I had. Soon after I met
my wonderful consultant, Dr George Nassim. What
a gem he is. Friendly, compassionate and funny, on
top of being a great surgeon. I felt like I was in
good hands. I didn't panic for more than a few
hours after I was told that I had cancer. They can
do loads of things to save cancer patients these
days. I was young and strong. I'd been a vegetarian
since I was 16. I ate mostly healthy foods, although
eating at night was a serious no-no when it came to
my weight. I went for walks a few times a week. I
felt I could beat this.

I was booked in for surgery to remove the tumour. I was given a stoma, which means I'll have to poop in a bag for the rest of my life. I found that really difficult to handle. More difficult than the cancer sometimes. I was in St Luke's Hospital for over 50 days last year. (I had to have a second surgery due to complications.) Recovery was hard, but I did it. I shared a room with two lovely women who also had cancer. They have since died. In another ward I was in I was next to another woman who had cancer. She died too. The staff at St Luke's in Kilkenny are the most kind, hardworking people I've ever met. In March, in between surgeries, I was sent to the Mater in Dublin and had a porto-cath put in for putting the chemo through, and a PET scan to see if the cancer had spread. If it hadn't, I'd live. If it had spread to other organs, I'd die. It had spread to my lungs.

I felt bad enough to go to the doctor. She did what she was supposed to do. She told them I had diarrhoea and blood from my rectum. But what could they do? So do lots of people. Should I have skipped the list ahead of those other people with the same symptoms? I don't think so. Should there be a list so long that it puts people at risk of dying? No. Definitely not.

I know in my heart and soul that when I started to feel really, really bad, especially from December to February 2006, is when the cancer broke through the wall of my bowel. Of course I can't prove it. But

I know. Because it broke through the bowel I have been given 2 to 4 years from diagnosis to live. The chemo is to prolong life, not to save it. I have 3 years, tops, to go. Despite that, I'm going to try my best to make it for 5 more, 'til my youngest turns 18. He needs me too much now. My husband has suffered right alongside of me in his own way knowing that the woman he loves will be dead soon. My 18-year-old daughter has been told and has gone quiet and doesn't want to talk about it. But I know she's scared. I haven't told my 13-year-old son yet. He's too young to handle it. The South East Cancer Foundation in Waterford have been very helpful and will help us when the time is right to do and say the 'right' things.

I don't blame the wonderful people who work in St Luke's in Kilkenny. They work with what they are given. St Luke's has the best A&E unit in the country. I had to use it three times in 2006 and twice with my son (nothing serious, thankfully). What did the government do? Threaten to shut it down. They also threatened to shut down the maternity unit *after* spending millions to improve it!! That would mean Carlow women would have to travel to already overcrowded hospitals in Dublin, and Kilkenny women would have to travel to Waterford, which is grand if you live in South Kilkenny. The rest could lump it and birth at the side of the road if necessary.

Twice I had to listen to two women die next to

me in hospital because there's no place for people nearing death and their loved ones to go to die and grieve in dignity.

My time in the Mater was dreadful. I was terrified I'd pick up MRSA, because it was filthy. I was put on a ward with cardiac patients, mostly men, who because of their ill health were unable to aim too well when they went to the toilet. Once when I used the toilet my pyjama bottoms soaked up urine up to my ankles. Even though I was still sick and weak I still tried to hover over the toilet so I wouldn't have to touch it. I wasn't able to hover and hold up my pyjama legs at the same time. I had just given my sister-in-law two sets of PJs to take home and wash and had nothing to change into. I rinsed them out in the grimy sink and wore them damp until she returned the next day with clean ones. There was excrement stuck to the sides of the toilet for days at a time. Water flooded the shower room, soaked my clean PJs and towel that were on the floor outside the shower and ran out into the hall. After that happened the first time, I learned to take a chair into the shower room to put my stuff on. At least I knew *that* floor got water and soap put on it regularly. The man in the bed next to me, who had suffered a triple by-pass, was served up a greasy fry for tea when he had specifically ordered fish because it was healthier. On the third day he refused to eat it when they wouldn't give him what he had ordered and went without eating on principle. I was vegetarian and so was served cheese on crackers and cheese sandwiches (fake cheese slices on white bread) for all but two meals. They brought one of the two nicer meals when I was fasting and not allowed to eat it. My suspicion is that the catering has been privatized, although I could be wrong. The staff, apart from one really nasty nurse, were lovely.

Should I blame anyone for my hard luck? I've thought about it over the last year and have tried to be reasonable about it. After all, I waited to get Christmas over with before I phoned the hospital for a second time asking to be seen. But today, when I heard that a very nice man who was in the same, if not worse condition, than me when he went to his GP is going to live because he had private health insurance and I'm going to die because I didn't, I had to bite my tongue. I'm happy he's going to live. He deserves to live. But so do I. Then I came home and watched that ad which told people to hurry up and get checked out for bowel cancer because it will save their lives, and I fucking lost it.

I've finally reached the angry stage, I guess. Who am I angry at? I'll tell you, Joe. The health service has been in the hands of Fianna Fáil and the PDs for years and all they can think to do is put resources into privatization. They don't have the ability to change structures in the public sector that would put more resources towards patient care. But it's not just the politicians. I'm also angry at every single voter who voted for Fianna Fáil and the PDs because they thought they'd get a few more shillings in their pockets but were too greedy and stupid to realize that that money they saved in wage taxes would be made up with stealth taxes. We all knew before the last election what their health policies were, and the majority of people ignored this and voted for them anyway. Maybe they thought this would never happen to them. Or maybe because so many have private health insurance they just didn't care because they were all right, Jack.

I never dreamed I'd get cancer, let alone die from it. But I was wrong. My message to anyone with symptoms of bowel cancer is, go to your GP immediately. If you, like me, don't have health insurance, pester them until they hate you, go to your politicians and beg them to help, go to the media, get a solicitor to threaten to sue the government and the hospital if they don't get you in soon for a colonoscopy. Otherwise, the people who love you might lose you and you'll not get to do all the things you planned in life.

I'm writing to you because the way this country is run leads me to believe that contacting a radio show is the only way to try to change things like this. I hope that when Ms SUV and Mr Builder go into the voting booth, they'll think about me, my husband and especially my children. My husband is a decent man. He works full time in a good job and I worked part time in a job I loved that helped people, but didn't pay well. It depended on government money to help women and children in crisis, so of course couldn't pay me well. We know what Bertie, Michael, Micheál and Mary's priorities are.

Despite 1½ incomes, we couldn't afford VHI or Bupa. But even if we could have, we wouldn't have gotten it because we believed (and still do) that all people should get good care despite their incomes. We thought jumping queues was wrong. We're socialists . . . just like Bertie. Ha Ha. Now I feel like vomiting and it's not the chemo!

From a Cancer Patient in Kilkenny.

We contacted Susie, and she agreed to go on the programme. She told her story, adopting the pseudonym 'Rosie', because her two teenage children were not fully aware of the dire prognosis. By the end of that programme, I was convinced that we should get Susie to read out the letter in full on air the next day. We asked her, she did, and it was one of the most powerful broadcasts I have ever heard.

Susie's story was by far the clearest, most searing illustration of the two-tier health system that had ever emerged in Ireland, and it rocketed through the public's imagination. It unleashed an avalanche of calls, with harrowing stories of people without private health insurance having to queue for necessary care. Is there any greater indictment of the inequality in our society than this two-tier health system, which has been consolidated during the last fifteen years?

As the weeks unfolded, Susie's condition was worsening. Her delayed diagnosis meant her next hospital stay would be in a hospice. But she continued to be a stalwart contributor to the programme. Six weeks after her initial call, she spoke again on *Liveline*, having decided to 'go public' and reveal her real name. She had spoken to her children Feargal and Aine and her ever-supportive husband Conor. She was buoyed by the level of support she had gathered – and the personal release she felt – following the initial broadcast.

During the programme we heard from philosopher John Moriarty, one of the most inspirational people I have ever met. I had first come across John back in the 1980s when a close friend of mine, Eoin Cooke, alerted me to his television programme, *The Blackbird and the Bell*. John was mesmeric; no other word could describe his radio presence and late-night television appearances. To me, he brought us to a new level of thinking, even transcendence. Since he had first been a guest on *Liveline*, alongside Professor Gerard Casey, in a discussion about the topic of happiness, John had become a regular on the programme, the timbre of his voice and his command of language making an instant connection with listeners. But then tragedy struck in February 2006 when he revealed on *Liveline* that he had been diagnosed with cancer.

Exactly a year later, John Moriarty and Susie Long spoke together on *Liveline* about their common battle. It was powerful, uplifting and deeply moving: two people who knew they would be dead by year's end openly talking about life. It wasn't maudlin, awkward or intrusive, but a rare glimpse of the depths of our humanity. John died on 1 June 2007.

I visited Susie in Our Lady's Hospice in Harold's Cross, Dublin. Meeting her in person for the first time, I was struck by how feisty she was. She was as bright and intelligent as I expected, if not even more so. Susie told me more about her life. Born in Ohio, shortly after finishing high school she had moved to Dublin alone in 1984, disillusioned by Reagan's America. She became involved in Amnesty International and left-wing politics, and met her future husband, Conor, on Grafton Street. She spoke of her love of Bob Dylan, her work for the women's refuge in Kilkenny and her belief in green politics.

The first thing Susie campaigned for in the hospice was a vegetarian option on the menu. The hospice chef visited her and came up with options, which I presume have remained on the menu. On a practical level, all we could offer were deliveries of her favourite vegetarian meals from the Bombay Pantry near by.

During Susie's final weeks, I was meeting her husband Conor more often, as Susie's visits were, rightly, limited to family. But her death, early on Saturday, 12 October 2007, still came as a shock.

Susie was one of the most remarkable people I have ever met. She had a large coterie of friends and family in Kilkenny and back home in the US. On principle, she refused to support or endorse a two-tier health service. When she became unwell she still would not sign up for private health care; of course, with a 'pre-existing' illness, she had not a hope in hell of being accepted into the VHI or Bupa.

She knew she was dying because of the system. She took part in whatever publicity she thought was needed, but she did not overdo, hype or manipulate her illness. Truly, her dignity and fortitude were stunning. What unimaginable pain she must have endured; what suffering and grief her family must have faced, and still face. I see Susie Long as being in the tradition of brave, ordinary, decent people who put cause before comfort. From our own heroes such as James Connolly to her fellow Americans Rosa Parks and Martin Luther King, Susie Long towers among us.

Whatever we say about the impact of Susie's story, the bottom line is that she is dead, swept away at forty-two. Truly a story from the rotten heart of the Celtic Tiger.

I had predicted that Brendan Gleeson's words on *The Late Late Show* would ring clear through to the election in 2007. But I was wrong; even after Susie Long's powerful letter, that election just turned into what every election had become for the past two decades: an 'advance auction of stolen goods', as the American journalist H. L. Mencken described them. It was a delusional election, a distraction from the real issues facing the country. A&E units didn't even get a mention.

But Susie's struggle did bring to the fore campaigners who are still among us. I first met Janette Byrne in

Ballymun in 1976 when I was running the Tír Na nÓg youth club, but I did not hear from her again until the A&E stories emerged in the early 2000s. Janette had been struck down by cancer and wanted publicly to describe how she had been treated, as well as her own mother's horrific experiences in A&E. She and her family, together with the Mulreany family, formed the lobby group Patients Together. From a working-class background, with little education or connections in the media or otherwise, Janette is a stunning communicator. When Susie Long raised issues, Janette was first in line to support her. She stood up and persevered in the face of a lot of opposition, including from some parts of the media. Incredibly, at one stage, a consultant asked her mother to move hospital, saying he felt unable to treat her because of the 'adverse' publicity her daughter was generating.

Janette Byrne is a heroine, and I am proud that I helped facilitate powerful broadcasts by her. I can say the same for cystic fibrosis campaigners such as Orla Tinsley and Gillian McNulty (about whom more below), clerical-abuse victim Andrew Madden, institutional-abuse survivor Michael O'Brien and donor-card advocate Frank Deasy, not to mention Susie Long and her husband Conor MacLiam.

Exactly one year after Susie Long made her call to *Liveline*, young cystic fibrosis sufferers took over the programme for a whole week to make a riveting, searing plea that struck deep into the heart of the nation. Strangely, it was the tragic death from drugs of model Katy French on 6 December 2007 that inadvertently ignited the firestorm of anger and outrage over the treatment of cystic fibrosis sufferers in Ireland.

I was reading the *Irish Times* in January 2008 and came across an article by Orla Tinsley, a young CF sufferer who had written before on the topic. I was struck by the bravery of her piece. Orla listed her young female friends – many the same age as Katy French – who had died quietly and unheralded, except of course by their family and friends, while the rest of Ireland, if you were to believe many of the newspapers, was consumed by the tragic loss of a beautiful young woman, one of Ireland's top models.

Moved by Orla's article, when I went down to studio at twelve forty to 'promo' *Liveline*, I simply read out the following paragraph:

As the public mourned Katy French and the lens on cocaine in Ireland started to get focused, I thought wildly that maybe if I got engaged and broke up with a slightly well-known person, did some lingerie modelling and then died, if I fought off my illness long enough, maybe something would be done. Maybe the Taoiseach's aide-de-camp would come to a cystic fibrosis funeral and see something he would remember, something that he might report back.

Within minutes, we were getting calls from young people, primarily women, who were suffering from cystic fibrosis. As soon as the programme started, it was clear to me that a volcano of pain, disappointment and betrayal had finally erupted.

Ireland has the highest rate of cystic fibrosis in the world. Apparently, it's in our Celtic DNA; indeed, one in nineteen Irish people carry the CF gene, something only spotted by screening, which is not widely available here. The average lifespan of a CF sufferer in Northern Ireland is ten years longer than someone living in the Republic. Indeed, in Canada, the average lifespan of a sufferer is forty-seven; in Ireland, it is twenty-one.

The simple demand of CF sufferers and their families is for individual en-suite rooms in hospital, which means that the life-threatening risk of infection is reduced significantly. Radio is an ideal medium for CF sufferers to tell their stories, as they are not allowed to meet each other for fear of infection. That week on *Liveline*, a group of young women emerged who lambasted the politicians and exposed maladministration in the HSE and hospitals. These young women knew, as sure as their young lives were ebbing away, that they could console each other and ensure that younger CF sufferers coming after them would not endure what they had to.

A week of searing and memorable stories, dominated by the breathless sounds of sufferers coughing uncontrollably, did have a major national impact. Anita Slowey, who rang us on the eve of her twenty-first birthday, noted that this milestone only brought her nearer to the life expectancy for CF sufferers in the Republic.

Anita died three weeks after her twenty-fourth birthday.

I refused a request to participate in *The Late Late Show* the following Friday, believing that my presence would only dilute the power of the sufferers and campaigners. I don't go along with the notion that my voice calling on the minister or the HSE to act adds much; it is the people who are directly affected who speak with the strongest voices.

A promise was extracted from the government to build a unit in the grounds of St Vincent's Hospital, the main national centre for adult CF sufferers, which would have individual rooms with en-suite facilities, to be completed by late 2010. This was January 2008. Despite constant campaigning, revisited on the programme on a number of occasions, the issue erupted again in October 2010, when we were contacted by CF patients in St Vincent's telling us once again of being corralled into six-bed wards with geriatric patients, some with dementia, whose erratic behaviour was exacerbating the condition of the young CF sufferers.

Gillian McNulty, Anita Slowey, Sacha Delaney and Orla Tinsley simply wanted a date for the turning of the sod and the arrival of construction machinery. After all, the date for the *completion* of the unit had arrived and building had not even started. During the same period, the state had spent €120 million building a new award-winning courts complex in central Dublin, which, by the way, has en-suite bathrooms and showers for every judge – none of whom, thankfully, has cystic fibrosis. Indeed, given that you usually have to be in your forties before you are appointed to the bench, very few if any CF sufferers ever reach that ripe old age.

It is shameful to watch the elite of this country, from the politicians to the judiciary, shell out our money on unwanted bidets, embroidered drapes, pointless tunnels under the Dáil and untrammelled personal pampering while young CF sufferers cough up pints of blood and tearfully support each other on the national airwaves in their dying days. All for the want of a basic en-suite room.

CHAPTER 28

Crime and Punishment

At the end of that awful year, 2007, we decided to do a full programme of poetry and reflection in the days leading up to Christmas. I asked Father Brian D'Arcy to say a prayer on the programme for those connected to *Liveline* who had died during the previous twelve months or so. Of course, I wanted Susie Long and John Moriarty mentioned, but there were two other callers to *Liveline* who had been brutally murdered subsequently: Baiba Saulite and John Daly.

Baiba Saulite, an immigrant from Latvia, had contacted *Liveline* on 6 January 2005 looking for help. Her sons had been abducted by her estranged husband in a custody row. Baiba made a very emotional appeal for the return of her two children, Ali and Mohammed, whom she believed were still in Ireland. Baiba received a lot of newspaper coverage after her *Liveline* appearance, posing with photographs of her two missing 'babies'. She did get her children back, and her

Lebanese husband Hassan Hassan subsequently pleaded guilty to their abduction. Hassan was sentenced to four years in prison in March 2006 for his part in exporting stolen cars to the Middle East. He was then sentenced to a further two years in December 2006 for the abduction.

On Sunday night, 19 November 2006, Baiba was brutally murdered as she stood at her hall door in Swords while her two young children slept in an upstairs bedroom. At that time in Ireland, we were enduring a gangland hit every two weeks on average, and the shooting in Swords was immediately bracketed into the same category. But once Baiba's name emerged, the savagery of the murder came into full focus.

Listening back to Baiba's plea, and her expressions of love for her two boys, during her *Liveline* call was heartbreaking. We replayed it in the hope that someone, somewhere, might know who ordered and carried out the assassination. Friends of Baiba pleaded with the public to come forward with information.

Baiba was buried in Latvia. I was subsequently asked by a local priest to do a short reading at a memorial service for her. It was a moving, understated service. The authorities refused to release her husband temporarily from Mountjoy to attend the service, though in the middle of the obsequies members of Hassan's family left flowers and a card at the foot of her coffin.

Nobody has yet been charged with Baiba's murder. In 2010, Hassan Hassan was released from Portlaoise

Prison, and it is believed he returned to his native Lebanon with his children.

Hassan Hassan's name also appeared in the papers when he was charged in December 2008 for having a mobile phone in his cell. The clampdown on mobile phones ironically began after an ill-fated phone call to *Liveline* from John Daly, an inmate in Portlaoise Prison, in May 2007, once again in the middle of that fateful election.

It was my interest in the Sheriff Street feud that led to this infamous incident, which shocked many people, sparked the minister for justice into action and apparently played a part in John Daly's subsequent assassination. The 'feud' had begun when one criminal, Christy Griffin, was sent to prison for raping an under-age girl over an eight-year period. Apparently, his allies split into two groups and began a deadly war which centred on a very tightly knit community in a small geographical area.

I had once spent a Trinity summer working as a youth leader in the local playground on Sheriff Street, and I had attended mass in the local church on a number of occasions, as a priest friend of mine was ministering there at the time. At one point, I spoke from the pulpit about the benefits of education. Thereafter, I was asked by Christy Burke, a local councillor, if I would allow my name to be used as part of a small group that would try to mediate in the dispute.

I read in the *Sunday World* in 2007 that its crime

editor, Paul Williams, believed that Christy Burke was a friend of Christy Griffin, so I suggested we ask both Paul Williams and Christy Burke to come on *Liveline*. They did, with Christy Burke denying he was a friend of Griffin (the *Sunday World* subsequently accepted this and apologized) and challenging the newspaper's contention that the republican movement had links with gangland crime. The argument became fairly animated. Then Alan 'Fatpuss' Bradley phoned in from his home in Finglas, accusing Williams of making false allegations against him and his family.

As this three-way phone row was being broadcast, producer Margaret Curley told me in my earpiece that a 'John Daly' was on the line from Portlaoise Prison. He had phoned a few minutes previously and, as we always do, we called him back on the number given – Daly had asked us to wait for a couple of minutes, as the signal was better on the other side of the cell! I had previously heard Daly's name mentioned in relation to crime in Finglas, but I knew little more about him.

John Daly admitted from the outset that he was phoning from inside Portlaoise Prison. He said a quick 'hello' to Alan Bradley, denied that there was a feud between them and thanked him for the postcard from a recent holiday. In florid language, he accused Paul Williams of trying to 'kick off a gang war'. I was determined at that moment just to keep my mouth shut and let Daly talk away, which he did for another five minutes, until he told me 'I can't stay long, I'm in a cell.' At that point, running feet could be heard in the background as prison officers came looking for the mobile phone, and John Daly hung up abruptly.

I knew it was unusual to get a call from inside a prison, but it wasn't the first time. Only a few weeks earlier, an inmate had phoned from Cloverhill to participate in a discussion on drugs. (Incidentally, he was agreeing with my long-standing contention that there is no such thing as a happy drug addict.) Following John Daly's call, Paul Williams commented on air that mobile phones were tolerated in Portlaoise Prison.

However, while I knew there would be newspaper coverage of Daly's call, I was unprepared for the reaction of RTÉ management at the time. We were sitting in the radio centre coffee shop for our daily debriefing when I was approached by Ian Noctor, who had been appointed a year previously as editor of current affairs in the station, having previously been head of communications for the Progressive Democrats. I had had few if any dealings with him. In a rather peremptory fashion, in front of the *Liveline* team, he instructed me to come into his office. I asked him what the purpose of the meeting was; he told me it was about the 'Daly phone call'. I reminded him that the series producer of the programme was beside me and I would be attending all meetings on programme content with her.

Ian Noctor then told me that the office of the minister for justice, Michael McDowell, had been in contact. The minister was outraged that RTÉ had allowed the call on air and he was demanding a right of reply. I was shocked when he informed me that Michael McDowell wanted to come into studio to rebut what was said on the programme about mobile phones in prisons.

The following day, the head of the prison service, Brian Purcell, who was himself once a victim of the infamous General's criminal gang, participated in *Liveline*, refuting what Paul Williams had said about the availability of mobile phones in Portlaoise. After that programme, we were told that the minister for justice would be on air in the studio from the start of the programme the next day about the issue, and would not take phone calls.

This was unprecedented on *Liveline*. Firstly, we seldom if ever have contributors in the studio, save in exceptional circumstances (for instance, once, when a cystic fibrosis sufferer left her sick bed in St Vincent's Hospital and arrived in the radio centre begging to be allowed to talk about the awful conditions there). Secondly, we always insist that all contributors are open to listener interaction; it is, after all, the bedrock of the programme. But it was made clear to us that the decision of the management was final. Everybody on the *Liveline* team was outraged.

I was tempted to resign. I felt that this was direct party-political interference in *Liveline*. I asked friends what I should do; the advice from one was: 'Choose your battles carefully.' There was a febrile atmosphere nationally, in the middle of an election, and they urged me: 'Don't lose the run of yourself,' adding, 'You're only a radio presenter!' I took the point.

So, the following day at 1.45, Michael McDowell marched in, obviously angered, and immediately stated on air that the allegations made about the regime in Portlaoise Prison were totally untrue. He was adamant that the prison regime was not lax, and that there was absolutely no tolerance of mobile phones being held by prisoners. I had made a decision not to 'rise' to the minister's arguments and simply let him talk. I was of the opinion that this was simply a party-political broadcast in the run-up to an election. I waited and waited, and eventually asked the minister for justice if he was finished. When he said he was, I said goodbye.

Of course, within weeks, hundreds of these non-existent mobile phones were confiscated from Irish prisons – along with plasma TVs and various other treasures, including a budgie!

John Daly was released from prison in August 2007 and murdered as he was getting out of a taxi eight weeks later; he was twenty-seven. When I saw the screaming headline on that day's *Evening Herald*, I got a shock: '*Liveline* Caller Shot Dead'.

I sent a card to his mother and sister; the latter spoke on the programme subsequently, and said that she didn't know if his phone call from his prison cell had contributed to his murder. But it is something I wonder and worry about to this day.

A few years earlier, in September 2003, I had spotted a very small piece in the *Sunday Business Post* about the upcoming Royal Hibernian Academy Art Exhibition, which mentioned that a new portrait of convicted killer Brian Meehan was to be shown and auctioned. The painting was executed by Mick O'Dea, a brilliant, well-respected artist who also happened to be a teacher in Portlaoise Prison, where Meehan was serving a life sentence for the murder of journalist Veronica Guerin seven years previously.

I had reported daily on Meehan's trial for *5-7 Live*, and I had no doubt that Meehan, Dutchy Holland and others were involved in the murder of the young journalist. That Brian Meehan should 'pose' for hours for his portrait by one of the country's foremost artists was sickening to me; that it should be offered for sale was mind-boggling. So, without hesitation, I mentioned this in the 'promo' I did with Ronan Collins at twelve forty that Monday.

The phones immediately lit up. We tried to get Mick O'Dea to come on the programme, but he declined, as did the organizers of the exhibition. But I was determined to highlight this insensitivity and, above all, to ensure that Meehan's portrait did not adorn some gangster's pimped-up pad. I later went into the Gallagher Gallery in Ely Place to see the painting, which convinced me even more that it should not be put up for sale. It portrayed a strident, defiant poser who was obviously wallowing in the prestige of being asked to pose for a portrait.

Sure enough, when people like Detective Gerry O'Carroll lent their voices and genuine outrage on *Liveline*, there was little doubt that the painting would not be offered for sale. The RHA withdrew the painting and *Liveline*, scourge of the powerful and the elite, had made yet more enemies. The usual commentators came out in force to say that the programme was anti-art – an insult to me personally.

Obviously, a programme like *Liveline*, which gives a voice to the powerless, does raise the ire of the judiciary from time to time. But the criticism by Judge Paul Carney has been hard to take. He criticized *Liveline* generally and me in particular in 2007 on two public occasions in relation to the 2005 Robert Holohan manslaughter trial. Wayne O'Donoghue, a near-neighbour of the 11-year-old victim, was eventually convicted by Judge Carney of the manslaughter in one of the most high-profile trials in recent years. He served three years in prison.

The then series producer, Margaret Curley, sent our only researcher on *Liveline* to the trial's final days. Because we have no reporting resources, we usually rely on listeners if a verdict comes in during our programme, but this was an exceptional case of public interest.

Speaking at a conference a few months later, Justice Carney had a go at me. 'Finally we got an interesting insight into how Mr Joe Duffy operates. In the explosive atmosphere after sentence being imposed, in ignorance of who he was, one of Mr Duffy's researchers approached a court official looking for a comment. This shatters the myth of Mr Duffy being a kindly old gentleman who sits by his telephone in Dublin waiting for it to ring.'

I wasn't there, so I don't know who said what to whom; but then again, Judge Carney wasn't there either. Apparently, our researcher did talk to a number of people and told them that we were covering the story on *Liveline*, asking them if they wanted to participate. This was not a problem as far as I was concerned. One of the people in the crowd happened to be a court official. The 'explosive atmosphere' after the manslaughter trial related to Majella Holohan's victim impact statement.

I chose not to respond to the judge then; after all, the Holohan family's grief should not be deflected by petty arguments. But Judge Carney revisited his 'kindly old gentleman' comments at another lecture some time later, and the *Sunday Independent* made hay out of them. Quoting unnamed sources, the *Sunday Independent* claimed that 'behind the scenes in RTÉ there is concern at the regularity with which *Liveline* fails to adhere to its marketed purpose as a phone-in programme' and whistled up a government spokesperson who said the criticism by Judge Carney 'must be taken seriously'.

Now, anyone who thinks that a serious programme on the national radio station could be simply based on taking phone calls and putting listeners on air has never worked in radio. We have producers whose first mammoth task is to decide which calls do not go on air. The decision about how to handle calls and why we deal with particular issues at particular times is also a critical part of the production process. *Liveline* does not have two million listeners each week by accident; we vary topics, try to pick the issues that will interest listeners and generate calls, while adding previous information or callers if needed. But live daily radio is the most transparent medium there is; false emotion and tricky editing will be spotted rapidly by listeners.

By the way, a couple of years later, *Liveline* featured in another court case, coincidentally also heard by Judge Paul Carney. On 13 March 2007, rape victim Mary Shannon phoned *Liveline*. Her assailant, Adam Keane, who had just been given a three-year suspended sentence, jeered, sneered and flipped a lit cigarette at her on her train journey home to Clare. Once Judge Carney heard about this incident, which was in clear breach of Keane's suspended sentence, he immediately brought him back to court and sent him to prison.

Another episode in May 2006 garnered me even more criticism from the bench, and quite a few 'liberal commentators' stuck the boot into *Liveline* while they were at it. The Supreme Court handed down a ruling that the law which stated that a man is automatically guilty of an offence if he has sex with a girl under seventeen was flawed. The court argued that there was a failure to allow the defence of 'genuine mistake'. The effect of this ruling was that all those sentenced to prison for having sex with an underage girl could argue that they had not been allowed this defence, so they would have to be freed – a massive legal loophole.

Initially, the politicians argued that it would not be interpreted in this way; but the following Tuesday, a

38-year-old man, 'Mr A', who was in prison for having sex with a 12-year-old girl, was brought before the High Court and freed under this loophole. This 'appalling vista' had been flagged the day before on *Liveline* by a caller, Monica Roe, who foresaw all child abusers being freed.

Looking at the screen that Tuesday, I knew from the number of callers who had been victims of child sexual abuse that a Pandora's box had been opened. The victims invariably argued that their assailants should finish their sentences. The rest of the programme was devoted to the issue. Monica Roe came back on the line to call for a protest march, a plea she had also made on *The Gerry Ryan Show* that morning.

Now, hardly a week goes by without some caller with a legitimate concern wanting to organize a demonstration, but I normally shy away from the demand. Simply put, it is incredibly hard to organize a public protest, especially for a weekday afternoon, and there are so many logistics involved, from Gardaí to public address systems, that it is too daunting a task. Most importantly, it is very hard to get a good attendance, leaving the organizers dispirited and some sections of the media gleeful! But Monica Roe was adamant that she wanted to proceed with a protest outside the Dáil, seventy-two hours later. We decided there and then to let her use the programme as a platform.

One victim knew that her own assailant, Simon Murphy from Ramsgrange in Wexford, was about to enter the High Court to seek his release under the loophole. She called *Liveline* and aired her distress at the situation and the effect it was having on her. It emerged that the judge in question, Justice Barry White, had been listening to the programme, but could not be swayed by it, as 'that would be repugnant to the oath I made in the Supreme Court on my appointment'. He did, however, put the case back to Friday afternoon at five.

Monica Roe decided to hold her 'white ribbon protest' outside the Dáil that Friday. Offers of free public address systems, lorries and other support flooded in. On Wednesday and Thursday, we broadcast more stories and updates on the organization of the demonstrations, which were gathering momentum by the hour.

By Friday afternoon at two o'clock, three thousand people – mainly women – had gathered in Dublin, and there were upwards of twenty other demonstrations at the same time around the country. We spoke to someone at nearly every protest and, through the programme, allowed the mother of the 12-year-old victim of Mr A (who was now free) to thank the protesters for their support.

That same afternoon, the Supreme Court overturned its decision. Mr A was promptly re-arrested, and it was left to a bewildered Dáil to sort out the loopholes.

But the vitriol that awaited me had to be read to be believed. I was genuinely shocked and embarrassed two days later to see the opinion piece on the front page of the *Sunday Independent* written by Brendan O'Connor which declared, 'We're all clowns in Duffy's circus.' It was an outrageous piece that accused *Liveline* of being 'a witch-hunt which in order to survive needs someone who is prepared to say something really crazy about someone else, the crazier the better for *Liveline* and Joe Duffy'.

It was one of many articles in the paper on the subject, all in the same tone; one even argued that Michael McDowell was 'a little tin man whose standards are set by the moral wasteland of Joe Duffy's nauseating leadership circus'.

CHAPTER 29

Crowd Control

FROM THE MUCK AND MADNESS AT THE BARBRA Streisand concert in Castletown House to the chaotic scenes at the Oasis Slane concert in 2009, *Liveline* has covered it all – but not in glory. As Barbra herself would sing – if she could have been heard above the pelting rain and irate punters clamouring to find their €270 seats – we've got nothing to be guilty of. I am more than happy that Irish people see *Liveline* as a quasi-ombudsman where they can lodge complaints when they feel they are not being listened to by the powers that be.

Irish punters, who often pay the highest prices for concert tickets in Europe, sometimes have a lot to complain about. The promoters usually choose one of three ways to react to calls from *Liveline*. Some try to ignore us completely, but that doesn't work. Some companies issue a bland statement, just as the banks do all the time, knowing full well that I won't waste the listeners' time reading out inanities. The third option is for them to come on air, which some do, ignoring the advice of their expensive public relations companies, and more times than not, they come out of it well.

Actually, there is a fourth route some companies take: sending us long, expensive solicitors' letters, usually rambling on about something that was never even alleged and sidestepping the main issue raised by our callers: can we have our money back, please?

The Barbra Streisand outdoor concert on 15 July 2007 was set to be a great occasion: one of the world's greatest singers, in the middle of an Irish summer, in the magnificent grounds of one of Ireland's greatest houses. Unfortunately, events conspired to derail the project, not least the typical Irish midsummer monsoon, and the roadworks and chaos at an untried venue.

Having shelled out up to €270 for a ticket, the least punters could have hoped for was a decent level of organization, from transport to seating. Having worked in daily frontline live radio for twenty-three years, I can at this stage spot the difference between a handful of complaints and a tsunami. When we rang the concert promoter, MCD, about the complaints, we were given the usual mantra: 'This was due to a small number of opportunistic fans taking seats which were not assigned to them and refusing to move when requested by authorities.'

MCD refused to come on air to answer the numerous complaints from concert-goers. But a few months later, when Justin Green, the public face of MCD, came on the programme to talk about another innocuous issue, I decided to ask him about the Barbra Streisand debacle. He was livid at this 'ambush' and undertook never to come on the programme again. In fairness, Justin Green and MCD eventually did compensate disgruntled ticket-holders, once they could prove their case.

The chaos at the Oasis concert at Slane in 2009 was another good example of how promoters react to *Liveline*. On Sunday morning, 21 June, I received a number of texts from friends who had been at the concert and thought it was dangerous. In particular, the complaints focused on the surge of people getting into the concert and the chaotic scenes at the end when buses disappeared.

Again, MCD refused to participate in the programme and immediately sent in a solicitor's letter. They used the same excuse as they had for the Barbra Streisand concert: that it was just a small number of complaints. When I did make one clarification the next day, MCD immediately issued a press statement saying *Liveline* had apologized.

As our callers repeatedly pointed out, ticket scanning was abandoned at one stage due to the crowd surge at the 'Dublin entrance' to the venue. Lord Henry Mountcharles, the owner of Slane Castle, came on *Liveline* and clearly indicated that he was 'far from happy' about the organization of the gig.

A subsequent court case between MCD and one of its senior employees, Sophie Ridley, the event controller at

Slane, demonstrated that there were serious safety concerns on the day. Ridley was subsequently dismissed by MCD, but claimed she was being scapegoated for problems at the concert. She took her employer to court for unfair dismissal and they settled before a verdict was reached.

One event in which I was directly involved did go smoothly from a crowd control point of view, but it is widely regarded as a disaster for me. Will we ever forget the 2002 World Cup in Japan? I won't.

Roy Keane, the captain of the Irish soccer team, walked out during the tournament preparations in Saipan because of his unhappiness with the management and facilities. There were many casualties from this debacle, and I was one of them. *Liveline* was at the heart of the debate for and against the manager Mick McCarthy and Roy Keane. You were either on one side or the other; there was no in-between. *Liveline* lit up for weeks over the controversy, while Roy stayed at home in the UK walking his dog, Triggs, and the rest of the team battled on. Ireland got knocked out in the second round, which, after the triumph of reaching the quarter-finals of Italia 1990, was a disappointment, though, in retrospect, looking at our absence from the last two World Cup finals, maybe we were a lot better than we gave ourselves credit for.

Our crunch game in 2002 was to be on Sunday, 16 June, when we faced Spain. The previous day, I was with the kids at a rugby training session when I got a call from the RTÉ sports department to ask if I would do live TV inserts before and after the Spanish game from the home of Damien Duff, Ireland's star player. My initial reaction was negative. But I had interviewed Damien's dad, Gerard, on *Liveline* and knew he was a very decent man who would give me a warm welcome, and the family had agreed to the TV intrusion.

Of course, my downfall in television has always been my inability to say no, so the following morning I turned up at the Duff family home in Stepaside. I was there way too early and spent most of the morning just sitting in the car as the family got on with their normal life. As I had predicted, I was given two one-minute inserts into the studio, with some nice words from Damien's parents, especially his mother, Mary, who revealed that she put a Padre Pio medal in Damien's football boots and that Ireland's star player had a special devotion to the saint-to-be with the stigmata.

As it happened, Damien had a wonderful game, performing magnificently on the right wing. His compadre Robbie Keane smashed home a penalty with twenty seconds of full time remaining to bring us level. The two of them were on fire against Spain and the game ended with a 1–1 draw after extra time before, sadly, we were knocked out on penalties. But it was a magnificent afternoon.

So our team were coming home. On Monday, I had a strange sense of foreboding that I was going to be asked to participate in the homecoming celebrations planned for Tuesday. By Monday morning, Dublin City Council was insisting that the event must not happen in the city centre but in the Phoenix Park. In terms of atmosphere, I thought this was a bad, bad idea, but the event was planned for the next day, so there was little chance of debate.

The whole shadow of the Saipan disaster was hanging over the event: the nation was divided and we had been knocked out. What would the reaction of the crowd be? Some argued that there should be no official 'party'; after all, we had not even won a game! So when I got the call from TV producer John Blackman, who was hastily organizing the live televising of the homecoming event, I bluntly asked him if the players were supportive of it. He told me that the Football Association of Ireland (FAI) had reassured him that the players would co-operate.

After that, things moved rapidly. I was to share the onstage duties with sports reporter Peter Collins. My role, in so far as I got any instruction, was to play to the crowd. I had asked John Blackman if I could bring radio producer Anne Farrell with me. I knew she would be brilliant at spotting angles and backstage organizing. I have not done much sports reporting, but I do know that, with a few exceptions, professional soccer players are paid for their football skills, not for their ability to communicate. That evening, I did a crash course in the Irish soccer team with my brother Peter and my brother-in-law, Patrick Meehan, both experts. I did up detailed 'cards' with photos and biographies of each player for my own reference.

After finishing *Liveline* on that Tuesday afternoon, I was surprised to be met by a team of Garda outriders who escorted me at great speed from Montrose to the Phoenix Park. This was very enjoyable for someone like me, obsessed with fire engines and Garda sirens, but it was a bit over the top nevertheless.

Over a hundred thousand people had turned up for the homecoming. When we arrived backstage in the Park, Westlife were just finishing a short concert, but the players were still over in Áras an Uachtaráin, and there was nobody from the FAI to be found. I was ushered onstage just as the team bus was arriving. I knew immediately that things were not all happy in the camp when one of the squad, alighting from the bus, told a young autograph hunter to 'fuck off'! They had endured a long flight home, welcomes at the airport and the Áras, and I think a couple of them were understandably tired and the worse for wear.

Then it struck me: these guys were living in dread of the type of reception they would get from the public. Would chants of 'Keano, Keano', in honour of the absent captain, come swirling from the crowd? Might they even be booed as they went onstage? I grabbed a couple of players backstage, who recoiled at the prospect of speaking on TV and nervously pointed to other players as I asked for volunteers. It's hard to describe the fear on their faces, or the anxiety in my stomach.

The FAI had asked me to introduce the players one by one, but it quickly became obvious that the players felt this might facilitate individual booing, so they just walked onstage en masse. I named every player out of courtesy anyway. I spoke to Damien Duff, who was standing beside me, and he visibly shied away at the prospect of being interviewed. I asked him about his mother's comments about the Padre Pio medal inside his football boots. He looked baffled; I might as well have told him he had poo on his shoe!

I knew Shay Given was affable, so I headed for him next. 'Given by name, Given by nature,' I intoned in honour of one of our stars of the competition, but my brilliant wit was lost in translation. Having discovered that it was Jason McAteer's thirty-first birthday, I asked Shay if he would lead the crowd in a rendition of that old Donegal number, 'Happy Birthday to You'.

The event was turning into a shambles. It was clear at this stage that the players simply were highly un-comfortable with the whole homecoming, while I was sitting in a metaphorical JCB digging a small landfill site.

I asked Robbie Keane to say a few words of thanks to the crowd. 'What do you want me to say?' responded Robbie. Oh Jaysus, I thought, get me out of here. Still, I soldiered on manfully – or kept digging, depending on your point of view.

In fairness, Mick McCarthy gave the crowd a decent thank-you. But I felt that the families present – includ-ing my own – had been short-changed. They had left home shortly after 1 p.m. and trekked a long distance to get a less than enthusiastic response from the players they looked up to. In my own mind, I blamed the FAI for not having the team on side for the celebrations. Nobody from the organization approached me before or after the event.

We mingled for a few drinks in a hospitality tent afterwards, but even then word was filtering through that the panel back in studio – Eamon Dunphy, John Giles and Ray Houghton – were already rubbishing my performance. Indeed, Dunphy wrote an especially nasty piece the following Sunday, comparing the similar backgrounds of myself and Robbie Keane and concluding that I was not worthy. I remember reading it halfway through and simply being so demoralized I threw down the paper, went off on holiday with my three seven-year-olds and seethed with anger in a small, sweltering mobile home in France for the fortnight.

I also felt I was hung out to dry by the FAI. It was a badly organized event and, in hindsight, I should probably have said no. I feel I did my best, but I misjudged the worries of the players and was roundly lambasted. Anyway, it was only a football game. But Google Saipan 2002 and it's not just Roy Keane and Mick McCarthy who get it in the neck – watch my ugly face jump out at you for the 'homecoming disaster'!

CHAPTER 30

What a Waste

WHILE IT WAS FLATTERING TO BE ASKED BY TWO leaders of different political parties over the past two years to 'put on the jersey' and stand for elected office, I have never felt that I am entitled in any way to such an accolade. Neither would I be presumptuous enough to believe that a successful campaigning radio programme would in any way provide adequate credentials for public office.

I also believe that, while political parties and individual politicians get full credit for achievements, mainly due to our media obsession with party politics, for some people *Liveline* has made a big difference. I firmly believe that our democracy is helped by having a recognized 'public discourse' radio programme; there is no equivalent with such a big audience in the UK, for instance.

Let me give a simple example of this power at work. When working widows had their sick pay abolished by minister for social welfare Mary Coughlan in the 2002 budget, the women turned to *Liveline* to highlight their case, giving a platform to another forgotten group in Irish society – widows, many of them quite young. The social welfare diktat that no one could receive two payments from the department for the same week meant that working widows were in effect barred from receiving statutory sick pay if they fell ill. They protested over a number of weeks, and the minister changed her mind.

One day, we even managed – inadvertently – to wipe billions off the share value of GlaxoSmithKline, one of the biggest pharmaceutical companies in the world. After a long-running discussion about the effects of the antidepressant Seroxat, one listener spotted that the multinational had failed to update the information on its packaging. The Irish Medicine Board, normally a fairly conservative body, ordered all stocks of the expensive drug to be removed immediately, and this set off a worldwide scare about the medicine. GSK shares plummeted, but bounced back within hours as the scare abated.

Politicians, I am told, do listen to *Liveline*, but dare not admit that they are influenced by a 'phone-in show'. I steer clear of the Dáil and indeed events involving politicians; I think it is better that I am not unduly friendly with any of them. I know that sounds odd, but most people in the country don't have powerful friends; that is the unique selling point of *Liveline*, and I cannot sacrifice that for a few friendly drinks in Buswell's Hotel or Doheny and Nesbitt's!

I have no doubt that politicians believe that the best response to issues raised on the programme by the public is silence and, if they are ever asked about *Liveline*, they feign indifference. After all, the programme unrelentingly highlights waste, rampant expenses, inadequate Dáil sittings, so it is hardly going to be nominated as their favourite listening. By this stage, the whole country knows the issues that animated the public and featured constantly on *Liveline* for more than two years up to the February 2011 election. Ministerial perks and mercs, foreign travel, personal expenses, extravagant pensions, cronyism and perceived arrogance – the list is endless. The government was rubbing its manicured, gloved hands in glee as ministers and their lackeys flounced around the world happily spending the taxpayers' money. There is some misconception that knowledge and criticism of all of this largesse only emerged after the economy collapsed. Not so.

Well before the crash of 2008, there were signs of rot at the heart of the Celtic Tiger. Callers to *Liveline* in August 2008 highlighted the cost, for example, of the curtains in the Ceann Comhairle's office. The Office of Public Works shelled out eleven thousand Euros of taxpayers' money for a pair of French-made drapes in John O'Donoghue's office. One of our intrepid callers, a curtain maker, told us that, using her most expensive material, she could hand-sew a pair of curtains for less than eight hundred Euros. More astonishing figures soon emerged about the cost of installing a new throne – of a sanitary kind – in the Ceann Comhairle's en suite.

This immediately unleashed a plethora of revelations from callers, including retired Gardaí who had driven ministerial Mercedes and had found themselves sent by various ministers on jobs ranging from collecting shopping from supermarkets, picking up the ministers' children from school and, in one famous case, transporting a lone passenger – a dog – in a state car from Dublin to Kerry during the Christmas holidays. Listeners also pointed out that the new glass sweet shop inside the railings of the Dáil – for those lucky enough to get beyond the ornate gates without the aid of a cement mixer – had cost the taxpayer over one million Euros. Of course, the glass walls ensured that the chocolate on sale melted quickly, just like our taxes.

On top of this, the same party held control over the massive tax income during the boom. Given that higher house prices meant more stamp duty for the state, at one stage, according to then minister Tom Parlon, 40 per cent of the full cost of every house to the buyer went to the state – a pyramid scheme if ever there was one. Even on a relatively minor note, the annual property tax on holiday homes was due to be levied on mobile homes and caravans until an eagle-eyed *Liveline* listener spotted this and successfully led the campaign against it. It was promptly dropped in May 2009.

Waste and the economy in general is a constant issue on *Liveline*. For instance, Irish taxpayers spend one million Euros a week on a privatized – and very good – search-and-rescue helicopter service, but there are eleven helicopters in the Aer Corps that could equally be tasked with this life-saving job. Another example is the early retirement of Gardaí, firefighters, teachers and prison officers. Many of them do not want to leave, and the flight of experience is heartbreaking. Perfectly fit, healthy and able men and women in their early fifties are being let go.

Then there is taxi regulation. The regulator increased fares in December 2008 as the recession began, despite the massive opposition by drivers who contacted *Liveline*. A family of four sees the meter hit eight Euros before the engine even starts – lunacy. The 'premium rate' taxi fares operate for a greater part of each week than the standard fare. Meanwhile, in 2010 the taxi regulator had a surplus of tweny million Euros from licensing and applying penalties. Many taxi drivers have expressed serious concern about stress and the drop-off in business caused by the recession is not helping.

Need I mention PPARS (Personnel, Payroll and Related Systems), a computer program that ran the HSE's personnel section? Estimated at nine million Euros, it eventually cost €220 million and was ultimately abandoned because it did not work. Similarly, what was the motivation behind the government's attempt to replace our perfectly functional voting systems with an electronic system that never got off the ground? We spent €51 million buying the voting machines, on top of the obligatory fees to the blessed PR companies, and that does not even cover the cost of storing the seven thousand unusable machines.

Small businesses have taken their issues to *Liveline*, especially in recent times; they complain about high rents, local authority rates and numerous extra charges for waste, water and various 'licences' they are obliged to purchase from different government quangos. Our 'Fiver Friday' campaign in July 2011, encouraging listeners to spend an extra five Euros locally, was a direct result of the pleas from small businesses around the country.

Is there anything as scandalous as the punishment – monetary and psychological – inflicted on the heavily taxed Irish motorist by toll roads? The Dublin Port Tunnel cost €752 million to build. It is toll-free for trucks, but the family motorists whose taxes paid for it are priced out. And having been completed just in time for the recession, the tunnel is the quietest place in the capital. Meanwhile, a private company, National Toll Roads, built the Westlink Bridge over the Liffey at a cost of €58 million. They collected the tolls for twenty years, netting them one billion Euros. The government then 'bought' back the bridge and guaranteed NTR fifty million Euros every year until 2020, a €1.5 billion bonanza. Week after week, *Liveline* listeners railed at the delays on the M50, some workers spending an extra five hours a week on the road, and at the lunacy of the original deal, signed on behalf of the taxpayer by then government minister Padraig Flynn and city manager George Redmond. So, the toll plaza bunged up the motorway for eighteen years; the taxpayer 'bought' our bridge from the private developer; and we pay higher tolls. As one listener described it, for NTR it was like winning the Lotto.

Speaking of the Lotto, the real winners are not the punters who buy the tickets and against the odds actually win a prize but the politicians who happen to be elevated to the Department of Arts, Sports and Tourism – in charge of the National Lottery – and their constituents. I have banged on about this scandal over the years in my newspaper columns, and on *Liveline*, to the point of boredom. A group of academics in University College Cork analysed the allocation of money from the National Lottery and discovered that the ministers' constituencies benefited most, regardless of population or spend on the tickets. The home constituencies of the three most recent (Fianna Fáil) ministers did extraordinarily well per capita: Kerry (John O'Donoghue), Donegal (Jim McDaid) and Waterford (Martin Cullen) all received, on average, twice as much from the Lotto per head of population as the likes of Carlow and Meath, while Dublin, which has never had a minister in this department since the Lotto began, did not fare much better. The capital, especially working-class areas, is the biggest contributor to the National Lottery.

The Eircom shares scandal was another hot *Liveline* issue. We were all urged to buy shares. They rose for three days, but only those with accounts in stockbrokers – i.e. the rich and connected – could sell them during this time. The ordinary punter was left high, dry and penniless when the shares crashed. But the government put their share of the money from the Eircom sale into the National Pension Reserve Fund – which in turn is being used to bail out the banks!

Perhaps one of the earliest signs of a government with

its priorities askew was the decentralization farce. At around 2 p.m. on Tuesday, 3 December 2003, we got a call from a listener who was driving through Laois and had spotted newly erected banners and posters proclaiming 'Welcome to Parlon country'. This was followed by other callers who spotted the mysterious banners in the then minister's constituency. All became clear within the hour as minister for finance Charlie McCreevy announced the transfer of 'complete departments, including their ministers and senior management, to provincial locations'. Minister Tom Parlon TD was simply jumping the gun and claiming credit for shifting public sector jobs from the capital.

McCreevy went on that afternoon to talk about eliminating the 'Dublin mindset' from the civil and public service – an outrageous comment. Decentralization was the beginning of the end of the Celtic Tiger. Hubris and arrogance meant that decent civil and public servants were terrorized or bribed into moving. Most did not go, so others were promoted to fill positions. A vast memory bank was lost, property prices in small towns shot up and empty offices in Dublin were still costing the taxpayers millions. State organizations such as the ESRI, which enthusiastically backed this government policy, should hang their heads in shame. Their offices, by the way, relocated from Dublin 4 to Dublin 2.

In late 2004, at the height of the Celtic Tiger, stories began to emerge in the newspapers highlighting the amount of money paid by the taxpayer to a freelance PR consultant, Monica Leech from Waterford, as an advisor to Martin Cullen, minister for the environment and Fianna Fáil TD for Waterford. In two years, she was paid three hundred thousand Euros for part-time work. Among other things, she advised on the Race Against Waste campaign. The media also alleged that, as part of her consultancy work, she had travelled on departmental delegations to the US.

I was in Waterford filming for RTÉ television in early December and happened to come across an interview with Martin Cullen on the local TV channel, Waterford City. Questioned about the ongoing controversy, he was adamant it was another attack on Waterford by the 'Dublin media' – an interesting angle, to say the least. This stuck in my head, and the following week, when the *Evening Herald* ran more stories about the PR contract, I put it to listeners in my 12.50 promo that maybe this was just that: a vendetta by the 'Dublin media' against a country TD.

The phones lit up. Even then, long before the crash, people were obsessed with perceptions of waste and alleged cronyism. During the programme, callers argued both sides of the debate. One caller, Ronan Petit, who claimed to be a member of the PDs, came on to 'defend' Martin Cullen. 'Defend away,' I said to him. And off he went.

Unfortunately, during his very short contribution, he made a vulgar remark about Ms Leech – six words that lasted less than three seconds. I immediately shouted

him down. I don't have the technology to cut off anyone; that happens in the control room, run by the
producer and sound operator. They cut Petit off, but it
was too late. I apologized to the listeners immediately,
took a commercial break and apologized again.

Ms Leech sued RTÉ. It was only when the case neared
a court date that I was asked to meet with the lawyers
for RTÉ. I was adamant that I had insisted that the
caller was cut off and that I had apologized twice. My
apologies had been intended for Ms Leech, but it
seemed to me that she may have felt they were not direct
enough. However, when I argued that I really believed
we should let a jury decide if we had done enough, it
was made clear to me that I would not be party to any
decision. And I wasn't.

When I arrived in court, I felt pretty alone. I had no
idea whether any talks were being pursued, but I fully
expected and was prepared for a court battle. However,
it was not to be. The case was quickly adjourned. I
rambled off to have a coffee, having been told I would
not be needed for an hour or two. When I returned, I
was told that Monica Leech had settled with RTÉ, for
an amount which was not divulged to me. A short statement of profound apology from RTÉ was read out, and
the court adjourned.

I was asked by the then head of RTÉ Radio, Adrian
Moynes, not to talk to the press. I was left to walk out
of the High Court and face the photographers alone. As
I walked by, the journalists were gathered around
Monica Leech. I could hear her declare that all she

wanted was an 'apology', and that she was 'disappointed that I had to wait two and a half years for that'. Cognisant of the RTÉ instruction that I should not talk to the media, I simply walked on by.

Ironically, when Ms Leech subsequently sued the *Irish Independent* for reprinting the words spoken on *Liveline*, she lost the case before a jury. The *Irish Independent* argued that the article, in which they had reported that 'RTÉ had cut off the caller immediately, apologized a number of times and had dissociated itself from the remarks', should be read as a whole.

In his summing-up, Judge Peter Charleton – who was also hearing the RTÉ case until it was settled out of court – clarified the law on the defence of public interest. He said such a defence meant the media could publish information, even if it turned out to be incorrect, as long as the public had a right to know and it was responsible journalism.

So we had the bizarre situation where RTÉ had paid Ms Leech a substantial out-of-court settlement, while Independent Newspapers won the case about the exact same words when it was decided by a jury. Subsequently, Ms Leech sued the *Evening Herald* for other articles they had written, and she won the case.

Ronan Petit was wrong in what he said about Ms Leech, and it was deeply upsetting to her, her husband and her young family, and I wish to take this opportunity to apologize to her again. He was also wrong about his inference about Minister Martin Cullen, and I apologize to him also.

* * *

'That *Liveline* programme on Thursday was absolutely its single most destructive broadcast ever.' So said an unnamed senior figure in Irish banking in mid-September 2008; it seems he was echoing the views of government ministers.

It had all begun rather innocuously. The previous weekend, I had heard minister for finance Brian Lenihan declare on *Saturday View* that the 'banks have been stress-tested by the regulator and they are all sound'. But with the Northern Rock closure still fresh in the public's memory, with pictures of people queuing for their deposits in Dublin's Harcourt Street, followed by the Lehman Brothers collapse in the US, there was a growing anxiety in the air and on the airwaves.

On Sunday, I was struck by the revelation from a contributor on *The Marian Finucane Show* that small depositors in Irish banks only had up to eighteen thousand Euros of their money guaranteed by the state. I discovered that the guarantee in the UK was more than double that, and that it was a hundred thousand Euros in Italy.

As someone whose first experience of saving was a post office savings book, I knew that money in the local post office at least was safe. So, a few days later, when I saw a call coming in from a rural postmaster about the dramatic increase in people moving their savings into their local post office, I knew there was something brewing. It would be a glorious opportunity to point out that the deposit guarantee in the banks was pathetic.

Was I open to allowing people to let rip at the banks? The straight answer is yes. I suspected the emperors had not a stitch of clothing between them. Firstly, banks and other big, powerful institutions have long held a coveted place in *Liveline* listeners' hearts, as was evident over the years in such scandals as the sale of unrealistic 'life' policies to older people, hidden charges or refusing to cash cheques for customers. Then there was the John Rusnak scandal at Allfirst, a branch of the AIB Group in the US, where the trader had managed to hide from his bosses $691 million in losses on 'bad bets'.

Secondly, a number of years earlier, *Liveline* had become the chosen forum for communities around the country witnessing the closure of local branches of their banks, from Ballymun to Tipperary, because they were not profitable enough.

Still, I did not expect the reaction we got when the rural postmaster pointed out – with my help – that people's money was safer in his little shop than in the big banks, where only eighteen thousand Euros was guaranteed. Listeners let loose and did not hold back on their distrust of the banks. There were stories of people carrying amounts of five thousand Euros in cash to their nearest post office. Again and again, I highlighted the small amount of the deposit guarantee and that it was the 'little person' who would get it in the neck if the banks went under; the big boys no doubt had their money elsewhere.

After the show, the main chatter in the radio centre was the shock news that our boss, Adrian Moynes, had decided to leave radio and move to administration within RTÉ. I sent him a text wishing him well. When I got a phone call from him that evening on a very poor mobile phone line at home, I simply presumed that he was acknowledging my message. He mentioned something about the need to be careful in the current climate. The dodgy line, coupled with my misunderstanding of the purpose of the call, meant that I was totally oblivious to the fact that the minister for finance had phoned the director general after *Liveline* to complain about the broadcast, which he alleged was causing panic in the financial system.

I only discovered the seriousness of the government intervention through the Sunday newspapers, which seemed to have been briefed by Brian Lenihan's office. Both the *Sunday Independent* and *Sunday Times* led with stories with headlines such as 'Lenihan Lash at Joe Duffy Bank Panic', peppered with anonymous quotes from shocked and upset 'senior bankers' and saying that 'concern began to sweep through RTÉ', with purported quotes from unnamed RTÉ management sources castigating my immaturity and recklessness. By the way, the Sunday newspapers buried the fact that, the previous day, Brian Lenihan had increased the deposit guarantee for savers to one hundred thousand Euros. Game, set and match to *Liveline* listeners; the little man and woman strike again.

Of course, that was not the end of it. The then chairman of the Financial Services Regulatory Authority, which as we now know exercised little regulation and even less authority, lost no opportunity to have a go at me for panicking the public in 2008. I laughed out loud when I heard minister Dick Roche exclaim on radio during September 2008 that I should be made to apologize publicly for allowing people to talk about moving their life savings from the banks. This call for my public humiliation was echoed that week by other politicians, senior bankers and economists, all because *Liveline* listeners had publicly expressed their mistrust of the banks. The people were worried; their instincts were that things were much worse than we were being told, and they were right.

The mantra that often rang out over the following three years was: 'Crisis? What crisis?' While the government cut social welfare payments, children's allowance and public servants' pay, and upped taxes, as well as introducing a few new ones, it seemed to be oblivious to the depth of the economic crisis.

I did not see the evening TV news on Bank Holiday Monday, 25 October 2010. But by the time I got into the office the following morning, I certainly knew about it. People were incensed beyond belief by the pictures of government ministers queuing up in their fleet of Garda-driven black Mercedes and lowering their windows to toss a few words about upcoming budget cuts to the baying media at the gates of Farmleigh. *Liveline* listeners were apoplectic; even though, time and time again in the years previously, we had covered the use and abuse of state cars, nothing ignited the public's anger like this display. The issue of 'perks and mercs' had bubbled under, but Farmleigh was a geyser of Icelandic proportions.

Many thought the Farmleigh footage was an iconic image of a government out of touch with reality, but to me the credibility of Fianna Fáil had collapsed a month beforehand with the infamous Ardilaun Hotel interview given by Taoiseach Brian Cowen on Tuesday, 14 September on *Morning Ireland*, when, to say the least, he sounded the worse for wear.

Here was the government, in the middle of the worst economic crisis in the history of the state, decamping to a plush hotel in Galway for a 'think in'. Even before the event began, we had callers protesting on air at the extravagance. It seemed that the people charged with rescuing us from a crisis, which many argued they had created and facilitated in the first place, were partying like there was no tomorrow. As *Liveline* approached, it was clear that the public had finally snapped, even before the Taoiseach mixed up the 'Croke Park deal' and the 'Good Friday Agreement' during the interview. It was Ursula Halligan of TV3 who put it straight to the Taoiseach when, later the same day, she asked him, 'Were you drunk, hung over or tired?' during the interview. The Taoiseach told her, 'Absolutely not.'

But the game was up. I wanted to do a ten-minute text poll on *Liveline*. Management was very nervous about it. RTÉ was in a very difficult position because of the power that the Cabinet has over it through the licence fee. I argued that, while we could fill the programme with irate callers, we needed to gauge the overall feeling on this one. I was convinced that it was a major turning point.

The twenty minutes before we went on air were more hectic than usual as we tick-tacked with senior management about the issue, eventually getting down to discussing the actual question to be asked. Just as the *Liveline* 'sig' was rolling, we agreed on a simple formula: 'Do you have confidence in the Taoiseach? Text "Y" for yes and "N" for no.'

I never flag these ten-minute text polls in advance – that is why they have proven to be so accurate. Shortly after two o'clock, I simply announced the poll and declared that the lines would be open for exactly ten minutes. There were over twenty-five thousand texts, the highest ever in an Irish radio programme in such a short space of time. The result was clear: 77 per cent did not have confidence in Brian Cowen as Taoiseach.

By the time the general election came around four months later, on Friday, 25 February 2011, you did not have to be a *Liveline* listener to know that havoc was about to be vengefully visited on the government. The Fianna Fáil vote dropped from 23 per cent in our poll to 17 per cent. The public were furious and, while they may have raised their angry voices on *Liveline*, they cast their ballots with even greater ferocity. The number of Fianna Fáil TDs fell from 78 to 20, and the Dáil seats of their Green Party partners were annihilated.

The people voted. Democracy worked.

CHAPTER 31

How *Liveline* Works

THE THEN HEAD OF RTÉ RADIO 1, ANA LEDDY, TOLD ME in 2010 that *Liveline* gave her more sleepless nights than any other programme. I get defensive when I hear such comments, and always try to remind whoever I'm talking to that the *Liveline* listeners – all four hundred thousand of them, every single day – are stakeholders in a programme that, per listener-minute, is easily the cheapest across the whole organization.

Still, I understand RTÉ management's concerns. In addition to Brian Lenihan phoning the director general, and Michael McDowell insisting on coming on air for his 'right of reply', I know that another minister even complained informally when *Liveline* was extended by fifteen minutes. But, in reality, there seldom any political interference in the day-to-day running of *Liveline*.

Liveline is a very unusual programme. It has for various reasons developed as the last – and sometimes first – port of call for those who feel unhappy with the way they have been treated by that most mysterious of Irish institutions, 'the powers that be'. While we try to ensure that the programme stays focused and balanced, there is no doubt that some people feel that *Liveline*, by its nature, is too negative. There are those, inside and outside RTÉ, who plead with the programme to be more 'positive'. Of course, I have been long enough in the business to know that issues are much more complex than that.

I encourage the production team only to put on stories that are interesting and have a chance of resolution; otherwise, critics will be justified when they call us the 'whineline'. But as for negativity, there is no point is us trying to magic up some Pollyanna-like programme with scented flowers and tranquil radio incense just for the sake of supposedly calming a raging nation. *Liveline* does a lot of positive stories but, more importantly, it proves its worth by helping listeners, and warning others, about problems with banks, insurance companies, dodgy builders and holiday-home salesmen. Our intervention, even when it starts from a 'complaint', often brings positive results for our listeners and helps prevent other calamities. People standing up for their rights is not in itself negative. It's the truth – and, let's face it, some people can't handle the truth!

Having said that, I am wary of being too negative, because we would lose listeners if we were. We watch the shape of the programme like a hawk, and I am acutely conscious of an ongoing tone and the need to change, vary and, above all, keep people listening; otherwise, my radio career is over.

Of course, we have to fill a seventy-five-minute programme every single weekday with live, interesting phone calls. We have no other choice some days but to simply let some people on the air who might be perceived as having an exaggerated sense of grievance.

I have never had an easy time from critics; that, I suppose, is the nature of the business, but some of the vitriol poured on me has hurt and rankled. Critics often accuse me and *Liveline* of 'dumbing down' Irish radio; to quote a recent review, I have 'lowered the level of public discourse in Ireland'. To me, this is a superficial, nonsensical claim with a snobbish tint which is refuted by the content and results of the programme, day in, day out. But one thing I learned early on about reviews is that you are never as good as they say you are, and you are never as bad either! Also, I learned not to carry the criticism around in my head; no one else does. Try to get your hands on a daily or Sunday newspaper a day later, and you can't, so why hold on to criticism?

A programme with an audience bigger than the daily sales of our four national newspapers is bound to be on their radar, in a positive and negative way. While every newspaper has followed up stories from *Liveline*, likewise they have been critical of me and the programme. Some of this criticism does hurt me personally – I have been called 'rabble rouser', 'mob orator', 'generator of hate mail and death threats'. I completely reject these criticisms, but from the instantaneous feedback that *Liveline* generates, I find out fairly quickly when I have lost the run of myself, which does happen, so I have tried to put trenchant criticism into perspective.

Of course, there is another side to *Liveline*. A daily programme such as this does not leave much time for reflection and analysis of successes and failures. The most important programme is today's *Liveline* and, by three o'clock today, the most important programme is tomorrow's. However, I am proud of the successes of *Liveline*. From building a house for a family with disabled children who were living in a garage in Wicklow town to shutting a hundred poisonous 'head shops'; from the campaign by cystic fibrosis sufferers to catapulting organ-donor cards to a new level in Ireland; from exposing pyramid schemes and other scams and tracking down rip-off conmen and companies, to giving a platform to the survivors of industrial schools and Magdalene laundries, *Liveline* has achieved an awful lot.

I am deeply proud of a number of programmes we did in February 2009 aimed at deaf people, with some of them participating for the first time ever in a radio debate. It came from a story I had read in the *Daily Telegraph* which told how a young woman being held captive was able to silently text her distress call to the police. It struck me that she could not do that in Ireland, so the next day I asked on air why the Irish emergency services don't have a texting facility. Within minutes, a listener pointed out that the main beneficiaries of such a service would be those with severe hearing difficulties.

I suggested that we try to talk to some deaf people with the aid of a signer, who would be with the caller and do the listening, signing and talking. But then we realized that we could use the texting technology ourselves, so we put out the word that we would type my on-air questions using Gmail, and the deaf caller could read them and respond.

It turned into a stunning programme, which gave many people a new glimpse into the world of the deaf community. We learned immediately that this absence of emergency texting was a serious issue, not just for those trying to contact the Gardaí, but for those trying to contact the ambulance and fire services. As a team, we had managed to do a series of programmes for, about and with the participation of deaf people. Radio for the deaf – wonderful.

In 2006, Newstalk Radio asked to meet me with a view to inviting me to join its team. I had three meetings with senior staff in the station at their request. I had never before seriously contemplated leaving RTÉ, but I respected Newstalk as serious 'talk radio', so I thought I would see what they had to say.

I met a management consultant friend of mine for advice. He brought me through all the reasons I should leave or stay. The most salient message he gave me at the end of our long session was that I would meet similar management structures elsewhere. It is the nature of the beast. Even when I was a probation officer, it became clear after a very short period that the organization was totally hierarchical. If you could not get your idea or proposal past your manager, it had little chance of going any further, because the system mistrusts anyone who challenges it.

The government has enormous power over RTÉ's finances and, with the recession and the drop in advertising revenue, RTÉ now rely on the licence fee more than ever. For years, they refused to increase the licence fee, until the Trojan work, led by my former direct boss Kevin Healy, eventually saw the fee rise to €160. I never hear people complaining about the amount; after all, people are now spending multiples of that on their Sky TV channels. From the licence fee and advertising revenue, RTÉ runs three TV stations, four national radio stations, two orchestras and numerous other free services such as digital radio channels and websites. By the way, according to RTÉ figures, Radio 1 gets just four cents a day from every licence-fee payer.

An old schoolmate who had emigrated to Sweden told me recently that he had asked his mother, 'What's yer man Joe Duffy doing now?' She promptly replied, 'Not much; he just answers the phones in RTÉ.'

I know that I have one of the best jobs in the world, and I still love it. I love knowing where the programme might begin but having no idea of where it might end. I often say to aspiring journalists that the wonderful thing about the job is that, no matter what you do, read or see, where you go or who you meet, it will at some stage be useful in the job. Simply being curious about society, or passionate about your interests – whether they include sports, politics or social affairs – means you are halfway to being a journalist.

I have to be up to speed with all that is happening in Ireland and abroad, whether I am on holiday or not. This is not a burden, as curiosity is my disposition in life anyway – after all, didn't my beloved Mr Long tell me when I was ten that I was the 'most curious boy' in his class!

People often ask me what time I have to start in the morning. I usually awake around six twenty and jump up straight away, slip into a fleece, sports shorts and trainers and head out the door for my early-morning swim at Westwood in Fairview – a ritual I have kept for nearly thirty years – muttering something incoherent to myself about my hard life. In the car, I tune into BBC Radio 4, the news channel, then a quick switch to grab the newspaper headlines on Newstalk, as their business programme starts at six thirty, before *Morning Ireland*. The gym usually has the daily newspapers, which I scan, page by page, to get a sense of what might dominate the day's news agenda. The 'letters pages' are crucial to try to spot what is exercising readers' minds.

The forty-minute swim is wonderful. I cannot open my mouth (except to exhale), watch telly, listen to the radio or, in my case, even see farther than my hand, so my mind goes off in all directions. My best and deepest ideas have often begun in the shallow end of the pool in Westwood – and vice versa! After my swim, it's back to *Morning Ireland*, Newstalk, Twitter and various news websites, with the same aim in mind: getting the zeitgeist of the day, trying to spot issues that might become search engines on that afternoon's *Liveline*.

Having read the morning papers and monitored the early radio output, I speak to the senior producer around 9 a.m. from home. I have one advantage in that I trained as a radio producer and held this role, sometimes combined with a reporting role, for over a decade, so I have a fair idea of what will work on radio. I make suggestions, mindful that some issues might be exhausted by lunchtime. We are on the air very late in the 'radio day' – nearly seven hours after *Morning Ireland* starts – so we have to presume that listeners will be very 'newsed-out' by one forty-five, when *Liveline* begins its rollercoaster ride.

I have a good memory for past shows, so I might spot an angle. The producer then lets me know what has come in overnight, and we agree generally what we will try to chase. Monday is the hardest day to produce *Liveline*; as the week progresses, items either fill themselves or thin out. The listeners are great producers.

There are six of us in the *Liveline* office, a combination of producers, a researcher, a broadcasting assistant and myself, who meet to toss around ideas and allocate tasks. We sit around two small groups of desks in an open-plan office, which also houses *The John Murray Show*, *Today with Pat Kenny*, *The Mooney Show*, *The*

Marian Finucane Weekend Show and *Drivetime* – all our talent in one room! Staff are changed on a regular basis between these programmes, too often for my liking. I am now the only person who has been on the programme for longer than two years. During my stint on *Liveline* I have been lucky to work with many staff who have given an incredible amount to the programme. Many of them – Anne Farrell, Anne Marie Power, Jane Murphy, Margaret Curley, Carol Louth, Rachel Graham, Kintilla Husseff, Liz Larraghy, Alice O'Sullivan, Emma Laffan, Elaine Carraher, Diarmuid Byrne, Jack Murphy, Sorcha Glackin, Siobhan Hough, Ger Philpott, Tim Desmond, Aidan Butler, Aidan Stanley, Kevin Reynolds, Leslie O'Connor, Nuala O'Neill, Elaine Conlan, Reg Looby, Tara Campbell and Cora Ennis – are all still creative and powerful players within RTÉ.

One of the most remarkable tools *Liveline* has at its disposal is the team's memory bank. We also have the most valuable database in Ireland; every day, hundreds of people contact *Liveline* on varying topics; most of them don't get on air. If the topic arises again, and it often does, we can alert previous callers to allow them to participate. The idea that the *Liveline* team simply sleepwalks through the day, just putting up calls as they come in, without any judgement in terms of the listen-ability of the programme, is nonsense. *Liveline* would not be where it is today if that was the case.

While we get many of our ideas from newspapers or from listening to other programmes, I am keen that *Liveline* is never driven by the editors of the national newspapers. Too many programmes on too many radio stations are simply truncated audio versions of the morning papers, which, in turn, usually don't get enough credit. If issues of the day, as decided by newspaper editors, are covered on *Liveline*, I always insist we add value, such as a new angle or new voices. But, in the main, I am more often heard exclaiming to the team, 'No reheats from the morning papers.'

By twelve fifteen, we normally have a fair idea of some items for that day, which I will mention when I do my live promo on the *Ronan Collins Show* at twelve forty. We don't do lunch on *Liveline*; it's a cup of soup or a sandwich at our desks. By one o'clock, we are normally peppering, gauging the calls to see what is catching the imagination, or acting as a good search engine. The mark of a good producer is someone who can say no easily and comfortably, can drop everything planned when a good call comes in, or has the confidence to spot a topic that will take off and begin the show with just one phone call.

I go down to studio at the exact same time each day – one thirty – with my flask of tea. I will always go to the bathroom beside Studio 7 and wash my face in cold water, do a few vocal exercises and repeat my daily *Liveline* mantra: 'Libel and entertainment.' In other words, listen like a hawk for libel and remember the importance of keeping people tuned in, so keep the show on the road, and keep it interesting!

The *Liveline* 'sig' is 'Over the Moor' by Stockton's Wing, which has been with the programme since 1985.

Once it rolls, it's all systems go. Three part-time call-takers in a separate room type up the listeners' comments, firstly asking if the caller is 'willing to go on air'. Upstairs, the remainder of the *Liveline* team monitors texts, answers calls and does research on the hoof, as callers often mention issues or people who need to be contacted immediately. We have been helped by text messages and emails, but sometimes these can just overwhelm the programme. In some of our *Liveline* ten-minute text polls, we get over two thousand votes every single minute!

Much of the team's day in the office is spent listening to people who never get on air. They may have a genuine story but often it just doesn't fit for that day. Of course, oftentimes, once *Liveline* makes one investigative call, the seemingly intractable issue is solved before one forty-five. This can be frustrating from a programme point of view, but it is heartening to know that *Liveline* does work – on and off the air.

The forwarded calls are flashed up on a screen in front of the producer in the studio control room. I don't see every call that comes into the programme, only those the producer decides to put up on air, and only when they are on the line and ready to go.

There is no 'delay mechanism' on *Liveline*, despite what people believe. Few people, even within RTÉ, are aware that the only microphone I can turn off is my own, the rest being controlled by a sound operator. After the Monica Leech case, it seemed that even some management were surprised that there was no 'delay', which would have allowed the sound operator to cut off the caller before his lewd comments went 'live'. There was a subsequent investigation into a possible mechanism, but I heard nothing about it again.

We have to be extra careful to alert our contributors to the limits of libel and taste, as they are mostly unseasoned media performers. But this to me is one of the strengths of the programme: the ability to facilitate ordinary people, and help them to feel comfortable and coherent on the national airwaves. Insisting that those who would not normally have a voice are given priority on *Liveline* is what distinguishes us. Those who are regulars on other programmes – politicians, journalists, trade unionists – and those with vested interests don't usually get a platform on *Liveline*, despite their best efforts. One of my main tasks on air is to create an atmosphere where many people, including the powerless, feel they will be treated properly and have some hope of redress, at best, if they have a grievance, or at least the opportunity to alert others to their predicament.

Liveline gives listeners their say, and this may in turn be picked up by other programmes or the following day's papers. Even before the programme finishes we often get calls from newspapers or news and current affairs programmes in RTÉ looking to talk to certain callers. We always ask them to hold on until the programme ends, as it can be rather hectic, and of course we cannot give out callers' details, but we do undertake to phone the listener with the message. The listener then has the choice to pursue their issue further or not.

Of course, while *Liveline* would not exist without the listeners, it is the staff who work every day on the programme and ensure it is on air every afternoon at one forty-five. Luckily, most of the staff on *Liveline* quickly develop an intense loyalty and commitment to the programme – one of the main reasons for its success.

I am taken aback when people ask me about callers I 'disliked'. I can genuinely say that I have a positive disposition to all our callers; I never try to save time by taking an instant dislike to people. Everyone who gets on the air has been vetted and deserves a hearing. Call it gratitude or a genuine interest in people, but I love *Liveline* callers!

Life is Short

CHAPTER 32

Holy Thursday

IT WAS A GLORIOUS SPRING MORNING, 9 APRIL 2009. THE family had just spent five days in London, where, as usual, we had run around all the attractions. I had led them like a hyperactive field marshal as we hit the Imperial War Museum, Brick Lane market, the Houses of Commons and Lords, the Queen musical *We Will Rock You*, and a load of other things. I had agreed for some reason to return to Dublin to work on Holy Thursday, after three days' leave, with the intention of later continuing on to Wexford for the Easter break.

Driving to work that day, I decided at the last minute to return a number of library books, all about London. The lure of the public library in my life is a strong one, ever since the dusty, dark makeshift library in Drumfin Avenue. But this day was going to be very different.

I parked opposite the wonderful Gilbert Library in Pearse Street, got out and went around the car to get the bag of books from the boot. I remember moving my laptop to one side and picking up the library books – and then I was hit. The car, a Fiat Punto, had pulled up alongside mine and was trying to reverse into the unoccupied parking space behind me, but it might as well have fallen from the sky for all I knew of it. As it reversed in, the front of the car swung sharply, barely missed the side of my car and hit my right leg with such force that I can still recall the sounds of the bonnet buckling, metal crushing and glass smashing. It was an unmerciful and violent smack.

I was still standing in disbelief, library books in hand, when I looked down at my right leg. It was literally swinging freely from below the knee. I had no control over it; it looked like the flopping leg of a shop dummy. The pain was excruciating, but I stayed upright, dropped the books back into the boot of the car and then fell to the ground, with my head towards the gutter. As I lay there I could see the front wheel of the car moving towards my head again; the driver subsequently revealed that she had pressed the accelerator in panic. I screamed and instinctively rolled out of the way of the oncoming wheel.

Seconds later, I looked up to see a young woman, dressed in floral pink pyjamas and slippers, standing over me and saying, 'I am sorry, I am sorry.' I begged people to help me. One young man ran into the nearby doctor's surgery. I kept asking, over and over, 'Why, why, why?'

A doctor quickly emerged from the surgery with a blanket in his hand. He asked me what had happened as

I begged him to do something about the pain. 'Are you Joe Duffy?' he asked. He must have been as surprised as I was, seeing this familiar but stupid-looking man in a suit, tie, white trenchcoat and trilby hat lying outside his surgery begging for help. He ran through a few questions about allergies and medications before he popped back into his surgery for a large syringe. He quickly pulled open my trousers and injected the painkiller into the top of my right leg.

As bystanders began to gather, I could hear their conversations. Someone craning for a view asked who the victim was and I heard someone mutter, 'It's just Joe.' Others asked, 'Is that Joe Duffy off the radio?' I cringed; embarrassment is a great painkiller. I even remember someone urging me to put a parking disc on my car so it wouldn't be clamped! Bizarrely, I tried to dial the office on my mobile phone to tell them I wouldn't be in. I also tried to call my wife June, but the number was constantly engaged.

I looked at my leg, doubled back in a direction it should never point. This was a mistake, as it is an image that still haunts me.

Then I remember the kerfuffle as an ambulance and a fire crew arrived. The paramedics told me they were going to have to move my leg back into position, and it was going to be painful. They produced an oxygen cylinder and asked me to bite on the rubber mouthpiece and take deep breaths. This seemed to have little effect, but I was getting more comfortable on the street; I think the painkiller was kicking in. The five paramedics debated how to move me safely; it took a long time for them to manoeuvre me delicately on to the stretcher and into the ambulance without making the leg worse.

As my shock gradually subsided, the pain began to take hold.

A firefighter asked for my car kes; he was going to move my car to their headquarters for safe-keeping. Another firefighter in a white helmet, a station officer, asked me for my home phone number. I could hear him talking to June, but he did not know at that stage which hospital I would be taken to.

At fifty-three years of age, I had never thankfully had any serious illness before; I was even born at home as I wanted to be near my mother. But here I was being carted off in an ambulance, sirens blazing. Though I was in pain, I was still totally conscious. I have very little memory of the journey to St James's, except being stretchered from the ambulance and looking up at what I thought was a warehouse roof. I was immediately met by a team of medics, who cut off my right shoe and trousers. I asked for more pain relief but they insisted I could not have any more medication until they 'righted' the leg – which they warned would be the most painful thing that would happen to me. Welcome to the real world!

June and my son Ronan arrived in the A&E cubicle around this time. They were calm and reassuring; I was mostly just embarrassed. The whole family, who were on their Easter break, had got a shock when they heard the news. Sean and Ellen were too anxious and upset to come straight to the hospital.

Una Geary, the consultant who led the brilliant team treating me in A&E, told me subsequently that she had no idea who I was at the time, though she did say that, at one stage during the team's efforts, somebody elbowed her in the ribs to tell her, 'It's your man, Joe Duffy.' June and Ronan were asked to leave. I braced myself as a couple of other medics gathered around. They gave my leg a quick turn in the correct direction. It was painful, but in truth I was so delirious and still in some shock, so it was more like a very sharp, stinging jolt than a persistent pain. I was to get more than my fair share of that later, as subsequent pain had a much greater impact, especially after the first operation on my leg.

I was X-rayed from every direction, while still conscious. I somehow still didn't realize the seriousness of what had happened. I had a notion that I would get out of hospital that evening and hobble around for the weekend before returning to work on Easter Tuesday.

Then a friendly face from my childhood arrived. It was the A&E consultant, Pat Plunkett, originally from Spiddal Road in Ballyfermot. I held Pat's hand and had my first cry as the extent of what lay ahead of me began to sink in. He told me what his colleague Una Geary had already intimated as she busily worked away on me. It was a serious accident: the two bones in my lower right leg, the tibia and fibula, had been snapped in two. I would need surgery. They were also still trying to establish if anything else had been damaged or broken. After that came more X-rays.

I was anxious not to unduly alarm anyone, especially my mother. I was deeply aware that the last car accident involving one of her sons had killed him, so I wanted to downplay the incident for her sake. June rang her later that evening and managed to convince her that it was a minor accident.

The following morning, Good Friday, I was brought down to be operated on. I remember being wheeled to the theatre at eight thirty and reawakening in the recovery room around four in the afternoon. The operation, which had lasted three hours, involved the surgeon Johnny McKenna opening my leg at the knee and hammering a 12-inch metal rod down through my tibia and securing it with six screws across the knee and the ankle. This would help the broken tibia to knit back together; the fibula would eventually heal itself. The metal rod was meant to be a permanent fixture, but the pain was so intense that the following year I had to have a second operation to have the foot-long 'nail' and the screws removed.

The shock of what happened to me was only sinking in at this stage. I was pumping morphine into myself and was zonked for days.

Gay Byrne once told me that, after his prostate operation, the general anaesthetic knocked him back for months. He reminded me that I was on the *Late Late Show* panel when he returned, and he revealed that he had wanted me there in case he forgot names and places, which of course he didn't. 'At one stage during that programme, I thought I was on the mail boat to Liverpool,' Gay confided.

* * *

I was released from hospital, after pestering them, five days after the operation. A bedroom had been prepared downstairs at home. The next few weeks were hell. I was in intense pain for at least six weeks after the accident, and to lesser degrees afterwards. For a long time I did not have one full night's sleep uninterrupted by pain and intense discomfort. I was claustrophobic, suffered persistent panic attacks and at times I felt hopeless with the pain and the prospect that I might never recover. Lying on the flat of my back for three weeks and peeing into a bottle was a new experience for me; but, boy, did it give me a lot of insight into how people who are in much worse situations than I can battle on.

Of course, given the fickle nature of our business, I was anxious to get back to work as soon as possible before they offered *Liveline* to someone else. Having missed nineteen editions of the programme, I hobbled back into RTÉ. For the next three months, I hired taxis to take me to work and home each day. With the help of a large box and a massive cushion I managed to rest my injured leg under my studio desk during the programme; it was uncomfortable, awkward and painful, as was crutching around the place.

I got a real sense of what people with disabilities have to put up with, particularly how inaccessible modern buildings are. Banisters were brilliant but might suddenly disappear; rain on cement and access ramps was treacherous. And why can no one invent a decent, comfortable pair of crutches?

Eight months later, when I informed my boss that I would have to undergo another operation requiring hospitalization and two weeks off, I was immediately handed a formal letter from RTÉ stating baldly that I was not now entitled to sick pay. When Gerry Ryan was informed of this new RTÉ interpretation of the sick-pay clause in our contracts, he was very angered and concerned. As he put it, it was 'deeply demoralizing and unfair' for workers who had been in RTÉ, man and boy, for up to thirty years, to be told in their fifties to get sick at their peril. Having said that, if, God forbid, one of us or a family member suffered serious illness, I am sure that the organization would be compassionate. However, the insecurity and worry is still huge. (By the way, in my twenty-three years in RTÉ, I only took one single day off sick prior to being knocked down, so I thought the decision to refuse me sick pay was unfair, to say the least.)

Unfortunately, the effects of the Holy Thursday accident have stayed with me. Two years later, I am still attending weekly acupuncture and physiotherapy for pain, around the knee in particular. I still get nightmares about lying on the road with my head in the gutter as the car jolted towards my head. But I treasure my good health and good fortune more than ever now!

Another side effect is that people tell me of their own awful road accidents, many much worse than I had to endure. I am a much more careful pedestrian; when I see a car reversing out of a driveway, I turn back and walk the other way to avoid the confusion dance where the driver and pedestrian wave each other on. No thanks, too risky. For a long time afterwards, I had a pathological fear of reversing my own car, in any circumstances. Oh, and parking sensors are to me the most important gadget you can have on a car.

I have total sympathy for the young woman who knocked me down. It was an accident. She had only been driving that car a couple of days. She called up to the hospital on the night of the accident and left a card telling me how sorry she was for what happened. There but for the grace of God go all of us.

CHAPTER 33

Gerry Ryan RIP

W HEN I SPOKE ABOUT GERRY RYAN ON *LIVELINE* ON Friday, 30 April 2010, I did not know that he was dead.

Brush Shiels, Sil Fox, Doc Savage, Paddy Cullivan, Bob Carley and Yann O'Brien were all in the studio for the usual manic end-of-month 'Funny Friday'. At one stage, someone mentioned Heather Mills and I interjected that I thought her interview on the previous night's *Ryan Confidential* was superb: 'Gerry was at his absolute best.'

I knew Gerry was absent that day; I had heard Fiona Looney presenting his programme that morning. However, I had gone over to his desk at noon, as I normally did, to leave a copy of that day's *Evening Herald* in his drawer, as it had an especially nice photo of his wife Morah and their five children taken at a movie premiere the previous night. On the way over, I met Gerry's long-time producer Siobhan Hough, who told me she was just about to ring him to see if he was all right.

At the end of that Friday's *Liveline*, when I saw the director general of RTÉ, Cathal Goan, and the head of radio, Clare Duignan, waiting to come in to the control room of the *Liveline* studio, I automatically blamed Gerry Ryan. There had been ongoing meetings with RTÉ about our contracts, and Gerry had encouraged us all to stand up for ourselves. I thought I was in trouble again.

Unusually, the producer Sorcha Glackin was hurriedly ushering all the guests out of the studio as my bosses waited to come in. But I knew from their faces this was not about stupid ruminations about pay and conditions. I could tell immediately that something catastrophic had happened.

Clare Duignan was pale and shaking as she told me quickly, 'I have some very bad news, Joe. Gerry Ryan died this morning.'

God knows, at fifty-four, I had seen enough death and grieving in my life, but this news knocked me back into my studio chair. Cathal Goan was ashen-faced, his head bowed in disbelief. Having seen Gerry only the day before, I kept asking Cathal, 'How do you know he's dead? Have you seen him?' I simply did not believe it. I know that disbelief is the textbook reaction to bad news, but this bombshell was so shocking, so unexpected, that I did not even cry. I just kept asking Cathal questions, begging him to check and re-check. The larger-than-life character, whom I had first come across in Trinity thirty years previously, who jumped on every health check going, could not be dead at fifty-four. 'Who have you spoken to?' 'Who found Gerry's body?' 'Are they sure it's him?'

But Cathal and Clare were sure. The news had filtered out shortly after noon, but RTÉ was not going to release it until they were absolutely sure all his family had been informed. A decision had been made not to tell me until after *Liveline* had aired.

Gerry had returned to his house on Leeson Street at around eleven o'clock the previous night. But, around noon, when he did not answer his phone, his girlfriend, Melanie Verwoerd, had arranged for the lock on the house to be broken; she found Gerry dead in his bedroom.

Although we were in Trinity around the same time, I hadn't known Gerry that well back then. He was more involved in the music end of college life, friendly with people such as Mark Storey and more interested in fun than in student politics. I do remember him flouncing around Trinity in his white trenchcoat, oozing confidence and good humour. He never changed. Ironically, while Gerry had gone straight to RTÉ from Trinity and was beavering away while I worked in the probation service, his big break only happened when he got his own daily prime-time show in March 1988, a month before I entered the radio centre.

In the early years at RTÉ, I seldom saw Gerry in the radio centre, as I was normally out doing reports for Gaybo. Gerry's three-hour programme was, I suppose, the competition. But I admired him tremendously as a broadcaster, marvelling at his fluency, humour, courage and audacity. Our paths seldom crossed, even in Clontarf, where we both lived. We would bump into each other occasionally at kids' rugby training or school meetings. When I was dropped from the morning radio schedule in 1996, Gerry contacted me and we met in Clontarf Castle. He was supportive, perceptive and wise, and as always gave great advice.

After that Friday-afternoon bombshell, I just wanted to talk about Gerry. I spoke about him on both *Drivetime* and the *Six One News*. After the TV news, I headed straight to the Ryan family home in Clontarf, a scene of unparalleled grieving. Family friend Moya Doherty and Gerry's two brothers Mike and Mano were trying to hold everyone together, but the uncontrollable weeping of Morah, Rex, Lottie, Eliot, Bonnie and Babette, in complete shock, is a sight I hope never to have to see again.

I got home just in time to go back out to RTÉ for the beginning of *The Late Late Show*'s tribute to Gerry, picking up Gay Byrne on the way. Gay was his usual stoical self. Indeed, he kept us all together that evening. I talked about Gerry's boldness, in every sense of the word, on the show. I remarked that I was struck by something he had said to Heather Mills in the interview I had referred to earlier on *Liveline*. Gerry had revealed to Heather that he had 'loads of regrets; two articulat-ed truckloads of regrets'. As usual, Gerry was giving as much in the interview as he got, but of course now that Gerry was dead, those words took on a very different meaning. For someone who lived for the day, I never thought regrets were part of Gerry's make-up or would slow him down.

After the show, Gay Byrne, Pat Kenny, Dave Fanning, Ryan Tubridy, myself and many others spent hours in the 'green room'. I remember it as a rollercoaster – lots of laughs, tears, anger, bafflement, stories about Gerry's love of good food, wine and whiskey, and some more laughs about the fact that, though obsessed with his health, and despite buying gym equipment, Gerry had a disdain of exercise. We reminisced about the occasion when a group of presenters went for a drink to the nearby Dylan Hotel; the barman knew Gerry's order, a vodka martini, even before he asked. I had tea, Pat Kenny had coffee and I think Ryan Tubridy ordered boiling water with a dash of lemon, as he was on a crash diet at the time!

But Gay was brilliant that night, like a father figure to us all: calming, reassuring and eventually just melting under all the emotion. Gay can come across as tough sometimes – he is reluctant to visit hospitals or go to funerals – but that night he again proved that wisdom does come with age. He truly is a most remarkable man.

I was genuinely taken aback the following morning with the extent of the newspaper coverage of Gerry's passing – dozens of pages devoted to his life and career. This continued for more than a full week.

On Saturday morning, I headed back to RTÉ with

flowers for the makeshift shrine; a book of condolence had also been set up in the Radio Centre. I was amazed at the queue of people and the genuine feelings of remorse and loss they expressed. I felt I owed a lot to Gerry and his bereaved family, especially for his advice over the previous difficult eighteen months. Of course, I was acutely conscious that we were the same age with young kids, so the empathy was even more intense.

On Sunday, we were invited to the home of Melanie Verwoerd, Gerry's girlfriend. I went without hesitation, though I was conscious of being sensitive to the wishes and feelings of Gerry's immediate family. As it happened, I met Gerry's brother Mike going into the house in Leeson Street, and his presence gave some blessing to the gathering.

The following day, being the May bank holiday Monday, I offered to do *Liveline* from the Mansion House in central Dublin, where people were queuing to sign a book of condolence, but management wisely decided against it. So I collected my mother and sister, and the three of us went into the Mansion House, where, again, I signed the book.

Liveline got many calls the next day from listeners about Gerry's radio programme and the contribution it made to their daily lives, a glimpse that we in RTÉ seldom get. Listeners spoke of how the intimacy of radio meant that Gerry, with fifteen hours of broadcasting a week, was a major part of their lives. Gerry's style of broadcasting and the format of his show allowed him to talk at length about his own family, escapades, holidays and experiences. He shared his life with his listeners to a greater extent than any other broadcaster.

On Wednesday, Gerry's remains were brought home to Castle Avenue in Clontarf. Father Brian D'Arcy, Marian Finucane and I met in nearby Clontarf Castle and arrived together. Taoiseach Brian Cowen had left just before we arrived, but Bertie Ahern was in the house. I knew Gerry was popular, but his wide circle of friends amazed me.

The funeral the following morning was not without its complications. St John's Church is quite beautiful but very small, the smallest church in Clontarf, so there was concern that many friends would not get in. Noel Kelly, Gerry's agent and close friend, rang me to say he was organizing a bus to bring people from the Four Seasons Hotel to the church.

The funeral mass was stunning, dignified and moving. Father Brian D'Arcy once again articulated what we all thought about Gerry: 'To say that Gerry was never arrogant or boastful . . . well, you never knew him if you were to say that. And if you said that he had overcome his anger or didn't take offence, then I'm afraid Gerry would have been as dull as the rest of us.' He commented on the outpouring of grief, love and admiration that followed Gerry's untimely death. 'Gerry would have been shocked at how popular he was.' But of course it was the words of Morah, Rex, Lottie and Gerry's brother Mano that we will all remember; they were eloquent, illuminating and respectful.

The composure of his children, the eloquence of Lottie and Rex, the elegance and generosity of Morah, all melded with the music of Westlife and the stunning audio tribute from U2 to turn the mass into a memorable and moving tribute to Gerry's life. U2, who were rehearsing in the US at the time, did a special version of 'With or Without You' which they sent from the States. (At the first-anniversary mass for Gerry, Bono told me he had once seen Gerry weeping as they performed the song on stage.)

Gerry's eldest son, Rex, who reminded me so much of how Gerry looked when I knew him in Trinity thirty years previously, said, 'He was a man who was too big for this world; he shone more brightly than anyone I have come across.'

The attendance at the funeral gave some insight into the power of his broadcasting and the breadth of his friendships: President Mary McAleese, government ministers, former Taoisigh, journalists, actors, businessmen, close friends like Harry and Rita Crosbie, John McColgan and Moya Doherty. The only downside was that the church was so full that many of Gerry's fans had to listen outside. But the reception from the crowd gathered outside on the Clontarf Road as we all left was uplifting and touching, a measure of how Gerry's radio programme had affected so many, so often and so deeply over so many years.

Eight months later, two days before the inquest, my line manager Tom Maguire called me into his office. 'About

Friday,' he began. I was confused, thinking he was talking about some political criticism or other on the previous Friday's programme. But then he went on: 'There will probably be some difficult things in Gerry's inquest.'

I asked him what he meant.

'Drink, prescription tablets and cocaine,' he murmured.

I was in total shock and got upset, blubbering through tears, 'Cocaine? Was he mad, using cocaine? And think of his kids.' Tom was a bit taken aback by my emotion, but he was considerate and he calmed me, and we sat down to absorb the information.

I knew that, even if only a small amount of cocaine was found at the post mortem (and, apparently, it was only a small amount), it would dominate the headlines. To those who say I was naïve not to know about cocaine and the so-called celebrity circuit, I can tell them honestly that I did not know. I can vaguely recall one or two references to the high living and the company Gerry was keeping, but I had just dismissed this as professional jealousy.

Sure enough, after the inquest, a firestorm of newspaper coverage was unleashed, catapulting Gerry's drug use into the stratosphere. The newspapers hung on to the utterings of those who said they knew and didn't feel able to tell – until now. Chief among these was former 2FM DJ Gareth O'Callaghan, who wrote an article revealing that he knew, and claiming that other friends also knew but did nothing about it. I was baffled by Gareth's claims; they seemed to me to be full of contradictions.

A troop of newspaper columnists used Gerry's inquest to continue their bashing of RTÉ. The focus then shifted to other RTÉ presenters. Was our silence somehow a sign of complicity? A day before the inquest, the managing director of radio had asked us not to comment publicly. I was clear anyway that my view of Gerry was as I knew him, and I had no intention of talking about the inquest, preferring to take the time to compose my own words before I put them on the record.

On the following Sunday's *Spirit Level* TV programme, I decided to react to the massive newspaper coverage about Gerry's 'drug use', some of it so ludicrous it was obviously made up – after all, you can't libel the dead. I said I was taken aback by the revelations and that I had never been naïve about the harm that drugs do at many levels in society. I pointed out that, in his public persona, Gerry did a lot of good. I was thinking of course of the positive impact of his daily programme. But, within an hour, these comments were being distorted and a cartoon was being circulated via Twitter portraying me as eulogizing Gerry and saying his drug use 'did no harm'. I knew then that the firestorm was out of control.

By the following Sunday, after a week of lunatic claims, including one commentator urging that the top stars in RTÉ be drug-tested, the story had galloped off into claims about daily drug deliveries to the RTÉ campus and supposed Garda collusion with 'Gerry's drug dealer'.

When I asked what calls were coming into *Liveline*, I was told that there was very little traffic on Gerry's inquest, and those calls fell into two categories: a small number asking why RTÉ was not covering the story, and an even smaller number of people with alcohol problems who wanted to talk about their addictions. I know from previous programmes about cocaine that the users of that particular drug don't call *Liveline*. When Katy French died a few years earlier, we did not get calls either.

On Thursday, Clare Duignan asked to see me and the *Liveline* series producer, Siobhan Hough, who had worked with Gerry for two decades. Clare was surprised to hear of the low number of calls on the topic, and their nature. She was obviously very cognizant of and worried about the unrelenting newspaper attacks on RTÉ.

I was surprised the following Sunday evening when radio colleagues rang me about an RTÉ statement which had just been issued about the 'cocaine' allegations, which praised a three-year-old *Prime Time* programme but said radio coverage the previous week of Gerry's inquest had 'fallen short'. Having been instructed not to comment on air, we really felt we were being treated unfairly.

Other news organizations and some politicians jumped on this RTÉ admission, but I thought it was grossly unfair to the radio staff who work so hard producing live programmes with massive audiences. Indeed, it is often forgotten, even within the organization, that Gerry Ryan did fifteen hours of live broadcasting every single week. Some much lauded and hyped RTÉ programmes don't do that in a full year.

The coverage of the aftermath of Gerry's death was massively unfair and tasteless. It is hard to believe that in their initial report of Gerry's sudden death, the *Irish Times* insisted on mentioning his salary. Can you think of any other public figures where a report of his or her death would be accompanied by a reference to their earnings?

I have learned much from Gerry's death. I am a different person. I don't bemoan extra work; after all, I can do charity events, Gerry can't. On another front, I have tried to worry less about the insecurity of the business, and Gerry was a strong, steady supporter in this, and nothing has replaced him in that.

As I wrote in a newspaper long before his death, Gerry was simply one of the best radio broadcasters Ireland has ever produced. His acting skills, his impersonations, his bravery, his ability to connect with the audience, his untrammelled belief in himself and what he was doing was gob-smacking. You had to admire his chutzpah, on air and off.

I know one thing about Gerry Ryan: his daily radio programme was a rich, valuable and vital part of the lives of so many people on this island and beyond, many of whom were the better for his broadcasts; their lives were enlivened, enriched and illuminated by his wisdom, his humour, his knowledge and his courage. And, for that, he should be publicly remembered.

He truly was a remarkable man, embracing enormous intelligence, unparalleled broadcasting gifts and unbounded confidence, embedded in a mischievousness that belied his age and worries. Genius Gerry.

EPILOGUE

One Life

'IF THE WORLD IS IN EACH ONE OF US, YOU HAVE THE power to change that world.' These are the inspirational words of my friend Frank Deasy, appealing on *Liveline* for more people to carry donor cards just days before his death while awaiting a liver transplant. His words sum up a truth that I have held to throughout my own life.

We are made of this world, not just through our parents and theirs; we are much closer to historical events than we imagine. In this age, while we may all 'live for the day', we are born and reborn of the countless days that went before. The links between today and our past are not forged in cold history books; they are forged with flesh-and-blood connections between real people who are part of what we are and what our children will be.

So it is with my story. My grandparents and parents

were all born into poor circumstances and lived most of their lives within a three-mile radius of the Liffey. My father was born in the same tenement where his own mother first saw the dusty, speckled light of day and which she would eventually leave only in the 1960s. My mother was born near her future husband and lived at nineteen different addresses before she got married aged twenty-one. There was a sense that, no matter how hard they tried, for them life was not a circle but a cul-de-sac.

If my mother, who is thankfully still alive, could have read on the day of her birth, 10 May 1929, she would have discovered that Dáil Éireann was debating a 'Poor Law', the first major change in the law since the Great Famine, when the only answer to poverty was the workhouse. Ten years after the foundation of the state, there were still over four thousand people in the workhouses of Dublin, with little if any aid for the destitute. The stew house, which many in Ballyfermot had to avail of, was a remnant of this system. But the dignity of Mrs Pender, who held her head high all those years ago, showed me the resilience of the human spirit.

In my case, I can clearly say that my desire for education was a product of my own mother's lack of it; but she saw and supported my efforts. While, for much of my journey, I did not know where I was going, I was driven by my perpetual desire to avoid the cul-de-sac, the dead end. I feel I have been lucky in discovering the transformative power of education. And in striving to better myself, I have always felt drawn to helping those around me.

If my three teenage children get a glimpse of the journey so many of us have made, they will see that, even in the midst of the economic and social turmoil which daily convulses us, there is hope – not forced, but real. The 'circle of life' is no such thing; it's a timeline, often crooked, sometimes looped, but always restless. The timelines of our lives are powered by the unquenchable desire to better ourselves and the lives of our children. Of all the things that separate us from other species, surely it is this that distinguishes us?

I hope that this book has shown that, throughout my life, I have kept faith in the power of the individual. I firmly believe that one person can make a difference; after all, 99 is not 100, and one *does* matter. One stranger added to another stranger does not make two strangers but a connection, a bond, that can spread out across the world. Everything interesting that happens in the world begins with one person in one place. And that one person has just one life to live.

The programme I present, *Liveline*, gives a voice to the voiceless. It begins with just one phone call. One voice *can* make a difference. And that's what gives me hope in people: that we can support each other to make that difference. We can delve into the past and try to influence the future; we can transcend the gap between us; we can feel, celebrate and grieve for the hurt and joy of others, regardless of physical distance.

In these times of great uncertainty and daily turmoil, of shifting earth and shifting values, our compasses are haywire; but we have to hold steady, as those who came before us held firm in different, often more difficult circumstances, so we might be here today. We must always remember our sense of self, our family, our friends, our communities, because it is these that will get us through times of no money better than money will ever get us through times of no family, friends, community or sense of self.

It is, after all, why we are here.

PICTURE ACKNOWLEDGEMENTS

All photographs not credited below were kindly supplied by the author. The publishers have made every effort to contact copyright holders where known. Copyright holders who have not been credited are invited to get in touch with the publishers.

First section:
pp. 4–5: JD in Junior Common Room © Derek Speirs; Group of expelled students courtesy of the *Irish Times*; JD talking to journalists © Derek Speirs
pp. 6–7: JD being removed from protest courtesy of the *Irish Times*; JD, June and triplets © Noel Gavin/Allpix/the *Star*; *RTÉ Guide* cover © RTÉ Stills Library

Second section:
pp. 6–7: JD with Outside Broadcast van © RTÉ Stills Library; Susie Long courtesy of Conor MacLiam; JD on crutches © Independent Newspapers
p. 8: JD with Eibhlín Ní Chonghaile, Gerry Ryan and

Miriam O'Callaghan © RTÉ Press Office; *Late Late Show* tribute © RTÉ Stills Library; Funny Friday crew © Cyril Fox/VideoMe

INDEX

Footprints in the Custard, Joe Duffy, 2011; oil on canvas.